LUCRETIUS ON THE NATURE OF THINGS

TRANSLATED BY

CYRIL BAILEY

FELLOW OF BALLIOL COLLEGE

OXFORD
AT THE CLARENDON PRESS

Oxford University Press, Amen House, London E.C.4

GLASGOW NEW YORK TORONTO MELBOURNE WELLINGTON
BOMBAY CALCUTTA MADRAS CAPE TOWN

Geoffrey Cumberlege, Publisher to the University

FIRST PUBLISHED 1910
REPRINTED 1920, 1921, 1923, 1924
1928, 1936, 1946, 1948, 1950
PRINTED IN GREAT BRITAIN

PREFACE

No one can set about translating Lucretius into English without finding his head full of the great work of H. A. J. Munro. It is not only that certain striking phrases ring in one's ears—*vitai claustra*, 'the fastnesses of life,' *alte terminus haerens*, 'the deepset boundary-mark,' &c.— but one is possessed with a strong feeling that he has finally set the tone or colour which Lucretius in English must assume. It might indeed be thought that with so fine a model in existence it is unnecessary and unprofitable to undertake the task again. But there are, I think, good reasons to justify the attempt. In the first place, the study of Lucretius has made considerable advances since Munro's edition : thanks largely to Dr. Brieger and still more to the late Professor Giussani,[1] the philo-sophy of Epicurus is far better understood than it was, and, as a consequence, much light has been thrown on many dark places in the poem, and its general grouping and connexion can be far more clearly grasped. Secondly, though Munro set the tone, he did not always keep it : in the more technical parts of the poem he is apt to drop almost into the language of a scientific textbook, and phrases and even passages of sheer prose give the

[1] In our own country Dr. Masson (Lucretius : Epicurean and Poet) has recently written a very suggestive, though not always accurate, sketch of Lucretius's relations to his predecessors and to modern scientific ideas, and has most successfully represented the spirit of the poem.

reader the idea that Lucretius's muse allowed him only a fitful inspiration. While acknowledging then my debt to Munro for the main spirit of the translation and often for words and phrases which seemed to me inevitable, I have tried at once to embody the results of more recent Lucretian scholarship, and to preserve a more equable level of style, which will, I hope, leave the impression that the De Rerum Natura, even in its most scientific discussions, is still poetry.

I have translated from my own text published in the Bibliotheca Oxoniensis in 1898, but in the—I fear—numerous places, where I have since altered my opinion, I have taken what I now believe to be the right reading or the best suggestion and added the warning of a footnote. I have appended some notes for the general reader, which are intended either to explain allusions or to elucidate what seemed to me difficult or obscure passages in the light of the general Epicurean theory.

I wish to thank the Rector of Lincoln for several valuable suggestions, and Professor H. H. Turner for much help in the elucidation of the astronomical problems raised in Book V.

C. B.

1910.

In the present reprint the translation has been adapted to the second edition of the text in the Bibliotheca Oxoniensis (1921).

C. B.

March, 1921.

INTRODUCTION

Of the three great Latin poets Lucretius seems to make the most peculiar appeal to our own age. Catullus and Virgil are for all time ; the passionate love-history of a genuine soul and a poet of marvellously wide range, the all-embracing yet finely pessimistic sympathy of a mind which could focus past and future in the consciousness of present crisis, will find their response in all generations. But Lucretius—possibly because from the point of view of universality he stands a little below the other two—seems to demand for full appreciation a rather special temper. His are not the interests of every man, nor is his a common attitude to life. A fierce hatred of conventional superstitions and a yearning for intellectual liberty coupled with a sense of awe—deeply religious in reality—in the presence of nature, a strong desire for scientific method and accuracy of observation combined with a profound feeling of the beauty of the world and its works, an unswerving consciousness of natural law and the sequence of cause and effect counteracted by an equal stubbornness in defence of man's moral freedom—these are qualities which may engage attention, but cannot at all times awaken a vital sympathy   Yet these are antitheses familiar enough to our generation, and this is an attitude of mind which we are peculiarly qualified to understand. The antagonism of Religion and Science, the relation of the investigation to the love of Nature, the opposition of Natural Law and Freewill are themes which seem very near to us.

Only we must be careful not to interpret the past by the present. To each generation its problems present themselves in their own peculiar manner, and we must endeavour to understand Lucretius not as a contemporary, but as an Epicurean of the last century B.C. It was eminently a period of disturbance and dissolution, intellectually as well as socially and politically. The Republican régime was breaking down, and with it the system of morals and beliefs on which it rested. The genuine Roman religion—the belief in the *numina*, the countless little impersonal 'spirits', always 'about man's path and about his bed', mostly hostile by instinct, but capable of pacification by simple gifts and easy acts of worship—had long ago lost its hold on the life of the city, or at the most lingered on here and there in the old-fashioned piety of a household cult. The imposing structure of the State-worship, raised as the primitive agricultural community developed into a commercial city, and consolidated when the great wave of Greek culture anthropomorphized *numina* into *dei*, gave them temples and statues, and organized ceremonials and priesthoods, remained still untouched in form, but the form was empty. Magistrates and priests duly sacrificed the appropriate victims, augurs watched for omens and blessed or stayed proceedings, the populace kept holiday on the festivals, but little real religious feeling remained, except a vague sense of the insecurity of life owing to the malevolent interference of divine beings, and an abiding fear of death and the punishments of a life to come. The more recent introduction of

Oriental cults, which had obtained a great influence over the popular mind, had but heightened these terrors, by adding an ecstatic and orgiastic form of worship, which through excitement and reaction gave an unnatural and intermittent character to religion, essentially foreign to the sober and straightforward temperament of the Roman.

Among the educated classes in consequence a profound scepticism prevailed. When Q. Mucius Scaevola [1] advocated the maintenance of religion among the populace as a political asset, he was but voicing what had for a generation been the practice of the ruling classes. Cicero, the Augur, could discuss [2] the fundamental assumptions of his art and arrive at a very unfavourable conclusion; Caesar, the acknowledged sceptic, was selected to direct the whole system of religious worship as Pontifex Maximus. But a pure scepticism cannot satisfy any type of mind, least of all the Roman, and Greek culture, which had introduced the disease, brought also the antidote in philosophy. Philosophy professed to place men above the conflict of religions and to give them what religion did not claim to offer, a guide to moral conduct. It seems strange at first sight that the two greatest philosophies of Greece—those of Plato and Aristotle— should have made so little impression on the Roman mind, attracting only a few strong intellects like Cicero's, and even then only to a very eclectic and almost dilettante study. But the reason is not really far to seek: not only were the idealism of Plato and the intellectualism of Aristotle alien to the plain Roman mind, but morally both systems rested essentially on the conception of the State, on the identification of the good man and the good

[1] St. Augustine, de Civ. Dei, iv. 27.   [2] De Divinatione.

citizen. It was just this conception which with the fall of the Republic was breaking down, and philosophy, if it was to help the sceptical Roman, must be individual-istic : he wanted to know about himself and his conduct as a single human being. In the corresponding period of the history of Athens, when the city-state had given place to the monarchy of Macedon, and that again had fallen into the disruption of the rule of the ' Successors ', two creeds had arisen to supply the need. Stoicism with its assertion of the divine element in the world and the mind of man had appealed to the more directly religious natures ; the doctrine of Epicurus, founded on the atomic materialism of Democritus, made its way with those more inclined to a matter-of-fact scientific outlook on life. And so now in Rome these two philosophies answered the demand, and as men drifted away from religion, they divided themselves almost unconsciously into the rival camps of the Stoics and Epicureans.

Into this atmosphere Lucretius grew up. Of his personal history we are singularly ignorant. By a comparison of an entry in Jerome's Fasti[1] and a casual note in Donatus's Life of Virgil,[2] and an attempt to reconcile their dis-agreement by considerations of probability, we can arrive at the conclusion that he was born in 94 B.C. and died in 55. We have a romantic story,[3] which has been very variously interpreted, that he was ' poisoned by a love-philtre, wrote some poems in his lucid intervals and finally committed suicide '. We are told that Cicero ' edited ' the poem—a statement whose meaning is again much vexed—and a recently discovered Renais-

---

[1] Chron. Euseb. [2] Reifferscheid, Sueton. reliq., p. 55.
[3] Jerome, l. c.

sance [1] 'Life' gives us what purport to be details of
his criticism:[2] we know for certain that by 54 B.C.
both Cicero and his brother had read the poem and
communicated to each other their opinions on it.
We are aware that the Lucretii were a family of good
standing in Rome, and Lucretius's friendship with
Memmius suggests that he too was—or might have been,
if he had wished it—in the society of his day: the 'Borgian
Life' gives us the names of others, prominent philosophers
and public men, with whom he was familiar. But
beyond that we must be content to know nothing, nor
indeed could any addition of external details add much
to the unmistakable picture of his personality which the
poem itself presents to us. A keen active mind, eager
in its pursuit of truth and not shrinking from hard
thought in the attainment of its end, or from intellectual
labour in the attempt to present it to others ; and
a profound poetic sensitiveness, alive at once to the
greatness and the beauty of nature, and instinct with
the feeling for accuracy in expression and the consciousness
of the revealing power of language in its ' sudden flashes ' [3]
—these are characteristics which strike one at once. And
the closer study of the poem seems to disclose another
feature almost equally marked. Whether or no we
accept the legend of the love-philtre and the idea of
insanity, we cannot refuse the testimony of the poem
itself to an abnormal and even morbid strain in its author's
character. The fierceness of the unceasing attack on
the religious point of view—even on its shadow in a

---

[1] See Masson. Lucretius : Epicurean and Poet, vol. i. pp. 38 ff. and
vol. ii. pp. 1–13.

[2] Cic. Ep. ad Q. Fr. ii. 11.   [3] *lumina ingenii*, Cic. l. c.

teleological interpretation of nature;[1] the unnatural
virulence of the onslaught on love;[2] the almost brooding
pessimism with which he anticipates the coming destruction of the world;[3] such are the signs which lead one to
think of Lucretius as a not quite normal personality—
perhaps even not quite sane.

Lucretius then approached the problems of his age
with a strongly-marked temper and a very decided bias.
It was not sufficient for him to take up, as did so many
of his contemporaries, a position of sceptical indifference
towards religion. Nor could he, like the Stoics, attempt
to get rid of the grosser elements of superstition and yet
retain a purified belief in the divine control of the world,
reconciling the conflicts of religion in a kind of religious
philosophy. Religion was his enemy and he could have
no truce with it, for he saw in it the cause of the greater
part of the sorrows and even the crimes[4] of human life.
The whole theological view must be eradicated from
men's minds before they could even begin to live a life
'worthy of the gods'.[5] Naturally enough then he turned
to the philosophy of Epicurus: he had had the same
battle to fight: it was he who, 'when the life of man
lay foul and grovelling upon the earth crushed by the
weight of religion . . . dared first to raise his mortal
eyes to meet her . . . and in mind and spirit traversed the
boundless whole:'[6] he was the real 'god',[7] who had
taught that the power of the gods over the world was
nought. In the philosophy of Epicurus Lucretius had
found his own rest, and it was the purpose of his life[8]

---

[1] iv. 823, v. 110, &c.   [2] iv. 1058 ff.   [3] v. 104 ff.
[4] i. 82 ff., iii. 59 ff.   [5] iii. 322.   [6] i. 62 ff.
[7] v. 8.   [8] i. 931.

to put that philosophy at the service of his countrymen and so deliver them too from the tyranny of religion.

But it would be the greatest mistake to think of Lucretius or his master as the author of a mere polemic against religion. Still less is Epicurus justly represented—as has sometimes been the case—as patching together from various sources a crude piecemeal view of the world to combat superstition and afford a plausible basis for a moral theory of doubtful moral tendency. If there is one point that modern work at Epicureanism tends to reveal, it is that it was a serious philosophy, a consistent whole derived from a single starting-point and following step by step with logical precision. As such Lucretius had learnt it, and as such he intended to present it, and many of the difficulties which modern critics have found in his detail, many of the puerilities at which they have scoffed, are to be explained by the perfectly consistent and relentless application of his fundamental principles. He has seemed trivial or inconsistent or obscure to his critics, because they would not take him seriously enough.

It will not be possible here to deal in any detail with the Epicurean system, and indeed, in most of its aspects it will gradually unfold itself in the De Rerum Natura, but it will be well to call attention to certain fundamental points with regard to it, which Lucretius has rather assumed than stated, but which are of vital importance for the understanding of his poem, and the comprehension of its essential unity. First, however, we must very briefly consider the origin of the system. It is commonly said that Epicurus adopted the atomic theory of Democritus to act as a physical basis for his moral theory that

the end of life was 'pleasure'. This is in a very limited
sense true. The long debate of the pre-Socratic physical
philosophers as to the ultimate constitution of the
universe had led up to the hypothesis, first propounded
by Leucippus and greatly strengthened and elaborated
by Democritus of Abdera (circ. 430 B.C.), that the physical
basis of the world was infinite atoms, tiny, eternal,
indivisible particles of matter, possessing and differing in
size, shape and weight,[1] and moving in infinite space.
This conclusion with many of the deductions from it
and much of Democritus's elaboration of detail Epicurus
accepted, and combined with it the theory that pleasure
was the highest good, but in no mere casual spirit of
eclecticism. He believed pleasure to be the moral end,
because that, as we shall see, was an immediate deduction
from his one fundamental principle; he accepted
Democritus's atomism, because that alone of all theories
of the world known to him was consistent with his
fundamental principle—and yet in his very maintenance
of that principle he most conspicuously differed from
Democritus.

The principle concerned the root-problem of meta-
physics : how do we get our knowledge ? are we to trust
our senses or our reason, or both or neither? The
question had been raised at a comparatively early stage
in pre-Socratic speculation, and had forced itself more
and more into prominence as theories of the world
became more and more remote from the experience of
every-day consciousness, until Parmenides, who believed

---

[1] There is, as a matter of fact, considerable doubt whether Democritus
attributed weight to the atoms, but I am inclined to believe that
he did.

the world to be a corporeal *plenum*, had declared whole-heartedly for reason and identified the 'way of the senses' with the 'way of error'. Democritus had pushed scepticism a step further: reason rested upon the senses, and if the senses were untrustworthy, still more so must reason be: 'wretched mind,' he represents the senses as saying, 'from us you received your belief, yet you overthrow us; your victory is your defeat.'[1] Epicurus approached the problem as the plain man: he must have a sure basis for the structure of his system, and no scepticism at the root. The keystone of the whole Epicurean philosophy is the simple assertion: 'sensation is true,' 'I know what I feel.' On this one foundation all is built. Wherever the senses give us evidence, we are to accept their evidence as finally and certainly true: where they do not, as for instance, in considering the ultimate constitution of the world,[2] they are still supreme; we must reject any hypothesis which is contradicted by the evidence of sense, and accept as equally probable any explanations that are consistent with it. Now Lucretius does not start with this fundamental principle: he does not even approach the discussion of it until the fourth Book.[3] But on the other hand he is always assuming it and acting on it, and to understand his line of thought it must always be borne in mind. The sun and the moon, for instance, are the same size as we see them to be:[4] there the senses

---

[1] Galen, de med. emp. 1259, 8; Diels B. 125. Democritus's exact position is very difficult to make out, but it seems that he accepted the evidence of the senses for the primary properties, size, shape, and weight, but regarded it with suspicion for all other qualities: in other words he held that touch alone among the senses could be trusted.

[2] Diogenes Laertius, x. 50, &c.   [3] iv. 469 ff.   [4] v. 564 ff.

give us evidence and we must not attempt to go behind it. The sequence of night and day,[1] the orbits of the heavenly bodies,[2] eclipses[3] may be explained in several ways, some of which to our mind appear trivial; but these are cases where the senses provide no direct evidence, and we must therefore accept as equally worthy of consideration all hypotheses which they do not contradict. Above all, it is this principle which prompts him again and again to appeal for support in his theories of imperceptible things to the analogy of the perceptible: the trust in the senses is the ultimate cause of those many illustrations from common experience, which are so largely responsible for the beauty and the poetic wealth of the whole poem.

Let us pursue this line of thought a little further. Of what do the senses give us evidence? Of nothing but a material world: matter then is the one reality. But can the existence of matter alone give us a world as we know it? No, for our senses tell us of a world of matter in motion,[4] and things cannot move without space to move in: there must then be empty space. And in what form does this matter exist? The section in the middle of the first Book,[5] in which Lucretius criticizes rival theories of the world, shows us how Epicurus applied his principle: some schools deny the existence of void, which makes motion impossible;[6] others permit infinite division, which precludes permanence;[7] some propose a fundamental matter that is unstable, for it changes into other things,[8] others one that is perishable, for it is

---

[1] v. 650 ff.   [2] v. 614 ff.   [3] v. 751 ff.
[4] Sextus Emp. adv. math. i. 213; cf. Lucr. i. 329 ff.   [5] i. 635–920.
[6] i. 655, 742, 843.   [7] i. 746, 844.   [8] i. 665, 763.

of the same nature as perceptible things.[1] The only theory which is found not to be contradicted, but rather supported by the evidence of the senses, is an atomic theory. Finally, lest the supply of matter should run short, the atoms must be infinite in number,[2] and, lest it should all congregate 'at the bottom', space must be infinite in extent.[3] Epicurus has then arrived at the atomism of Democritus, not, however, as an arbitrary choice, but as a direct deduction from the primary assertion of the infallibility of sense-perception.

And in this atomic system Epicurus and Lucretius find their refutation of the pretensions of religion, the release from the two great terrors which beset man's mind, the fear of the arbitrary intervention of the gods in life, and the fear of the punishment of an immortal soul after death. For the atomic system, capable of being worked out in detail throughout the whole realm of the universe, can show how every phenomenon is but the result of natural causes. The atoms in the void, obeying the law of their own nature, falling down-wards owing to their weight,[4] meeting and clashing,[5] form first into little molecules, then into larger masses, and ultimately build up the whole universe of worlds, planted about here and there in infinite space, and all things, down to the smallest, contained in them. Nature, acting by law and yet without purpose—'for not by design did the first-beginnings of things place them-selves each in their order with foreseeing mind . . . but by trying movements and unions of every kind, at last they fall into such dispositions as those, whereby our world

[1] i. 753, 847.   [2] i. 1008.   [3] i. 988.
[4] ii. 184.   [5] ii. 216.

of things is created '[1]—acting indeed blindly and occasionally with a kind of spontaneity which seems like chance,[2] Nature made all the worlds and 'all that in them is '. There is no need for the aid of the gods, there is not even room for their interference. They are rather a part of nature's creation, immortal creatures,[3] of a body of infinitely subtle formation,[4] dwelling apart in the 'interspaces between the worlds ',[5] in regions 'where falls not hail or rain or any snow, nor ever wind blows loudly',[6] an example and an ideal in their untroubled calm to man, but utterly unconcerned with the movements of the world or human affairs. As for the soul, it is, like all other things, a corporeal aggregate of atoms,[7] which owes its sensation to the shape and movements of its constituents,[8] and its union with the body :[9] neither can exist without the other, at death the soul is dissolved just like the body,[10] and it can have nothing to fear for all time to come.[11] Nature then has freed man alike from the tyranny of the gods and the fear of death, and in the knowledge of nature he will find not only the guarantee of his freedom, but the highest pleasure of his free life.

But is man 'free'? The exclusion of the gods from the workings of the universe has been accomplished by the establishment of law, the demonstration of the natural sequence of cause and effect from the first downward movement of the atoms to the formation of the newest 'thing' in the remotest world. Is man then

---

[1] i. 1021 ff.   [2] 'Be it by the chance or the force of nature,' vi. 31.   [3] v. 1175.   [4] v. 146 ff.   [5] Cic. de Nat. Deor. i. 8. 18.   [6] iii. 19.   [7] iii. 161.   [8] ii. 894.   [9] iii. 323. [10] iii. 417–829.   [11] iii. 838.

alone exempt from this chain of causation ? has he the power to direct his own actions, or is he too ruled by this inexorable destiny, so that his smallest act is but the inevitable outcome of all that has preceded? Democritus had already been confronted with this problem and had boldly answered it with an absolute determinism : man's actions are no exception to the universal law, free-will is but a delusion. But for Epicurus this answer would not do : man's conduct was his primary interest, and it is no use, he thought, telling a man what he ought to do, unless he is free to do it. Even the tyranny of religion is better than the tyranny of destiny.[1] Besides, Epicurus on his own fundamental principles had a good reason to fight for free-will ; for it is a matter of immediate consciousness : ' we know '[2] that from time to time we assert our independence of the great claim of causation : ' we feel ' our freedom and it cannot therefore be denied. Yet how is it to be preserved? Is man to be an exception to the universal law, or can it be otherwise accounted for? Epicurus's answer, the ' swerve '[3] of the atoms, has always been ridiculed, but, whatever may be thought of it, it is not to be regarded as a weak admission, but rather as a cardinal point in the system, second only in importance to the infallibility of the senses, and again reached by a strict logical deduction. For if man's will is free, it cannot be by special exemption granted him, but because of some principle inherent in the very first-beginnings : man can do what he will because there is an element of spontaneity—not of course conscious spontaneity—in the atoms. It is the ' swerve ' then which enables the atoms to meet in their downward

---

[1] Diog. Laert. x. 134.   [2] ii. 261.   [3] ii. 216 ff.

fall, it is the 'swerve' which preserves in inorganic
nature that curious element of spontaneity which we
call chance,[1] and it is the 'swerve', become conscious
in the sensitive aggregate of the atoms of the mind,
which secures man's freedom of action and makes it
possible to urge on him a theory of conduct.

Lastly then—for though Lucretius never explicitly
deals with it, it emerges to the surface again and again
in the poem—we must very shortly consider the moral
theory of Epicurus. Let us go back once more to the
fundamental principle. In the sphere of conduct, of
action and suffering, has immediate sensation any evidence
to give us comparable to the evidence of sense-perception
in the field of knowledge? Clearly it has in the immediate
perceptions of pleasure and pain : we all feel them,
we all instinctively seek pleasure and avoid pain. Epicurus
then has his answer at once : pleasure is the moral good ;
sensation tells us so, and we cannot attempt to go behind
it. But what does 'pleasure' mean? to what practical
conduct will its adoption as the aim of life lead us? Two
points in the physical theory are here of importance : firstly,
that man, in Epicurus's idea, is always essentially a compound of body and soul ; secondly, that pain is dislocation
of atomic arrangements and motions, pleasure, their
readjustment and equilibrium. Pleasure then must be
of body and soul alike, and it will show itself in the
calm that denotes atomic equilibrium. It is seen at once
that Epicurus's doctrine is no recommendation of mere
vulgar pleasures of sensuality, as it has sometimes been
represented. The body must have its pleasure, but the

---

[1] This point is much disputed, but see Guyau, La Morale
d'Épicure, pp. 70 ff.

true pleasure is not such as brings attendant pain in the form either of anticipation or reaction : rather, we shall secure its pleasure best by maintaining its health and restricting its desires within the narrowest possible limits. Lucretius has given us a pleasing picture of the Epicurean ' picnic '—a full satisfaction of the bodily needs : ' men lie in friendly groups on the soft grass near some stream of water under the branches of a tall tree and at no great cost delightfully refresh their bodies, above all when the weather smiles on them and the season of the year bestrews the green grass with flowers.'[1] And with the pleasures of the soul the principle is the same. First it must be relieved of its peculiar pains, the fear of the gods and the fear of death : and then it may give itself up to its own particular pleasure, the study—not of rhetoric,[2] for in the private life of the individual that has no place, not of mathematics,[3] or literature,[4] for they deal with mere words, not things— but of nature : and so the highest pleasure of the mind is the acquisition of that knowledge which will incidentally free it from its pains. Epicurean pleasure is indeed simple of acquisition, and men are strangely blind that they do not recognize it : ' to think that ye should not see that nature cries aloud for nothing else but that pain may be kept far sundered from the body, and that, withdrawn from care and fear, the mind may enjoy the sense of pleasure.'[5]

The ideal for the individual then is not far to seek, and Epicurus is above all an individualist. But a man cannot live his life quite alone and he must have relations with his fellows : how are they to be regulated? As

---

[1] ii. 29 ff. [2] Quintilian, Inst. Or. ii. 17, 15. [3] Proclus in Eucl. elem. 322. [4] Plut. contr. Ep. beat. 13. 1095ᵉ. [5] ii. 16 ff.

one would expect, Epicurus treats the 'other-regarding'
virtues with scant respect : they are but of secondary
importance and necessary only in so far as they secure
the individual from interruption in the pursuit of his
own pleasure.   Justice, the summing up of the relations
between man and man, is a convention : Lucretius
describes to us how, when primitive man came to unite
in a common life, 'neighbours began eagerly to form
friendship with one another, not to hurt or be harmed.'[1]
The individual retains his freedom by a compact, and for
his own sake respects his neighbours.   But beyond that
he is but little concerned with them.   He will not enter
public life or attempt to hold office, for ambition and the
cares of rule are among the most disturbing influences
which can beset the mind : 'it is far better to obey in
peace than to long to rule the world with kingly power
and to sway kingdoms.'[2]   Even in private life he will
learn not to trust too much to others, for his life must
be independent.   Friendships he will form, for friendship
based on the common study of philosophy is one of
the highest blessings of life : such friendship Lucretius
hopes for with Memmius.[3]   But love—the giving up of
oneself to one's affections and the complete dependence
on another's will—the philosopher will of all things
eschew : Lucretius's denunciations in the fourth Book [4]
are unmistakable.   It is not perhaps a very attractive
picture of the philosopher in isolation, pursuing his own
pleasure and disregarding others, but it is again a relentless deduction from first principles, and it explains many
casual touches in Lucretius.

These hints may serve to make clear some of the

[1] v. 1019.   [2] v. 1129.   [3] i. 140.   [4] iv. 1058 ff.

salient points in the Epicurean theory which in Lucretius's own treatment are somewhat obscured, and to show how the whole system is really knit together by the single principle of the certainty of sensation. For those who like to find in antiquity the anticipation of modern ideas and hypotheses [1] Lucretius is of course instinct with interest. The physicist will find in him the germs of the modern atomic theory, which in its most recent development seems more likely than ever to come back to the notion of uniform homogeneous 'first-beginnings': the biologist will find notable anticipations of the hypothesis of the formation of species by evolutionary experiments and the survival of the fittest,[2] and in the idea of the spontaneous 'swerve' of the atoms a supposition not far remote from the modern speculations of W. K. Clifford and Haeckel: the anthropologist will see a picture of primitive man startlingly like that to which modern investigation has led,[3] and all the more noticeable in that the current notions of Lucretius's time looked back to a primitive 'Golden Age': the moral philosopher will discover the foundation both of Hedonism and Utilitarianism, and the political scientist will recognize the familiar description of the Social Contract.[4] But to the general reader what will come home most is the spirit of the whole, the problems with which Lucretius is faced and the general attitude in which he goes to meet them. And if one is to appreciate this fully, it is more than all else necessary to have the clear conception of the main principles and their fearless application.

---

[1] Several interesting and suggestive chapters on this subject will be found in Masson's Lucretius: Epicurean and Poet.

[2] v. 837-77. [3] v. 925-1104. [4] v. 1019.

It is often asked whether a didactic work can be real poetry, and certainly didactic poetry must stand or fall by the answer given in the case of Lucretius, for not even Hesiod or the Georgics can put forward a higher claim. It is easy, of course, to point to long tracts of scientific discussion, to call them ' arid ', or to characterize them as ' scanning prose ' : it is just to urge that a few or even many great passages of sustained poetic beauty cannot in themselves save a poem, if they are sundered by such deserts. It is not difficult to reply by pointing, as Cicero did,[1] to the ' flashes of genius ' in the poem, whether they be the wonderful descriptions, such as that of the cow who has lost her calf,[2] or the distant view of the flock on the hillside,[3] or those quieter ' flashes ' of poetic painting,—the ' flower of flame ',[4] ' the ice of brass,'[5] the shells ' painting the lap of the earth '[6]—which in a moment transform argument with imagination. It might be maintained rather more subtly that there is high poetic quality in the very exactness of the expression of the intricate theories and abstruse arguments— a quality which is the more appreciated, the more we realize the genius with which almost every word in the poem is chosen to do precisely its own work and no more. But surely a didactic poem, more than any other, must not be judged piecemeal in this way by isolated phrases or even continuous passages of poetic imagination. Its claim to rank as true poetry will rest rather on the spirit of the whole—the depth of intention underlying the work and giving life to the parts. And this is the supreme claim of the De Rerum Natura ; there may be portions

[1] ad Q. Fr. ii. 11. [2] ii. 352 ff. [3] ii. 317 ff.
[4] i. 900. [5] i. 493. [6] ii. 375.

of it, which judged separately by superficial students would seem to fall beneath the dignity of poetry, but it is knit into a whole and vivified through all its parts by the fearless desire for truth, the consciousness of a great purpose, and a deep reverence for nature—felt almost as a personal presence—which has caused this bitter opponent of religion to be universally recognized as one of the most truly religious of the world's poets.

SHORT ANALYSIS OF THE POEM

Book I deals with the ultimate constitution of the universe, which consists of infinite atoms moving in infinite space.

   Introduction: Invocation to Venus and appeal to Memmius; 1–145.

     A. *General principles;* 146–482.

       (*a*) The existence of 'first-bodies', or fundamental matter in the form of particles; 146–328.

       (*b*) The existence of void, or empty space; 329–417.

       (*c*) Everything else is either property or accident of these two; 418–82.

     B. *The 'first-bodies'* are atoms: solid, eternal and indivisible particles; 483–634.

     C. *Refutation of rival theories;* 635–920.

       (*a*) Heraclitus; 635–704.

       (*b*) Empedocles; 705–829.

       (*c*) Anaxagoras; 830–920.

     D. *The universe is infinite;* 921–1117.

Book II deals with the motion and forms of the atoms, and their combination in things.

   Introduction: The blessings of philosophy; 1–61.

     A. *The motion of the atoms;* 62–332.

       (*a*) The incessant movement of the atoms; 80–141.

       (*b*) The velocity of their motion; 142–164.

       (*c*) Universal downward motion due to weight; 184–215.

       (*d*) The swerve of the atoms; 216–293.

       (*e*) The permanence of matter and motion; 294–332.

     B. *The forms of the atoms and their effects in combination;* 333–729.

       (*a*) The variety of atomic forms and their effects on sensation; 333–477.

       (*b*) This variety not infinite; 478–521.

       (*c*) Atoms of any given form infinite; 522–580.

       (*d*) Variety of combinations: differences within species; 581–729.

    C. The atoms are without secondary qualities ; 730–990.
      (*a*) Colour ; 730–841.
      (*b*) Heat, Sound, Taste, Smell ; 842–64.
      (*c*) Sensation ; 865–990.
      (*d*) Summary ; 991–1022.
    D. The infinite worlds and their formation and destruction ;
        1023–1174.

Book III deals with the soul, its nature, and its fate.
   Introduction : Praise of Epicurus and effect of the fear of
        punishment after death ; 1–93.
    A. Nature and formation of the Soul ; 94–416.
      (*a*) Distinction between mind and soul, or vital
         principle ; 94–160.
      (*b*) Their corporeal nature and composition ; 161–257.
      (*c*) Their relation to one another and to the body ;
         258–416.
    B. Proofs of the Mortality of the Soul ; 417–829.
  (This section cannot be satisfactorily subdivided, but
may roughly be classified as follows :)
      (*a*) Proofs from the structure of the soul ; 425–58.
      (*b*) Proofs from disease and its cure ; 459–547.
      (*c*) Proofs from connexion of soul and body ; 548–623.
      (*d*) Proofs from absurdity of separate existence of
         soul ; 624–829.
    C. The folly of the fear of death ; 830–1094.

Book IV deals mainly with the psychology of sensation and
   thought, and also with certain biological functions.
   Introduction : Lucretius's Mission ; 1–25.
    A. Existence and nature of the ' idols ' ; 26–216.
      (*a*) Their existence ; 26–109.
      (*b*) Their fineness of texture ; 110–42.
      (*c*) Swiftness of their formation ; 143–75.
      (*d*) Rapidity of their motion ; 176–216.
    B. Sensation and Thought ; 217–822.
      (*a*) Sight and phenomena connected with it ; 217–378.
      (*b*) False inferences of the mind and infallibility of
         the senses ; 379–521
      (*c*) Hearing ; 522–614.
      (*d*) Taste ; 615–72.
      (*e*) Smell ; 673–721.
      (*f*) Thought, i. e. mental images, both in sleep and
         waking life ; 722–822.
    C. Some functions of the Body ; 823–1057.
      (*a*) Refutation of teleological view ; 823–57.

    (*b*) Food; 858–76.
    (*c*) Walking : the act of will; 877–906.
    (*d*) Sleep and dreams; 907–1036.
    (*e*) Love; 1037–57.
  D. *Attack on the passion of Love ;* 1058–1287.

Book V deals with our world and its formation, astronomy,
    the beginnings of life and civilization.
  Introduction : Praise of Epicurus ; 1–54.
    Argument of the book; 55–109; attack on the
    theological and teleological view; 110–234.
  A. *The world had a beginning and is mortal ;* 235–415.
  B. *Formation of the world ;* 416–508, 534–64.
  C. *Astronomy ;* 509–33, 564–770.
    (*a*) Motions of heavenly bodies ; 509–33.
    (*b*) Size of sun, moon and stars ; 564–613.
    (*c*) Cause of orbits of heavenly bodies ; 614–49.
    (*d*) Causes of night and day, and their variations ;
      650–704.
    (*e*) Cause of the moon's light ; 705–50.
    (*f*) Cause of eclipses ; 751–70.
  D. *The youth of the world ;* 772–1010.
    (*a*) Origin of vegetable and animal life ; 772–924.
    (*b*) Origin of human life and primitive man ; 925–1010.
  E. *The beginnings of civilization* ; 1011–1457.

Book VI explains from the atomic point of view a variety of
    occurrences, partly meteorological phenomena, partly
    terrestrial curiosities.
  Introduction : Praise of Epicurus : the gods ; 1–95.
  A. *Celestial phenomena* ; 96–534.
    (*a*) Thunder, lightning and thunderbolts ; 96–422.
    (*b*) Waterspouts ; 423–50.
    (*c*) Clouds and Rain ; 451–534.
  B. *Terrestrial phenomena ;* 535–1137.
    (*a*) Earthquakes ; 535–607.
    (*b*) Constant size of the sea ; 608–38.
    (*c*) Volcanoes ; 639–711.
    (*d*) The Nile ; 712–37.
    (*e*) Pestilential lakes, &c. ; 738–847.
    (*f*) Curious fountains ; 848–905.
    (*g*) The Magnet ; 906–1089.
    (*b*) Pestilences ; 1090–1137.
  C. *The Plague at Athens ;* 1138–1286.

LUCRETIUS

ON THE NATURE OF THINGS

BOOK I

MOTHER[n] of Aeneas's sons, joy of men and gods, Venus
the life-giver, who beneath the gliding stars of heaven
fillest with life the sea that carries the ships and the land
that bears the crops; for thanks to thee every tribe of
living things is conceived, and comes forth to look upon
the light of the sun. Thou, goddess, thou dost turn to
flight the winds and the clouds of heaven, thou at thy
coming; for thee earth, the quaint artificer, puts forth
her sweet-scented flowers; for thee the levels of ocean
smile, and the sky, its anger past, gleams with spreading
light. For when once the face of the spring day is
revealed and the teeming breeze of the west wind is
loosed from prison and blows strong, first the birds in
high heaven herald thee, goddess, and thine approach,
their hearts thrilled with thy might. Then the tame
beasts grow wild and bound over the fat pastures, and
swim the racing rivers; so surely enchained by thy
charm each follows thee in hot desire whither thou goest
before to lead him on. Yea, through seas and mountains
and tearing rivers and the leafy haunts of birds and ver-
dant plains thou dost strike fond love into the hearts of
all, and makest them in hot desire to renew the stock of
their races, each after his own kind. And since thou alone
art pilot to the nature of things, and nothing without
thine aid comes forth into the bright coasts of light, nor
waxes glad nor lovely, I long that thou shouldest be my

helper in writing these verses, which I essay to trace on
the nature of things for the son of the Memmii, my
friend, whom thou, goddess, through all his life hast willed
to be bright with every grace beyond his fellows.   Therefore the more, goddess, grant a lasting loveliness to my
words.   Bring it to pass that meantime the wild works of
warfare may be lulled to sleep over all seas and lands.
For thou only canst bless mortal men with quiet peace,
since 'tis Mavors, the lord of hosts, who guides the wild
works of war, and he upon thy lap oft flings himself back,
conquered by the eternal wound of love ; and then pillow-
ing his shapely neck upon thee and looking up he feeds
with love his greedy eyes, gazing wistfully towards thee,
while, as he lies back, his breath hangs upon thy lips.   Do
thou, goddess, as he leans resting on thy sacred limbs,
bend to embrace him and pour forth sweet petition from
thy lips, seeking, great lady, gentle peace for the Romans.
For neither can we in our country's time of trouble [n] set
to our task with mind undistressed, nor amid such doings
can Memmius's noble son [n] fail the fortunes of the state.

.   .   .   .   [1]

Appeal to
Memmius.
for the rest, do thou (Memmius), lend empty ears and
a keen mind, severed from cares, to true philosophy, lest,
before they are understood, you should leave aside in dis-
dain my gifts set forth for you with unflagging zeal.   For
of the most high law of the heaven and the gods I will
set out to tell you, and I will reveal the first-beginnings
of things, from which nature creates all things, and increases and fosters them, and into which nature too
dissolves them again at their perishing : these in rendering

[1] Some lines are lost here, in which he passed from addressing
Venus to Memmius.

our account it is our wont to call matter or the creative bodies of things, and to name them the seeds of things, and again to term them the first-bodies, since from them first all things have their being.

When the life of man lay foul to see and grovelling upon the earth, crushed by the weight of religion, which showed her face from the realms of heaven, lowering upon mortals with dreadful mien, 'twas a man of Greece [n] who dared first to raise his mortal eyes to meet her, and first to stand forth to meet her : him neither the stories of the gods nor thunderbolts checked, nor the sky with its revengeful roar, but all the more spurred the eager daring of his mind to yearn to be the first to burst through the close-set bolts upon the doors of nature. And so it was that the lively force of his mind won its way, and he passed on far beyond the fiery walls of the world,[n] and in mind and spirit traversed the boundless whole ; whence in victory he brings us tidings what can come to be and what cannot, yea and in what way each thing has its power limited, and its deepset boundary-stone. And so religion in revenge is cast beneath men's feet and trampled, and victory raises us to heaven.

Herein I have one fear, lest perchance you think that you are starting on the principles of some unholy reasoning, and setting foot upon the path of sin. Nay, but on the other hand, again and again our foe, religion, has given birth to deeds sinful and unholy. Even as at Aulis [n] the chosen chieftains of the Danai, the first of all the host, foully stained with the blood of Iphianassa the altar of the Virgin of the Cross-Roads.[n] For as soon as the band braided about her virgin locks streamed from her either cheek in equal lengths, as soon as she

(marginal notes) Epicurus and Religion. · The impiety of Religion. · Sacrifice of Iphigenia.

saw her sorrowing sire stand at the altar's side, and near
him the attendants hiding their knives, and her country-
men shedding tears at the sight of her, tongue-tied with
terror, sinking on her knees she fell to earth. Nor could
it avail the luckless maid at such a time that she first had
given the name of father to the king. For seized by
men's hands,[n] all trembling was she led to the altars, not
that, when the ancient rite of sacrifice was fulfilled, she
might be escorted by the clear cry of 'Hymen', but in
the very moment of marriage, a pure victim she might
foully fall, sorrowing beneath a father's slaughtering
stroke, that a happy and hallowed starting might be
granted to the fleet. Such evil deeds could religion
prompt.

The fear of death and its cure.

You yourself sometime vanquished by the fearsome
threats of the seer's sayings, will seek to desert from us.
Nay indeed, how many a dream may they even now
conjure up before you, which might avail to overthrow
your schemes of life, and confound in fear all your fortunes. And justly so: for if men could see that there
is a fixed limit to their sorrows, then with some reason
they might have the strength to stand against the scruples
of religion, and the threats of seers. As it is there is no
means, no power to withstand, since everlasting is the

The nature of the soul.

punishment they must fear in death. For they know not
what is the nature of the soul, whether it is born or else
finds its way into them at their birth, and again whether
it is torn apart by death and perishes with us, or goes to
see the shades of Orcus and his waste pools, or by the
gods' will implants itself in other breasts, as our own
Ennius[n] sang, who first bore down from pleasant Helicon
the wreath of deathless leaves, to win bright fame among

the tribes of Italian peoples. And yet despite this, Ennius sets forth in the discourse of his immortal verse that there is besides a realm of Acheron, where neither our souls nor bodies endure, but as it were images pale in wondrous wise ; and thence he tells that the form of Homer, ever green and fresh, rose to him, and began to shed salt tears, and in converse to reveal the nature of things. Therefore we must both give good account of the things on high, in what way the courses of sun and moon come to be, and by what force all things are governed on earth, and also before all else we must see by keen reasoning, whence comes the soul and the nature of the mind, and what thing it is that meets us and affrights our minds in waking life, when we are touched with disease, or again when buried in sleep, so that we seem to see and hear hard by us those who have met death, and whose bones are held in the embrace of earth. _{Problems to be dealt with.}

Nor does it pass unnoticed of my mind that it is a hard task in Latin verses to set clearly in the light the dark discoveries of the Greeks, above all when many things must be treated in new words, because of the poverty of our tongue and the newness of the themes ; yet your merit and the pleasure of your sweet friendship, for which I hope, urge me to bear the burden of any toil, and lead me on to watch through the calm nights, searching by what words, yea and in what measures, I may avail to spread before your mind a bright light, whereby you may see to the heart of hidden things. _{Lucretius' difficulty.}

This terror then, this darkness of the mind, must needs be scattered not by the rays of the sun and the gleaming shafts of day, but by the outer view and the inner law of nature ; whose first rule shall take its start for us from _{A. General principles. The first law : nothing is}

made of
nothing.

this, that nothing is ever begotten of nothing [n] by divine will. Fear forsooth so constrains all mortal men, because they behold many things come to pass on earth and in the sky, the cause of whose working they can by no means see, and think that a divine power brings them about. Therefore, when we have seen that nothing can be created out of nothing, then more rightly after that shall we discern that for which we search, both whence each thing can be created, and in what way all things come to be without the aid of gods.

Proof :
all things
require
fixed seeds.

For if things came to being from nothing, every kind might be born from all things, nought would need a seed. First men might arise from the sea, and from the land the race of scaly creatures, and birds burst forth from the sky ; cattle and other herds, and all the tribe of wild beasts, with no fixed law of birth, would haunt tilth and desert. Nor would the same fruits stay constant to the trees, but all would change : all trees might avail to bear all fruits. Why, were there not bodies to bring each thing to birth, how could things have a fixed unchanging mother ? But as it is, since all things are produced from fixed seeds, each thing is born and comes forth into the coasts of light, out of that which has in it the substance and first-bodies of each ; and 'tis for this cause that all things cannot be begotten of all, because in fixed things there dwells a power set apart. Or again, why do we see the roses in spring, and the corn in summer's heat, and the vines bursting out when autumn summons them, if it be not that when, in their own time, the fixed seeds of things have flowed together, then is disclosed each thing that comes to birth, while the season is at hand, and the lively earth in safety brings forth the fragile

For 1. they
have fixed
substance,

2. and
fixed
seasons of
birth.

things into the coasts of light? But if they sprang from
nothing, suddenly would they arise at uncertain intervals
and in hostile times of year, since indeed there would be
no first-beginnings which might be kept apart from
creative union at an ill-starred season. Nay more, there
would be no need for lapse of time for the increase of
things upon the meeting of the seed, if they could grow
from nothing. For little children would grow suddenly
to youths, and at once trees would come forth, leaping
from the earth. But of this it is well seen that nothing
comes to pass, since all things grow slowly, as is natural,
from a fixed seed, and as they grow preserve their kind :
so that you can know that each thing grows great, and is
fostered out of its own substance. There is this too, that
without fixed rain-showers in the year the earth could
not put forth its gladdening produce, nor again held apart
from food could the nature of living things renew its kind
or preserve its life ; so that rather you may think that
many bodies are common to many things, as we see letters
are to words, than that without first-beginnings anything
can come to being. Once more, why could not nature
produce men so large that on their feet they might wade
through the waters of ocean or rend asunder mighty
mountains with their hands, or live to overpass many
generations of living men, if it be not because fixed substance has been appointed for the begetting of things,
from which it is ordained what can arise? Therefore, we
must confess that nothing can be brought to being out
of nothing, inasmuch as it needs a seed for things, from
which each may be produced and brought forth into the
gentle breezes of the air. Lastly, inasmuch as we see

Marginal notes:

3. and require fixed periods for increase,

4. and fixed nourish-ment ;

5. they have too a fixed limit of growth;

6. and
culture
makes the
soil more
fertile.

that tilled grounds are better than the untilled, and when worked by hands yield better produce, we must know that there are in the earth first-beginnings of things, which we call forth to birth by turning the teeming sods with the ploughshare and drilling the soil of the earth. But if there were none such, you would see all things without toil of ours of their own will come to be far better.

The second
law :
nothing is
resolved
into
nothing.
Otherwise
1. all
things
would be
destroyed
at once ;

Then follows this, that nature breaks up each thing again into its own first-bodies, nor does she destroy ought into nothing.[n] For if anything were mortal in all its parts, each thing would on a sudden be snatched from our eyes, and pass away. For there would be no need of any force, such as might cause disunion in its parts and unloose its fastenings. But as it is, because all things are put together of everlasting seeds, until some force has met them to batter things asunder with its blow, or to make its way inward through the empty voids and break things up, nature suffers not the destruction of

2. nor
could the
world be re-
plenished ;

anything to be seen. Moreover, if time utterly destroys whatsoever through age it takes from sight, and devours all its substance, how is it that Venus brings back the race of living things after their kind into the light of life, or when she has, how does earth, the quaint artificer, nurse and increase them, furnishing food for them after their kind? how is it that its native springs and the rivers from without, coming from afar, keep the sea full? how is it that the sky feeds the stars? For infinite time and the days that are gone by must needs have devoured all things that are of mortal body. But if in all that while, in the ages that are gone by, those things have existed, of which this sum of things consists and is replenished, assuredly they are blessed with an immortal nature ; all things

cannot then be turned to nought. And again, the same
force and cause would destroy all things alike, unless an
eternal substance held them together, part with part
interwoven closely or loosely by its fastenings. For in
truth a touch would be cause enough of death, seeing
that none of these things would be of everlasting body,
whose texture any kind of force would be bound to break
asunder. But as it is, because the fastenings of the first-
elements are variously put together, and their substance
is everlasting, things endure with body unharmed, until
there meets them a force proved strong enough to overcome the texture of each. No single thing then passes
back to nothing, but all by dissolution pass back into the
first-bodies of matter. Lastly, the rains pass away, when
the sky, our father, has cast them headlong into the lap
of earth, our mother ; but the bright crops spring up,
and the branches grow green upon the trees, the trees
too grow and are laden with fruit ; by them next our
race and the race of beasts is nourished, through them we
see glad towns alive with children, and leafy woods on
every side ring with the young birds' cry ; through them
the cattle wearied with fatness lay their limbs to rest
over the glad pastures, and the white milky stream trickles
from their swollen udders ; through them a new brood
with tottering legs sports wanton among the soft grass,
their baby hearts thrilling with the pure milk. Not
utterly then perish all things that are seen, since nature
renews one thing from out another, nor suffers anything
to be begotten, unless she be requited by another's
death.

Come now, since I have taught you that things cannot
be created of nought nor likewise when begotten be called

[margin notes:]
3. the same force could destroy all things alike ;

4. as it is, the loss of one thing means the increase of another.

The existence of

C 2

invisible
particles is
supported
by other
invisible
bodies.

1. Wind.

back to nothing, lest by any chance you should begin
nevertheless to distrust my words, because the first-
beginnings of things cannot be descried with the eyes,
let me tell you besides of other bodies, which you must
needs confess yourself are among things and yet cannot
be seen. First of all the might of the awakened wind
lashes the ocean and o'erwhelms vast ships and scatters
the clouds, and anon scouring the plains with tearing
hurricane it strews them with great trees, and harries the
mountain-tops with blasts that rend the woods : with
such fierce whistling the wind rages and ravens with
angry roar. There are therefore, we may be sure, unseen bodies of wind, which sweep sea and land, yea, and
the clouds of heaven, and tear and harry them with
sudden hurricane ; they stream on and spread havoc in
no other way than when the soft nature of water is borne
on in a flood o'erflowing in a moment, swollen by a great
rush of water dashing down from the high mountains
after bounteous rains and hurling together broken branches
from the woods, and whole trees too ; nor can the strong
bridges bear up against the sudden force of the advancing
flood. In such wise, turbid with much rain, the river
rushes with might and main against the piles : roaring
aloud it spreads ruin, and rolls [1] and dashes beneath its
waves huge rocks and all that bars its flood. Thus then
the blasts of wind too must needs be borne on ; and when
like some strong stream they have swooped towards any
side, they push things and dash them on with constant
assault ; sometimes in eddying whirl they seize them up
and bear them away in swiftly swirling hurricane. Wherefore again and again there are unseen bodies of wind,

[1] Read *ruitque et quidquid.*

inasmuch as in their deeds and ways they are found to
rival mighty streams, whose body all may see. Then
again we smell the manifold scents of things, and yet we   2. Scent.
do not ever descry them coming to the nostrils, nor do
we behold warm heat, nor can we grasp cold with the   3. Heat.
eyes, nor is it ours to descry voices ; yet all these things   4. Cold.
   5. Sound.
must needs consist of bodily nature, inasmuch as they can
make impact on our senses. For, if it be not body,
nothing can touch and be touched. Once more, gar-   6. Moisture.
ments hung up upon the shore, where the waves break,
grow damp, and again spread in the sun they dry. Yet
never has it been seen in what way the moisture of the
water has sunk into them, nor again in what way it has
fled before the heat. Therefore the moisture is dispersed into tiny particles, which the eyes can in no way
see. Nay more, as the sun's year rolls round again and   7. The
again, the ring on the finger becomes thin beneath by   evidence of
   Decay.
wearing, the fall of dripping water hollows the stone,
the bent iron ploughshare secretly grows smaller in the
fields, and we see the paved stone streets worn away by
the feet of the multitude ; again, by the city-gates the
brazen statues reveal that their right hands are wearing
thin through the touch of those who greet them ever and
again as they pass upon their way. All these things then
we see grow less, as they are rubbed away : yet what
particles leave them at each moment, the envious nature
of our sight has shut us out from seeing. Lastly, what-   8. and
ever time and nature adds little by little to things,   Growth.
impelling them to grow in due proportion, the straining
sight of the eye can never behold, nor again wherever
things grow old through time and decay. Nor where
rocks overhang the sea, devoured by the thin salt spray,

could you see what they lose at each moment. 'Tis then by bodies unseen that nature works her will.

The Void.

And yet all things are not held close pressed on every side by the nature of body; for there is void in things.[n] To have learnt this will be of profit to you in dealing with many things; it will save you from wandering in doubt and always questioning about the sum of things, and distrusting my words. There is then a void, mere space untouchable and empty. For if there were not, by no means could things move; for that which is the office of body, to offend and hinder, would at every moment be present to all things; nothing, therefore, could advance, since nothing could give the example of yielding place. But as it is, through seas and lands and the high tracts of heaven, we descry many things by many means moving in diverse ways before our eyes, which, if there were not void, would not so much be robbed and baulked of restless motion, but rather could in no way have been born at all, since matter would on every side be in close-packed stillness. Again, however solid things may be thought to be, yet from this you can discern that they are of rare body. In rocky caverns the liquid moisture of water trickles through, and all weeps with copious dripping: food spreads itself this way and that into the body of every living thing: trees grow and thrust forth their fruit in due season, because the food is dispersed into every part of them from the lowest roots through the stems and all the branches. Noises creep through walls and fly through the shut places in the house, stiffening cold works its way to the bones: but were there no empty spaces, along which each of these bodies might pass, you would not see this come to pass by any means. Again, why do we see one thing surpass another in weight, when

1. Without void motion is impossible.

2. Void accounts for the perviousness of seeming solids,

3. and differences

its size is no whit bigger? For if there is as much body
in a bale of wool as in lead, it is natural it should weigh
as much, since 'tis the office of body to press all things
downwards, but on the other hand the nature of void
remains without weight. So because it is just as big, yet
seems lighter, it tells us, we may be sure, that it has more
void; but on the other hand the heavier thing avows
that there is more body in it and that it contains far less
empty space within. Therefore, we may be sure, that
which we are seeking with keen reasoning, does exist
mingled in things—that which we call void. in weight in
bodies of
equal size.

Herein lest that which some vainly imagine[n] should
avail to lead you astray from the truth, I am constrained
to forestall it. They say that the waters give place to
the scaly creatures as they press forward and open up
a liquid path, because the fishes leave places behind, to
which the waters may flow together as they yield: and
that even so other things too can move among themselves
and change place, albeit the whole is solid. In very
truth this is all believed on false reasoning. For whither,
I ask, will the scaly creatures be able to move forward,
unless the waters have left an empty space? again, whither
will the waters be able to give place, when the fishes cannot
go forward? either then we must deny motion to every
body, or we must say that void is mixed with things, from
which each thing can receive the first start of movement.
Lastly, if two broad bodies leap asunder quickly from
a meeting, surely it must needs be that air seizes upon all
the void, which comes to be between the bodies. Still,
however rapid the rush with which it streams together
as its currents hasten round, yet in one instant the whole
empty space cannot be filled: for it must needs be that

The false
theory of
motion
without
void.

1. How can
things move
without
room to go
to?

2. There is
a momen-
tary void
between
two re-
bounding
bodies.

it fills each place as it comes, and then at last all the

False idea of
the con-
densation
of air:

room is taken up. But if by chance any one thinks [n] that
when bodies have leapt apart, then this comes to be
because the air condenses, he goes astray ; for in that
case that becomes empty which was not so before, and

which is
impossible
without
void.

again that is filled which was empty before, nor can air
condense in such a way, nor, if indeed it could, could it,
I trow, without void draw into itself and gather into
one all its parts.

The
growth of
knowledge.

Wherefore, however long you hang back with much
objection, you must needs confess at last that there is
void in things. And besides by telling you many an
instance, I can heap up proof for my words. But these
light footprints are enough for a keen mind : by them
you may detect the rest for yourself. For as dogs rang-
ing over mountains often find by scent the lairs of wild
beasts shrouded under leafage, when once they are set
on sure traces of their track, so for yourself you will be
able in such themes as this to see one thing after another,
to win your way to all the secret places and draw out
the truth thence. But if you are slack or shrink a little
from my theme, this I can promise you, Memmius, on
my own word : so surely will my sweet tongue pour forth
to you bounteous draughts from the deep well-springs
out of the treasures of my heart, that I fear lest sluggish
age creep over our limbs and loosen within us the fastenings of life, before that the whole store of proofs on one
single theme be launched in my verses into your ears.

The two
natures,
matter and
void.

But now, to weave again at the web, which is the task
of my discourse, all nature then, as it is of itself, is
built of these two things : for there are bodies and the

void, in which they are placed and where they move
hither and thither. For that body exists is declared by
the feeling which all share alike ; and unless faith in this
feeling be firmly grounded at once and prevail, there will
be naught to which we can make appeal about things
hidden, so as to prove aught by the reasoning of the
mind. And next, were there not room and empty space,
which we call void, nowhere could bodies be placed, nor
could they wander at all hither and thither in any direction ; and this I have above shown to you but a little
while before. Besides these there is nothing which you *There is no*
could say is parted from all body and sundered from void, *third*
which could be discovered, as it were a third nature in *nature.*
the list. For whatever shall exist, must needs be something *1. Touch*
in itself ; and if it suffer touch, however small and light, it *shows*
will increase the count of body by a bulk great or maybe *matter,*
small, if it exists at all, and be added to its sum. But *intangi-*
if it is not to be touched, inasmuch as it cannot on *bility void.*
any side check anything from wandering through it and *2. Body*
passing on its way, in truth it will be that which we call *acts or*
empty void. Or again, whatsoever exists by itself, will *suffers :*
either do something or suffer itself while other things *void is the*
act upon it, or it will be such that things may exist and *field of*
go on in it. But nothing can do or suffer without body, *action.*
nor afford room again, unless it be void and empty space.
And so besides void and bodies no third nature by itself
can be left in the list of things, which might either at
any time fall within the purview of our senses, or be
grasped by any one through reasoning of the mind.

For all things that have a name, you will find either *Properties*
properties linked to these two things or you will see them *and*
to be their accidents. That is a property which in no *Accidents.*

case can be sundered or separated without the fatal disunion of the thing, as is weight to rocks, heat to fire,
moisture to water, touch to all bodies, intangibility to
the void.   On the other hand, slavery, poverty, riches,
liberty, war, concord, and other things by whose coming
and going the nature of things abides untouched, these
Time is not we are used, as is natural, to call accidents. Even so
a separate
existence, time exists not by itself,[n] but from actual things comes
but an
accident of a feeling, what was brought to a close in time past, then
things. what is present now, and further what is going to be hereafter.   And it must be avowed that no man feels time
by itself apart from the motion or quiet rest of things.
False Then again, when men say [n] that ' the rape of Tyndarus's
argument
from past daughter ', or ' the vanquishing of the Trojan tribes in
events,
because the war ' are things, beware that they do not perchance con-
persons,
whose strain us to avow that these things exist in themselves, just
accidents
they were, because the past ages have carried off beyond recall those
are no more. races of men, of whom, in truth, these were the accidents.
But For firstly, we might well say that whatsoever has happened
1. they
may be is an accident in one case of the countries, in another even
called
accidents of the regions of space. Or again, if there had been no sub-
of places ; stance of things nor place and space, in which all things
2. without
matter and are carried on, never would the flame of love have been
space, they fired by the beauty of Tyndaris, nor swelling deep in the
could not
have Phrygian heart of Alexander have kindled the burning
occurred ; battles of savage war, nor unknown of the Trojans would
the timber horse have set Pergama aflame at dead of
night, when the sons of the Greeks issued from its womb.
So that you may see clearly that all events from first to
last do not exist, and are not by themselves like body,
nor can they be spoken of in the same way as the being

of the void, but rather so that you might justly call them the accidents of body and place, in which they are carried on, one and all.

Bodies, moreover, are in part the first-beginnings of things, in part those which are created by the union of first-beginnings. Now the true first-beginnings of things, no force can quench; for they by their solid body prevail in the end. Albeit it seems hard to believe that there can be found among things anything of solid body. For the thunderbolt of heaven passes through walled houses, as do shouts and cries; iron grows white hot in the flame, and stones seethe in fierce fire and leap asunder; then too the hardness of gold is relaxed and softened by heat, and the ice of brass yields beneath the flame and melts; warmth and piercing cold ooze through silver, since when we have held cups duly in our hands we have felt both alike, when the dewy moisture of water was poured in from above. So true is it that in things there is seen to be nothing solid. But yet because true reasoning and the nature of things constrains us, give heed, until in a few verses we set forth that there are things which exist with solid and everlasting body, which we show to be the seeds of things and their first-beginnings, out of which the whole sum of things now stands created.

First, since we have found existing a twofold nature of things far differing, the nature of body and of space, in which all things take place, it must needs be that each exists alone by itself and unmixed. For wherever space lies empty, which we call the void, body is not there; moreover, wherever body has its station, there is by no means empty void. Therefore the first bodies are solid and free from void. Moreover, since there is void in

B. The ultimate particles are solid and eternal atoms.

Proofs.

1. Void and body are mutually exclusive.

2. Body must be solid to enclose void.

things created, solid matter must needs stand all round, nor can anything by true reasoning be shown to hide void in its body and hold it within, except you grant that what keeps it in is solid. Now it can be nothing but a union of matter, which could keep in the void in things. Matter then, which exists with solid body, can be ever-lasting, when all else is dissolved. Next, if there were nothing which was empty and void, the whole would be solid; unless on the other hand there were bodies determined, to fill all the places that they held, the whole universe would be but empty void space. Body, then, we may be sure, is marked off from void turn and turn about, since there is neither a world utterly full nor yet quite empty. There are therefore bodies determined, such as can mark off void space from what is full. These cannot be broken up when hit by blows from without, nor again can they be pierced to the heart and undone, nor by any other way can they be assailed and made to totter; all of which I have above shown to you but a little while before. For it is clear that nothing could be crushed in without void, or broken or cleft in twain by cutting, nor admit moisture nor likewise spreading cold or piercing flame, whereby all things are brought to their end. And the more each thing keeps void within it, the more is it assailed to the heart by these things and begins to totter. Therefore, if the first bodies are solid and free from void, as I have shown, they must be everlasting. Moreover, if matter had not been everlasting, ere this all things had wholly passed away to nothing, and all that we see had been born again from nothing. But since I have shown above that nothing can be created from nothing, nor can what has been begotten be summoned

3. Body is that which distin-guishes the full from the void;

it cannot be broken and is there-fore eternal.

4. Other-wise all things would ere now have perished.

back to nothing, the first-beginnings must needs be of immortal body, into which at their last day all things can be dissolved, that there may be matter enough for renewing things. Therefore the first-beginnings are of solid singleness, nor in any other way can they be preserved through the ages from infinite time now gone and renew things.

Again, if nature had ordained[n] no limit to the breaking of things, by now the bodies of matter would have been so far brought low by the breaking of ages past, that nothing could be conceived out of them within a fixed time, and pass on to the full measure of its life; for we see that anything you will is more easily broken up than put together again. Wherefore what the long limitless age of days, the age of all time that is gone by, had broken ere now, disordering and dissolving, could never be renewed in all time that remains. But as it is, a set limit to breaking has, we may be sure, been appointed, since we see each thing put together again, and at the same time fixed seasons ordained for all things after their kind, in the which they may be able to reach the flower of their life. There is this too that, though the first-bodies of matter are quite solid, yet we can give account of all the soft things that come to be, air, water, earth, fires, by what means they come to being, and by what force each goes on its way, when once void has been mingled in things. But on the other hand, if the first-beginnings of things were to be soft, it will not be possible to give account whence hard flints and iron can be created; for from the first all nature will lack a first-beginning of foundation. There are then bodies that prevail in their

5. If there were no limit to division, things could not reach maturity in due season, and destruction would now have gone past repair.

6. Solid bodies with void can make soft things: the reverse is impossible.

solid singleness, **by** whose more close-packed union all things can be riveted and reveal their stalwart strength.

7. If there are not atoms, things themselves must be eternal, which is clearly untrue. Moreover, if no limit has been appointed to the breaking of things, still it must needs be that all the bodies of things survive even now from time everlasting, such that they cannot yet have been assailed by any danger. But since they exist endowed with a frail nature, it is not in harmony with this that they have been able to abide for everlasting time harried through all the ages by countless blows.

8. Eternal atoms account for the persistence of species. Once again, since there has been appointed for all things after their kind a limit of growing and of maintaining life, and inasmuch as it stands ordained what all things severally can do by the laws of nature, and what too they cannot, nor is anything so changed, but that all things stand so fast that the diverse birds all in their due order show that the marks of their kind are on their body, they must also, we may be sure, have a body of unchanging substance. For if the first-beginnings of things could be vanquished in any way and changed, then, too, would it be doubtful what might come to being, what might not, yea, in what way each thing has its power limited and its deepset boundary-stone, nor could the tribes each after their kind so often recall the nature, habits, manner of life and movements of the parents.

9. The analogy of perceptible extremities Then, further, since there are extreme points [n], one after another ⟨on bodies, which are the least things we can see, likewise, too, there must be a least point⟩[1] on

---

[1] Two lines are probably lost here, the sense of which has been admirably restored by Munro :

corporibus, quod iam nobis minimum esse videtur,
debet item ratione pari minimum esse cacumen

that body, which our senses can no longer descry ; that point, we may be sure, exists without parts and is endowed with the least nature, nor was it ever sundered apart by itself nor can it so be hereafter, since it is itself but a part of another and that the first single part : then other like parts and again others in order in close array make up the nature of the first body, and since they cannot exist by themselves, it must needs be that they stay fast there whence they cannot by any means be torn away.   The first-beginnings then are of solid single-ness ; for they are a close dense mass of least parts, never put together out of a union of those parts, but rather prevailing in everlasting singleness ; from them nature, keeping safe the seeds of things, suffers not anything to be torn away, nor ever to be removed.   Moreover, if there be not a least thing, all the tiniest bodies will be composed of infinite parts, since indeed the half of a half will always have a half, nor will anything set a limit.   What differ-ence then will there be between the sum of things and the least of things?   There will be no difference ; for however completely the whole sum be infinite, yet things that are tiniest will be composed of infinite parts just the same.   And since true reasoning cries out against this, and denies that the mind can believe it, you must be vanquished and confess that there are those things which consist of no parts at all and are of the least nature. And since these exist, those first-beginnings too you must needs own are solid and everlasting.   And again, if nature, the creatress, had been used to constrain all things to be dissolved into their least parts, then she could not again renew aught of them, for the reason that things which

Marginal notes:

proves the solid single-ness of the atoms.

10. Unless there is a ' least part ' the universe and the smallest thing are equal.

11. The least parts, if separated, could not produce things.

are not enlarged by any parts, have not those powers which must belong to creative matter, the diverse fastenings, weights, blows, meetings, movements, by which all things are carried on.

C. False
theories.
That one
element is
the primal
substance.
Heraclitus's
doctrine of
fire.

Wherefore those who have thought that fire is the substance of things, and that the whole sum is composed of fire alone, are seen to fall very far from true reasoning. Heraclitus[n] is their leader who first enters the fray, of bright fame for his dark sayings, yet rather among the empty-headed than among the Greeks of weight, who seek after the truth. For fools laud and love all things more which they can descry hidden beneath twisted sayings, and they set up for true what can tickle the ear with a pretty sound and is tricked out with a smart ring.

1. It does
not account
for the
variety of
things.

For I am eager to know how things could be so diverse, if they are created of fire alone and unmixed. For it would be of no avail that hot fire should condense or grow rare, if the parts of fire had the same nature which the whole sum of fire has as well. For fiercer would be the flame, if the parts were drawn together, and weaker again, were they sundered and scattered. But further than this there is nothing which you can think might come to pass from such a cause, far less might the great diversity of things come from fires condensed and rare.

2. He
denies the
void and so
vitiates his
own theory.

This too there is : if they were to hold that void is mingled in things, the fires will be able to condense or be left rare. But because they see many things to thwart them, they hold their peace and shrink from allowing void unmixed among things ;[1] while they fear the heights, they lose the true track, nor again do they perceive that, if void be removed from things, all things must condense

[1] Read *mussant* and place semicolon after *purum*, l. 658.

and be made one body out of many, such as could not
send out anything from it in hot haste ; even as fire that
brings warmth casts abroad light and heat, so that you
may see that it has not parts close-packed. But if per- **3. Fire ever**
chance they believe that in some other way fires may be **changing to**
other things
quenched in union and alter their substance, in very **means**
truth if they do not spare to do this at any point, then, **ultimate**
destruction.
we may be sure, all heat will perish utterly to nothing,
and all things created will come to be out of nothing.
For whenever a thing changes and passes out of its own
limits, straightway this is the death of that which was
before.   Indeed something must needs be left untouched
to those fires, lest you find all things returning utterly to
nothing, and the store of things born again and growing
strong out of nothing. As it is then, since there are **The true**
certain bodies most determined which keep nature safe **atomic**
view.
ever the same, through whose coming and going and shifting order things change their nature and bodies are
altered, you can be sure that these first-bodies of things
are not of fire. For it would be no matter that some
should give place and pass away, and others be added,
and some changed in order, if despite this all retained
the nature of heat ; for whatever they might create
would be in every way fire. But, I trow, the truth is
this ; there are certain bodies, whose meetings, movements, order, position, and shapes make fires, and when
their order changes, they change their nature, and they
are not made like to fire nor to any other thing either,
which is able to send off bodies to our senses and touch
by collision our sense of touch.

Moreover, to say that fire is all things, and that there **4. Hera-**
is no other real thing in the whole count of things, but **clitus**

impugns the
senses.
only fire, as this same Heraclitus does, seems to be raving frenzy. For on behalf of the senses he fights himself against the senses, and undermines those on which all that he believes must hang, whereby he himself has come to know that which he names fire. For he believes that the senses can know fire aright, but not all other things, which are no whit less bright to see. And this seems to me alike idle and frenzied. For to what shall we appeal? What can be surer for us than the senses themselves, 5. Why
choose fire? whereby we may mark off things true and false? Besides, why should any one rather annul all things, and wish to leave only the nature of heat, than deny that fire exists, and grant in its stead that another nature exists? For it seems equal madness to say the one or the other.

That (a)
other ele-
ments are
the primal
substance,
Wherefore those who have thought that fire is the substance of things, and that the whole sum may be built of fire, and those who have set up air as the first-beginning for the begetting of things, or again all who have thought that moisture fashions things alone by itself, or that earth creates all and passes into all the natures of things, or (b) a combination of
two, or (c)
of four. seem to have strayed very far away from the truth. Add to them too those who make the first-beginnings of things twofold, linking air to fire or earth to water, and those who think that all can grow up out of four things, fire, earth, wind, and rain. Of them in the forefront comes Empe-
docles. Empedocles of Acragas; him that island [1] bore within the three-cornered coasts of its lands, around which flows the Ionian ocean, with many a winding inlet, splashing salt foam from its green waves, while with narrow strait a tearing sea sunders with its waves the coasts of Italy's lands from the island-borders. Here is devastating Charybdis, and here the rumblings of Aetna threaten

to gather once more the flames of its wrath, that again
in its might it may belch forth the fires bursting from its
throat, and once more dash to the sky its flashing flames.
And though this mighty country seems in many ways
marvellous to the tribes of men, and is said to deserve
seeing, rich in goodly things, and strengthened with
a mighty wealth of men, yet it is seen to have held nothing
in it more glorious than this man, nothing more holy,
more marvellous and loved. Nay, the songs of his godlike heart lift up their voice and set forth his glorious
discoveries, so that he seems scarce born of human
stock.[n]

Yet he and those whom I named before, weaker than
he by exceeding many degrees, and far beneath him,
though they discovered much in good, nay godlike fashion,
and gave answers as from the shrine of their hearts in
more holy wise and with reasoning far more sure than
the Pythian priestess who speaks out from the tripod and
laurel of Phoebus, yet in the first-beginnings of things
they came to grief : great were they, and great and heavy
their fall therein. First because they take away the void
from things, but suppose movement, and leave things
soft and rare, air, sunlight, fire, earth, beasts, and crops,
and yet mingle no void in their body. Then because they
hold that there is no limit at all to the cutting of bodies,
that no halting-place is set to their breaking, nor again is
there any least among things. And that when we see
that there is that extreme point in each thing, which is
seen to be the least to our senses, so that you can infer
from this that the extreme point in things which you
cannot see is the least in them. Then follows this

Errors of Empedocles and his school :

1. they deny the void ;

2. they set no limit to division ;

3. their
elements
are soft

that, since they suppose the first-beginnings of things
soft, things which we see come to birth and endowed
throughout with a mortal body, the whole sum of things
must then return to naught, and the store of things be
born again, and grow strong out of nothing. And how
far both this and that are from the truth, you will know

4. and
pernicious
to one
another.

by now. Then again, these things are in many ways
hostile, nay poison, the one to the other ; therefore
either when they meet they will pass away, or they will
so fly apart, as when a storm gathers we see the thunderbolts and rain and wind fly asunder.

5. Why not
call things
the primal
substance
of the
elements ?

Again, if from four things all are created and all again
are dissolved into those things, how can they be called
the first-beginnings of things any more than things the
first-beginnings of them, with our thought reversed ? For
they are begotten turn by turn, and change their colour
and all their nature one with the other from all time

6. or, if the
elements do
not change
in com-
pounds,
what else
could they
create ?

onward. But if perchance you think that the body of
fire and the body of earth and the breezes of the air and
the dewy moisture so unite, that in union no one of them
changes its nature, you will see that nothing can be
created out of them, no, not a living thing, nor one with
lifeless body, like a tree. Indeed in the mingling of this
diverse mass each thing will reveal its own nature, and air
will be seen to be mixed together with earth, and heat to
cleave to moisture. But first-beginnings ought in the
begetting of things to bring to bear a secret and unseen
nature, that nothing may stand out which might bar and
thwart whatever is created from existing with its own
true being.

7. The
flux of the

But indeed they trace it back to heaven and heaven's
fires, and hold that fire first turns itself into the breezes

of the sky, that thence is begotten rain, and of rain is elements
destroys
perma-
nence; created earth, and then all things pass back again from earth, first moisture, next air, then heat, and that these things never cease their mutual changes, in their path from heaven to earth, from earth to the stars of the firmament. But the first-beginnings ought in no wise to do this. For it must needs be that something abides unchangeable, that all things be not altogether brought to naught. For whenever a thing changes and passes out of its own limits, straightway this is the death of that which was before. Wherefore since the things we have named a little before pass into a state of interchange, they must needs be made of other things, which cannot in any case be altered, lest you find all things returning altogether to naught. Why not rather suppose that there are certain bodies endowed with such a nature, and that, if by chance they have created fire, they can too, when a few are removed and a few added, and their order and movement is changed, make the breezes of the sky, and that thus all things are changed one into another?

'But,' you say, 'the facts show clearly that all things are nourished and grow from the earth up into the breezes of the sky; and unless the season at a propitious time fosters them with rain, so that the trees rock beneath the outpouring of the storm-clouds, and the sun for its part cherishes them, and bestows its heat on them, crops, trees, living creatures, none could grow.' Yes, in very truth, unless we too were nurtured by dry food and soft moisture, we should lose our flesh, and all the life too would be loosened from all our sinews and bones. For beyond all doubt we are nurtured and nourished upon things determined, and other things again, each in their turn, 8. the
argument
from the
presence of
the four
elements in
growth; its true
atomic ex-
planation.

on things determined.   Yea, we may be sure, it is because
many first-beginnings common in many ways to many
things are mingled among things, that so diverse things
are nourished on diverse food.   And often it is of great
matter with what others those first-beginnings are bound
up, and in what position, and what movements they
mutually give and receive ; for the same build up sky,
sea, earth, rivers, sun, the same too crops, trees, living
creatures, but only when mingled with different things
and moving in different ways.   Indeed scattered abroad
in my verses you see many letters common to many
words, and yet you must needs grant that verses and
words are unlike both in sense and in the ring of their
sound.   So great is the power of letters by a mere change
of order.   But the first-beginnings of things can bring
more means to bear, by which all diverse things may be
created.

The homoeo-meria of Anaxa-goras :

Now let us also search into the homoeomeria of Anaxagoras,[n] as the Greeks term it, though the poverty of our
country's speech does not suffer us to name it in our
own tongue ; nevertheless the thing itself it is easy to
set forth in words.   First—what he calls the homoeo-
meria of things—you must know that he thinks that
bones are made of very small and tiny bones, and flesh
of small and tiny pieces of flesh, and blood is created of
many drops of blood coming together in union, and that
gold again can be built up of grains of gold, and the earth
grow together out of little earths, that fire is made of fires,
and water of water-drops, and all the rest he pictures and

1. he denies the void ;

imagines in the same way.   And yet he does not allow
that there is void in things on any side, nor that there is
a limit to the cutting up of bodies.   Therefore in this

point and that he seems to me to go astray just as they
did, of whom I told above. Add too to this that he
pictures his first-beginnings too weak : if indeed those
are first-beginnings, which exist endowed with a nature
like things themselves, which suffer none the less, and
pass away, nor does anything rein them back from their
destruction. For which of them all will hold out beneath
strong pressure, so as to escape death in the very jaws of
destruction? fire or moisture or breeze? which of these?
blood or bones? Not one, I trow, when everything alike
will be altogether as mortal as the things we see clearly
before our eyes vanquished by some violence and passing
away. But that things cannot fall away into nothing,
nor again grow from nothing, I call to witness what
I have before now proved. Moreover, since 'tis food
that increases and nourishes the body, you may know that
our veins and blood and bones ⟨and sinews are created of
parts alien in kind⟩ ;[1] or if they say that all foods are of
mingled substance, and have in them little bodies of
sinews, and bones and indeed veins and portions of gore,
then it will be that all food, both dry, yes and liquid too,
must be thought to consist of things alien in kind, of
bones and sinews and matter and blood mingled together.
Moreover, if all bodies that grow from out the earth are
in the earth, the earth must be composed of things alien
in kind, which rise up out of the earth. Shift this to
another field, you may use the same words again. If in
logs flame lurks hidden, and smoke and ash, it must needs
be that the logs are composed of things alien in kind.
Moreover, all the bodies which the earth nourishes, it

*2. he sets
no limit to
division ;*

*3. his first
particles are
soft ;*

*4. he does
not account
for change.*

---

[1] Lambinus supplied the sense of a missing verse :
et nervos alienigenis ex partibus esse.

increases ⟨from things alien in kind, which rise up out
of the earth. So too the bodies which logs emit, are
nourished⟩ [1] upon things alien in kind, which rise up out
of the logs.

*Anaxa-
goras's eva-
sion : ' all
things are
in all
things ' ;*

Herein there is left a slight chance of hiding from
justice, which Anaxagoras grasps for himself, to hold that
all things are mingled, though in hiding, in all things,
but that that one thing comes out clear, whereof there are
most parts mingled in, stationed more ready to view and
in the forefront. But this is very far banished from true
reasoning. For it were right then that corn also, when

*then they
ought to
appear.*

crushed by the threatening strength of rock, should often
give out some sign of blood, or one of those things which
are nourished in our body, and that when we rub it with
stone on stone, gore should ooze forth. In the same way
it were fitting that blades of grass too and pools of water
should often give out sweet drops with a savour like the
richness of the milk of fleecy beasts, and that often when
sods of earth are crumbled, kinds of grasses and corn and
leaves should be seen, hiding in tiny form, scattered about
among the earth, lastly that ash and smoke should be seen
in logs, when they were broken off, and tiny flames in
hiding. But since facts clearly show that none of these
things comes to pass, you may be sure that things are not
so mingled in other things, but that seeds common to
many things lie mingled and hidden in things in many
ways.

*The argu-
ment from
forest con-
flagrations.*

' But often on mighty mountains it comes to pass,'
you say, ' that the neighbouring tops of tall trees rub

[1] Two lines seem to be lost here, of which Munro has supplied the
sense :

> ex alienigenis, quae terris exoriuntur.
> sic itidem quae ligna emittunt corpora, aluntur

together, when the strong south winds constrain them
to it, until at last a flowery flame gathers, and they blaze
with fire.' And yet you must know that fire is not
implanted in their wood, but there are many seeds of
heat, which when they have flowed together through the
rubbing, create fires in the forests. But if the flame had
been hidden away ready-made in the forests, the fires
could not have been concealed for any time, they would
consume the forests one and all, and burn the trees to
ashes. Do you not then see now, what I said but a little
while ago, that it is of very great matter often with what
others those same first-beginnings are bound up, and in
what position, and what movements they mutually give
and receive, and that the same a little changed with one
another can create beams or flames? Even as the words
themselves have their letters but little changed, when
with sound distinct we signify beams or flames. Once
again, if you think that all that you can descry in things
clear to be seen cannot come to being, but that you must
suppose first-bodies of matter endowed with a nature
like the whole, by this reasoning you see the first-beginnings of things pass away. Nay, it will come to be that
they will be shaken with quivering mirth and laugh aloud,
and wet face and cheeks with salt tears.

The true atomic explanation.

Reductio ad absurdum.

Come now, learn what remains, and listen to clearer
words. Nor do I fail to see in mind how dark are the
ways; but a great hope has smitten my heart with the
sharp spur of fame, and at once has struck into my breast
the sweet love of the muses, whereby now inspired with
strong mind I traverse the distant haunts of the Pierides,
never trodden before by the foot of man. 'Tis my joy
to approach those untasted springs and drink my fill, 'tis

D. Lucretius's mission.

my joy to pluck new flowers and gather a glorious coronal for my head from spots whence before the muses have never wreathed the forehead of any man. First because I teach about great things, and hasten to free the mind from the close bondage of religion, then because on a dark theme I trace verses so full of light, touching all with the muses' charm. For that too is seen to be not without good reason ; but even as healers, when they essay to give loathsome wormwood to children, first touch the rim all round the cup with the sweet golden moisture of honey, so that the unwitting age of children may be beguiled as far as the lips, and meanwhile may drink the bitter draught of wormwood, and though charmed may not be harmed, but rather by such means may be restored and come to health ; so now, since this philosophy full often seems too bitter to those who have not tasted it, and the multitude shrinks back away from it, I have desired to set forth to you my reasoning in the sweet-tongued song of the muses, and as though to touch it with the pleasant honey of poetry, if perchance I might avail by such means to keep your mind set upon my verses, while you come to see the whole nature of things, what is its shape and figure.

The problem of infinity.

But since I have taught that the most solid bodies of matter fly about for ever unvanquished through the ages, come now, let us unfold, whether there be a certain limit to their full sum or not ; and likewise the void that we have discovered, or room or space, in which all things are carried on, let us see clearly whether it is all altogether bounded or spreads out limitless and immeasurably deep.

There is no limit to the sum of things.

a. The universe is

The whole universe then is bounded in no direction of its ways ; for then it would be bound to have an extreme

point.   Now it is seen that nothing can have an extreme
point, unless there be something beyond to bound it,
so that there is seen to be a spot further than which the
nature of our sense cannot follow it.   As it is, since we
must admit that there is nothing outside the whole sum,
it has not an extreme point, it lacks therefore bound and
limit.   Nor does it matter in which quarter of it you
take your stand ; so true is it that, whatever place every
man takes up, he leaves the whole boundless just as much
on every side.   Moreover, suppose now[n] that all space
were created finite, if one were to run on to the end, to
its furthest coasts, and throw a flying dart, would you
have it that that dart, hurled with might and main, goes
on whither it is sped and flies afar, or do you think that
something can check and bar its way?   For one or the
other you must needs admit and choose.   Yet both shut
off your escape and constrain you to grant that the
universe spreads out free from limit.   For whether there
is something to check it and bring it about that it arrives
not whither it was sped, nor plants itself in the goal, or
whether it fares forward, it set not forth from the end.
In this way I will press on, and wherever you shall set the
furthest coasts, I shall ask what then becomes of the dart.
It will come to pass that nowhere can a bound be set and
room for flight ever prolongs the chance of flight.   Lastly,
before our eyes one thing is seen to bound another ; air
is as a wall between the hills, and mountains between
tracts of air, land bounds the sea, and again sea bounds
all lands ; yet the universe in truth there is nothing to
limit outside.

Moreover, if all the space in the whole universe were
shut in on all sides, and were created with borders deter-

(marginal notes)

infinite :
1. for it has no bound-ing point ;

2. experi-ment of the hurled dart;

3. the sensible world bears no analogy.

b. Space is infinite :

otherwise
matter
would
collect at
the bottom.

mined, and had been bounded, then the store of matter
would have flowed together with solid weight from all
sides to the bottom, nor could anything be carried on
beneath the canopy of the sky, nor would there be sky at
all, nor the light of the sun, since in truth all matter
would lie idle piled together by sinking down from limitless time.   But as it is, no rest, we may be sure, has been
granted to the bodies of the first-beginnings, because
there is no bottom at all, whither they may, as it were,
flow together, and make their resting-place.   All things
are for ever carried on in ceaseless movement from all
sides, and bodies of matter are even stirred up and
supplied from beneath out of limitless space.   The nature
of room then and the space of the deep is such that neither
could the bright thunderbolts course through it in their
career, gliding on through the everlasting tract of time,
nor bring it about that there remain a whit less to traverse
as they travel ; so far on every side spreads out huge room
for things, free from limit in all directions everywhere.

c. Matter
is infinite:

Nay more, nature ordains that the sum of things may
not have power to set a limit to itself, since she constrains
body to be bounded by void, and all that is void to be
bounded by body, so that thus she makes the universe
infinite by their interchange, or else at least one of the
two, if the other of them bound it not, yet spreads out
immeasurable with nature unmixed.   〈But space I have

otherwise
things
could not
last

taught above spreads out without limit.   If then the
sum of matter were bounded,〉[1] neither sea nor earth nor
the gleaming quarters of heaven nor the race of mortal

---

[1] Munro again has well supplied the sense of two lost lines :

> sed spatium supra docui sine fine patere.
> si finita igitur summa esset materiai,

men, nor the hallowed bodies of the gods could exist for the short space of an hour. For driven apart from its unions the store of matter would be carried all dissolved or even through the great void, or rather in truth it could never have been have grown together and given birth to anything, since created. scattered abroad it could not have been brought to meet For in very truth, not by design did the first-beginnings Our world of things place themselves each in their order with fore- was not seeing mind, nor indeed did they make compact what formed by movements each should start, but because many of them but by the shifting in many ways throughout the world are harried movements and buffeted by blows from limitless time, by trying of atoms. movements and unions of every kind, at last they fall into such dispositions as those, whereby our world of things is created and holds together. And it too, pre- served from harm through many a mighty cycle of years, when once it has been cast into the movements suited to its being, brings it about that the rivers replenish the greedy sea with the bounteous waters of their streams, and the earth, fostered by the sun's heat, renews its in- crease, and the race of living things flourishes, sent up from her womb, and the gliding fires of heaven are alive; all this they would in no wise do, unless store of matter might rise up from limitless space, out of which they are used to renew all their losses in due season. For even as the nature of living things, robbed of food, loses its flesh and pines away, so all things must needs be dissolved, when once matter has ceased to come for their supply, turned aside in any way from its due course. Nor can blows Its preser- from without on all sides keep together the whole of each vation by world which has come together in union. For they can without. smite on it once and again, and keep a part in place, until others come, and the sum may be supplied. Yet sometimes they are constrained to rebound and at once afford space and time for flight to the first-beginnings of things, so that they can pass away freed from union. Therefore, again and again, it must be that many things rise up, yea, and in order that even the blows too may not fail, there must needs be limitless mass of matter on all sides.

Necessity of infinity of matter.

Herein shrink far from believing,[n] Memmius, what some say: that all things press towards the centre of a sum, and that 'tis for this cause that the nature of the world stands fast without any blows from outside, and that top and bottom cannot part asunder in any direction, because all things are pressing upon the centre (if indeed you can believe that anything can stand upon itself) : and that all heavy things which are beneath the earth press upwards, and rest placed upside down upon the earth, like the images of things which we see, as it is, through water. And in the same way they maintain that living things walk head downwards, and cannot fall off the earth into the spaces of heaven beneath them any more than our bodies can of their free will fly up into the quarters of heaven : that when they see the sun, we are descrying the stars of night, and that they share with us turn by turn the seasons of the sky, and pass nights equal to our days.[1] But empty error has commended these false ideas to fools, because they embrace and hold a theory with twisted reasoning. For there can be no centre, since the universe is created infinite. Nor, if indeed there were a centre, could anything at all rest there any more for

False theory of Stoics: the world is held together by centripetal force.

Its absurdities.

---

[1] The next eight lines are omitted or mutilated in the MSS., but once more Munro's restoration must give the sense, and probably something very near the actual words.

that, rather than be driven away for some far different reason : for all room and space, which we call void, must through centre or not-centre give place alike to heavy bodies, wherever their motions tend. Nor is there any place, to which when bodies have come, they can lose the force of their weight and stand still in the void ; nor must aught that is void support anything, but rather hasten to give place, as its own nature desires. It cannot be then that things can be held together in union in such a way, constrained by a yearning for the centre.

Moreover, since they do not pretend that all bodies press towards the centre, but only those of earth and liquid, the moisture of the sea and mighty waters from the mountains, and those things which are, as it were, enclosed in an earthy frame ; but on the other hand, they teach that the thin breezes of air and hot fires at the same time are carried away from the centre, and that for this cause all the sky around is twinkling with stars, and the flame of the sun is fed through the blue tracts of heaven, because all the heat fleeing from the centre gathers itself together there : nor again can the topmost branches grow leafy upon trees, unless from the earth little by little each has food ⟨supplied by nature, their thoughts are not at harmony with themselves. There must then be an infinite store of matter⟩,[1] lest after the winged way of flames the walls of the world suddenly fly apart, dissolved through the great void, and lest all else follow them in like manner, or the thundering quarters of

Its inconsistency ; for not all things seek the centre.

Without infinite matter, the world would be destroyed.

---

[1] The best MS. marks eight lines lost here, corresponding to the mutilation above : the words in brackets would give the general sense, as suggested by Munro.

the sky fall down from above, and the earth in hot haste withdraw itself from beneath our feet, and amid all the mingled ruin of things on earth and of the sky, whereby the frames of bodies are loosed, it pass away through the deep void, so that in an instant of time not a wrack be left behind, except emptied space and unseen first-beginnings. For on whatever side you maintain that the bodies fail first, this side will be the gate of death for things, by this path will all the throng of matter cast itself abroad.

Progress in learning.

These things you will learn thus, led on with little trouble ; for one thing after another shall grow clear, nor will blind night snatch away your path from you, but that you shall see all the utmost truths of nature : so shall things kindle a light for others.

BOOK II

Sweet it is, when on the great sea the winds are buffet- Introducing the waters, to gaze from the land on another's great tion : the
struggles ; not because it is pleasure or joy that any one calm
should be distressed, but because it is sweet to perceive heights of
from what misfortune you yourself are free. Sweet is it philosophy.
too, to behold great contests of war in full array over the
plains, when you have no part in the danger. But nothing
is more gladdening than to dwell in the calm high places,
firmly embattled on the heights by the teaching of the
wise, whence you can look down on others, and see them
wandering hither and thither, going astray as they seek
the way of life, in strife matching their wits or rival claims
of birth, struggling night and day by surpassing effort to
rise up to the height of power and gain possession of the
world. Ah ! miserable minds of men, blind hearts ! in
what darkness of life, in what great dangers ye spend
this little span of years ! to think that ye should not see
that nature cries aloud for nothing else but that pain may Nature's
be kept far sundered from the body, and that, withdrawn needs
from care and fear, she may enjoy in mind the sense of
pleasure ! And so we see that for the body's nature but for the
few things at all are needful, even such as can take away body
pain. Yea, though pleasantly enough from time to time
they can prepare for us in many ways a lap of luxury, yet
nature herself feels no loss, if there are not golden images
of youths about the halls, grasping fiery torches in their
right hands, that light may be supplied to banquets at

night, if the house does not glow with silver or gleam with gold, nor do fretted and gilded ceilings re-echo to the lute.   And yet, for all this, men lie in friendly groups on the soft grass near some stream of water under the branches of a tall tree, and at no great cost delightfully refresh their bodies, above all when the weather smiles on them, and the season of the year bestrews the green grass with flowers.   Nor do fiery fevers more quickly quit the body, if you toss on broidered pictures and blushing purple, than if you must lie on the poor man's plaid. Wherefore since in our body riches are of no profit, nor high birth nor the glories of kingship, for the rest, we *and for the* must believe that they avail nothing for the mind as *mind.* well; unless perchance, when you see your legions swarm- *Earthly* ing over the spaces of the Campus,[n] and provoking a mimic *power and* war, strengthened with hosts in reserve and forces of *the terrors* cavalry,[1] when you draw them up equipped with arms,[2] *of Religion.* all alike eager for the fray, when you see the army wander- ing far and wide in busy haste, then alarmed by all this the scruples of religion fly in panic from your mind, or that the dread of death leaves your heart empty and free from care.   But if we see that these thoughts are mere mirth and mockery, and in very truth the fears of men and the cares that dog them fear not the clash of arms nor the weapons of war, but pass boldly among kings and lords of the world, nor dread the glitter that comes *Religion* from gold nor the bright sheen of the purple robe, can *and* you doubt that all such power belongs to reason alone, *Philosophy.* above all when the whole of life is but a struggle in dark- ness?   For even as children tremble and fear everything

---

[1] Read with Munro, *et ecum vi.*
[2] Read with Munro, *ornatasque armis statuas.*

in blinding darkness, so we sometimes dread in the light things that are no whit more to be feared than what children shudder at in the dark, and imagine will come to pass. This terror then, this darkness of the mind, must needs be scattered not by the rays of the sun and the gleaming shafts of day, but by the outer view and the inner law of nature.

Come now, I will unfold by what movement the creative bodies of matter beget diverse things, and break up those that are begotten, by what force they are constrained to do this, and what velocity is appointed them for moving through the mighty void : do you remember to give your mind to my words. For in very truth matter does not cleave close-packed to itself, since we see each thing grow less, and we perceive all things flow away, as it were, in the long lapse of time, as age withdraws them from our sight : and yet the universe is seen to remain undiminished, inasmuch as all bodies that depart from anything, lessen that from which they pass away, and bless with increase that to which they have come ; they constrain the former to grow old and the latter again to flourish, and yet they abide not with it. Thus the sum of things is ever being replenished, and mortals live one and all by give and take. Some races wax and others wane, and in a short space the tribes of living things are changed, and like runners hand on the torch of life.

If you think that the first-beginnings of things can stay still, and by staying still beget new movements in things, you stray very far away from true reasoning. For since they wander through the void,[n] it must needs be that all the first-beginnings of things move on either by their own weight or sometimes by the blow of another

A. Motion of the atoms :

the cause of successive growth and decay.

Their incessant movement Its two causes :

movement
of free
atoms in
the void;

For when quickly, again and again, they have met and
clashed together, it comes to pass that they leap asunder
at once this way and that; for indeed it is not strange,
since they are most hard with solid heavy bodies, and
nothing bars them from behind. And the more you
perceive all the bodies of matter tossing about, bring it
to mind that there is no lowest point in the whole universe, nor have the first-bodies any place where they may
come to rest, since I have shown in many words, and it
has been proved by true reasoning, that space spreads
out without bound or limit, immeasurable towards every
quarter everywhere. And since that is certain, no rest,
we may be sure, is allowed to the first-bodies moving
through the deep void, but rather plied with unceasing,
diverse motion, some when they have dashed together
leap back at great space apart, others too are thrust but

movement
of atoms in
compounds.

a short way from the blow. And all those which are
driven together in more close-packed union and leap back
but a little space apart, entangled by their own close-
locking shapes, these make the strong roots of rock and
the brute bulk of iron and all other things of their kind.
Of the rest which wander through the great void,
a few leap far apart, and recoil afar with great spaces
between; these supply for us thin air and the bright
light of the sun. Many, moreover, wander on through
the great void, which have been cast back from the unions
of things, nor have they anywhere else availed to be taken
into them and link their movements. And of this truth,
as I am telling it, a likeness and image is ever passing
presently before our eyes. For look closely, whenever

Illustration
from the

rays are let in and pour the sun's light through the dark
places in houses : for you will see many tiny bodies mingle

in many ways all through the empty space right in the motes in the
light of the rays, and as though in some everlasting strife sunbeam;
wage war and battle, struggling troop against troop, nor
ever crying a halt, harried with constant meetings and
partings; so that you may guess from this what it means
that the first-beginnings of things are for ever tossing in
the great void. So far as may be, a little thing can give a picture
a picture of great things and afford traces of a concept.[n] and an indication
And for this reason it is the more right for you to give of the unseen
heed to these bodies, which you see jostling in the sun's movements
rays, because such jostlings hint[n] that there are movements of the atoms.
of matter too beneath them, secret and unseen. For you
will see many particles there stirred by unseen blows
change their course and turn back, driven backwards on
their path, now this way, now that, in every direction
everywhere. You may know that this shifting movement comes to them all from the first-beginnings. For
first the first-beginnings of things move of themselves;
then those bodies which are formed of a tiny union, and
are, as it were, nearest to the powers of the first-beginnings,
are smitten and stirred by their unseen blows, and they in
their turn, rouse up bodies a little larger. And so the
movement passes upwards from the first-beginnings, and
little by little comes forth to our senses, so that those
bodies move too, which we can descry in the sun's light;
yet it is not clearly seen by what blows they do it.

Next, what speed of movement is given to the first- Velocity
bodies of matter, you may learn, Memmius, in a few words of the atoms.
from this. First, when dawn strews the land with new Compari-
light, and the diverse birds flitting through the distant son with sunlight,
woods across the soft air fill the place with their clear
cries, we see that it is plain and evident for all to behold

how suddenly the sun is wont at such a time to rise and
clothe all things, bathing them in his light.   And yet that
heat which the sun sends out, and that calm light of his,
is not passing through empty space ; therefore, it is constrained to go more slowly, while it dashes asunder, as it
were, the waves of air.   Nor again do the several particles[n]
of heat move on one by one, but entangled one with
another, and joined in a mass ; therefore they are at once
dragged back each by the other, and impeded from without, so that they are constrained to go more slowly.   But
the first-beginnings, which are of solid singleness, when
they pass through the empty void, and nothing checks
them without, and they themselves, single wholes with
all their parts, are borne, as they press on, towards the
one spot which they first began to seek, must needs, we
may be sure, surpass in speed of motion, and be carried
far more quickly than the light of the sun, and rush
through many times the distance of space in the same
time in which the flashing light of the sun crowds the sky.

.   .   .   .
                                                                        1

nor to follow up each of the first-beginnings severally, to
see by what means each single thing is carried on.

    Yet a certain sect, against all this, ignorant ⟨that the
bodies⟩ of matter ⟨fly on of their own accord, unvanquished
through the ages,⟩[2] believe that nature cannot without the

Marginal notes (left):
which yet
is impeded
by external
opposition

and
internal
vibration,

whereas the
atoms are
quite
unchecked.

False
theory that
the world
is made for

---

[1] A considerable number of lines seems to be lost here, in which
Lucretius probably first gave other reasons for the atoms' velocity, and
then fulfilled the promise of line 62 to explain how the atoms by their
motion created and dissolved things : the next two lines read like
a conclusion of such a section.

[2] A line is probably lost here, of which Hoerschelmann has restored
the sense : corpora sponte sua volitare invicta per aevum.

power of the gods, in ways so nicely tempered to the needs of men, change the seasons of the year, and create the crops, and all else besides, which divine pleasure wins men to approach, while she herself, the leader of life, leads on and entices them by the arts of Venus to renew their races, that the tribe of mankind may not perish. But when they suppose that the gods have appointed all things for the sake of men, they are seen in all things to fall exceeding far away from true reason. For however little I know what the first-beginnings of things are, yet this I would dare to affirm from the very workings of heaven, and to prove from many other things as well, that the nature of the world is by no means made by divine grace for us : so great are the flaws with which it stands beset. And this, Memmius, I will make clear to you here-after. Now I will set forth what yet remains about the movements.

Now is the place, I trow, herein to prove this also to you, that no bodily thing can of its own force n be carried upwards or move upwards ; lest the bodies of flames give you the lie herein. For upwards indeed the smiling crops and trees are brought to birth, and take their increase, upwards too they grow, albeit all things of weight, as far as in them lies, are borne downwards. Nor when fires leap up to the roofs of houses, and with swift flame lick up beams and rafters, must we think that they do this of their own will, shot up without a driving force. Even as when blood shot out from our body spirts out leaping up on high, and scatters gore. Do you not see too with what force the moisture of water spews up beams and rafters? For the more we have pushed them straight down deep in the water, and with might and main have

men by divine power ;

but it is made so badly.

Causes of atomic motion :

1. the universal motion downwards : upward motion is always due to force ;

pressed them, striving with pain many together, the more eagerly does it spew them up and send them back, so that they rise more than half out of the water and leap up. And yet we do not doubt, I trow, but that all these things, as far as in them lies, are borne downwards through the empty void. Just so, therefore, flames too must be able when squeezed out to press on upwards through the breezes of air, albeit their weights are fighting, as far as in them lies, to drag them downwards. And again, the nightly torches of the sky which fly on high, do you not see that they trail long tracts of flames behind towards whatever side nature has given them to travel? do you not descry stars and constellations falling to earth? The sun too from the height of heaven scatters its heat on every side, and sows the fields with his light; 'tis towards the earth then that the sun's heat also tends. And you descry, too, thunderbolts flying crosswise through the rain; now from this side, now from that the fires burst from the clouds and rush together; the force of flame everywhere falls towards the earth.

2. the swerve of the atoms. Herein I would fain that you should learn this too, that when first-bodies are being carried downwards straight through the void by their own weight, at times quite undetermined and at undetermined spots they push a little from their path:[n] yet only just so much as you could call a change of trend. But if they were not used to swerve, all things would fall downwards through the deep void like drops of rain, nor could collision come to be, nor a blow brought to pass for the first-beginnings: so nature would never have brought aught to being.

But if perchance any one believes [n] that heavier bodies, because they are carried more quickly straight through the void, can fall from above on the lighter, and so bring about the blows which can give creative motions, he wanders far away from true reason. For all things that fall through the water and thin air, these things must needs quicken their fall in proportion to their weights, just because the body of water and the thin nature of air cannot check each thing equally, but give place more quickly when overcome by heavier bodies. But, on the other hand, the empty void cannot on any side, at any time, support anything, but rather, as its own nature desires, it continues to give place; wherefore all things must needs be borne on through the calm void, moving at equal rate with unequal weights. The heavier will not then ever be able to fall on the lighter from above, nor of themselves bring about the blows, which make diverse the movements, by which nature carries things on. Wherefore, again and again, it must needs be that the first-bodies swerve a little; yet not more than the very least, lest we seem to be imagining a sideways movement, and the truth refute it. For this we see plain and evident, that bodies, as far as in them lies, cannot travel sideways, since they fall headlong from above, as far as you can descry. But that nothing at all swerves from the straight direction of its path, what sense is there which can descry? [1]

Once again, if every motion is always linked on, and the new always arises from the old in order determined, nor by swerving do the first-beginnings make a certain start of movement to break through the decrees of fate,

Marginal notes: False theory that heavier atoms fall faster than lighter. This is not true in the void. A slight swerve is necessary, and is not contradicted by phenomena. The swerve accounts for the power of free motion in living beings.

[1] Read *sensus* for *sese* with Bernays.

so that cause may not follow cause from infinite time; whence comes this free will for living things all over the earth, whence, I ask, is it wrested from fate, this will whereby we move forward, where pleasure leads each one of us, and swerve likewise in our motions neither at determined times nor in a determined direction of place, but just where our mind has carried us? For without doubt it is his own will which gives to each one a start for this movement, and from the will the motions pass flooding through the limbs. Do you not see too how, when the barriers are flung open, yet for an instant of time the eager might of the horses cannot burst out so suddenly as their mind itself desires? For the whole store of matter throughout the whole body must be roused to movement, that then aroused through every limb it may strain and follow the eager longing of the mind; so that you see a start of movement [n] is brought to pass from the heart, and comes forth first of all from the will of the mind, and then afterwards is spread through all the body and limbs. Nor is it the same as when we move forward impelled by a blow from the strong might and strong constraint of another. For then it is clear to see that all the matter of the body moves and is hurried on against our will, until the will has reined it back throughout the limbs. Do you not then now see that, albeit a force outside pushes many men and constrains them often to go forward against their will and to be hurried away headlong, yet there is something in our breast, which can fight against it and withstand it? And at its bidding too the store of matter is constrained now and then to turn throughout the limbs and members, and, when pushed forward, is reined

It starts from the will and then passes through all the limbs.

It is very different from motion under compulsion.

back and comes to rest again. Wherefore in the seeds too you must needs allow likewise that there is another cause of motion besides blows and weights, whence comes this power born in us, since we see that nothing can come to pass from nothing. For weight prevents all things coming to pass by blows, as by some force without. But that the very mind feels not some necessity within in doing all things, and is not constrained like a conquered thing to bear and suffer, this is brought about by the tiny swerve of the first-beginnings in no determined direction of place and at no determined time. *It is due to the second cause of motion, the swerve of the atoms.*

Nor was the store of matter ever more closely packed nor again set at larger distances apart. For neither does anything come to increase it nor pass away from it. Wherefore the bodies of the first-beginnings in the ages past moved with the same motion as now, and hereafter will be borne on for ever in the same way; such things as have been wont to come to being will be brought to birth under the same law, will exist and grow and be strong and lusty, inasmuch as is granted to each by the ordinances of nature. Nor can any force change the sum of things; for neither is there anything outside, into which any kind of matter may escape from the universe, nor whence new forces can arise and burst into the universe and change the whole nature of things and alter its motions. *The sum of motion, like that of matter, is unchangeable.*

Herein we need not wonder why it is that, when all the first-beginnings of things are in motion, yet the whole seems to stand wholly at rest, except when anything starts moving with its entire body. For all the nature of the first-bodies lies far away from our senses, below their purview; wherefore, since you cannot reach to look upon them, they must needs steal away their motions *Though a whole body seems at rest, the atoms are in unseen motion.*

from you too; above all, since such things as we can look upon, yet often hide their motions, when withdrawn from us on some distant spot. For often the fleecy flocks cropping the glad pasture on a hill creep on whither each is called and tempted by the grass bejewelled with fresh dew, and the lambs fed full gambol and butt playfully; yet all this seems blurred to us from afar, and to lie like a white mass on a green hill. Moreover, when mighty legions fill the spaces of the plains with their chargings, awaking a mimic warfare, a sheen rises there to heaven and all the earth around gleams with bronze, and beneath a noise is roused by the mighty mass of men as they march, and the hills smitten by their shouts turn back the cries to the stars of the firmament, and the cavalry wheel round and suddenly shake the middle of the plains with their forceful onset, as they scour across them. And yet there is a certain spot on the high hills, whence all seems to be at rest and to lie like a glimmering mass upon the plains.

Parallels in experience.

Now come, next in order learn of what kind are the beginnings of all things and how far differing in form, and how they are made diverse with many kinds of shapes, not that but a few are endowed with a like form, but that they are not all alike the same one with another. Nor need we wonder; for since there is so great a store of them, that neither have they any limit, as I have shown, nor any sum, it must needs be, we may be sure, that they are not all of equal bulk nor possessed of the same shape. Moreover, the race of men, and the dumb shoals of scaly creatures which swim the seas, and the glad herds and wild beasts, and the diverse birds, which throng the gladdening watering-places all around the

B. The shapes of the atoms. Their variety,

which arises from the infinite number of the atoms,

and is the cause of the distinction of individuals in the same species.

riverbanks and springs and pools, and those which flit
about and people the distant forests; of these go and take
any single one you will from among its kind, yet you will
find that they are different in shape one from another.
Nor in any other way could the offspring know its mother,
or the mother her offspring; yet we see that they can,
and that they are clearly not less known to one another
than men. For often before the sculptured shrines of Illustra-
the gods a calf has fallen, slaughtered hard by the altars tions : the
cow and her
smoking with incense, breathing out from its breast the calf;
hot tide of blood. But the mother bereft wanders over
the green glades and seeks [1] on the ground for the footprints marked by those cloven hoofs, scanning every spot
with her eyes, if only she might anywhere catch sight of
her lost young, and stopping fills the leafy grove with
her lament: again and again she comes back to the stall,
stabbed to the heart with yearning for her lost calf, nor
can the tender willows and the grass refreshed with dew
and the loved streams, gliding level with their banks,
bring gladness to her mind and turn aside the sudden
pang of care, nor yet can the shapes of other calves
among the glad pastures turn her mind to new thoughts
or ease it of its care : so eagerly does she seek in vain for
something she knows as her own. Moreover, the tender kids and
kids with their trembling cries know their horned dams lambs and
their
and the butting lambs the flocks of bleating sheep : mothers;
so surely, as their nature needs, do they run back always
each to its own udder of milk. Lastly, take any kind of grains of
corn, you will not find that every grain is like its fellows, corn ;
each in its several kind, but that there runs through all

---

[1] This should be the sense, but the reading is uncertain : possibly
quaerit.

some difference between their forms.   And in like manner
we see the race of shells painting the lap of earth, where
with its gentle waves the sea beats on the thirsty sand
of the winding shore.   Wherefore again and again in
the same way it must needs be, since the first-beginnings
of things are made by nature and not fashioned by hand
to the fixed form of one pattern, that some of them fly
about with shapes unlike one another.

It is very easy by reasoning of the mind for us to read
the riddle why the fire of lightning is far more piercing
than is our fire rising from pine-torches on earth.   For
you might say that the heavenly fire of lightning is made
more subtle and of smaller shapes, and so passes through
holes which our fire rising from logs and born of the pine-
torch cannot pass.   Again light passes through horn-
lanterns, but the rain is spewed back.   Why? unless it
be that those bodies of light are smaller than those of
which the quickening liquid of water is made.   And we
see wine flow through the strainer as swiftly as you will;
but, on the other hand, the sluggish olive-oil hangs back,
because, we may be sure, it is composed of particles
either larger or more hooked and entangled one with the
other, and so it comes about that the first-beginnings
cannot so quickly be drawn apart, each single one from
the rest, and so ooze through the single holes of each thing.

There is this too that the liquids of honey and milk
give a pleasant sensation of the tongue, when rolled in
the mouth; but on the other hand, the loathsome
nature of wormwood and biting centaury set the mouth
awry by their noisome taste; so that you may easily
know that those things which can touch the senses
pleasantly are made of smooth and round bodies, but

Marginal notes:

shells.

It is owing to this variety that some things pass through, where others are checked.

To it are due differences of taste,

that on the other hand all things which seem to be bitter and harsh, these are held bound together with particles more hooked, and for this cause are wont to tear a way into our senses, and at their entering in to break through the body.

Lastly, all things good or bad to the senses in their touch fight thus with one another, because they are built up of bodies of different shape; lest by chance you may think that the harsh shuddering sound [n] of the squeaking saw is made of particles as smooth as are the melodies of music which players awake, shaping the notes as their fingers move nimbly over the strings; nor again, must you think that first-beginnings of like shape pierce into men's nostrils, when noisome carcasses are roasting, and when the stage is freshly sprinkled with Cilician saffron, and the altar hard by is breathing the scent of Arabian incense; nor must you suppose that the pleasant colours of things, which can feed our eyes, are made of seeds like those which prick the pupil and constrain us to tears, or look dreadful and loathly in their hideous aspect. For every shape, which ever charms the senses, has not been brought to being without some smoothness in the first-beginnings; but, on the other hand, every shape which is harsh and offensive has not been formed without some roughness of substance. Other particles there are, moreover, which cannot rightly be thought to be smooth nor altogether hooked with bent points, but rather with tiny angles standing out a little, insomuch that they can tickle the senses rather than hurt them; and of this kind is lees of wine and the taste of endive. Or again, that hot fires and cold frost have particles fanged in different ways to prick the senses of the body, is proved

and all differences of sensation in hearing,

smell,

and sight.

Pleasure and pain are determined by the shapes of the particles;

for touch
is the
ultimate
cause of all
sensation.

to us by the touch of each. For touch, yea touch, by the holy powers of the gods, is the sense of the body, either when something from without finds its way in, or when a thing which is born in the body hurts us, or gives pleasure as it passes out, or else when the seeds after collision jostle within the body itself and, roused one by another, disturb our sense: as if by chance you should with your hand strike any part of your own body and so make trial. Therefore the first-beginnings must needs have forms far different, which can produce such diverse feelings.

Further
differences
and the
atomic
shapes
which
cause
them:
hard
things;

Or, again, things which seem to us hard and compact, these, it must needs be, are made of particles more hooked one to another, and are held together close-fastened at their roots, as it were by branching particles. First of all in this class diamond stones stand in the forefront of the fight, well used to despise all blows, and stubborn flints and the strength of hard iron, and brass sockets, which scream aloud as they struggle against the bolts.

liquid
things;

Those things indeed must be made of particles more round and smooth, which are liquid with a fluid body: for indeed a handful of poppy-seed moves easily just as a draught of water; for the several round particles are not checked one by the other, and when struck, it will roll downhill just like water.

pungent
and
evanescent
things;

Lastly, all things which you perceive flying asunder, like smoke, clouds and flames, it must needs be that even if they are not made entirely of smooth and round particles, yet they are not hampered by particles closely linked, so that they can prick the body, and pass into rocks, and yet not cling one to another: so that you can easily learn that, whatever we see ⟨borne asunder by the

tearing winds and⟩ meeting our senses ⟨as poison⟩,[1] are of
elements not closely linked but pointed. But because
you see that some things which are fluid, are also bitter,
as is the brine of the sea, count it no wonder. For
because it is fluid, it is of smooth and round particles,
and many rugged bodies mingled in it give birth to pain;
and yet it must needs be that they are not hooked and
held together : you must know that they are nevertheless
spherical, though rugged, so that they can roll on together
and hurt the senses. And that you may the more think
that rough are mingled with smooth first-beginnings,
from which is made the bitter body of the sea-god, there
is a way of sundering them and seeing how, apart from
the rest, the fresh water, when it trickles many a time
through the earth, flows into a trench and loses its harsh-
ness; for it leaves behind up above the first-beginnings
of its sickly saltness, since the rough particles can more
readily stick in the earth.[2]

And since I have taught this much, I will hasten to
link on a truth which holds to this and wins belief from it,
that the first-beginnings of things are limited in the tale
of their varying shapes. If it were not to be so, then
once again certain seeds must needs be of unbounded
bulk of body. For, within the same tiny frame of any
one single seed, the shapes of the body cannot be very
diverse. For suppose the first-bodies [n] to be of three

Marginal notes:
liquid but bitter things.

Differences of shapes of atoms limited in number. Otherwise 1. some atoms would be of vast size;

---

[1] The text is corrupt and a line is probably lost : the translation
follows Brieger's restoration :

> ventis differri rapidis, nostrisque veneno
> sensibus esse datum,

[2] It is likely that a paragraph is here lost in which Lucretius showed
that the size of the atoms was limited : otherwise some would be
perceptible. To this he probably refers in lines 479, 481 and 499.

least parts, or if you will, make them larger by a few more ;
in truth when you have tried all those parts of one body
in every way, shifting top and bottom, changing right
with left, to see what outline of form in that whole
body each arrangement gives, beyond that, if by chance
you wish to make the shapes different, you must needs
add other parts ; thence it will follow that in like manner
the arrangement will ask for other parts, if by chance
you still wish to make the shapes different : and so
greater bulk in the body follows on newness of forms.
Wherefore it is not possible that you can believe that
there are seeds with unbounded difference of forms,
lest you constrain certain of them to be of huge vastness,

2. all
extremes
in our
experience
would be
surpassed.

which I have taught above cannot be approved.[1] At
once you would see barbaric robes and gleaming Meli-
boean purple, dyed with the colour of Thessalian shells,
and the golden tribes of peacocks, steeped in smiling
beauty, lie neglected and surpassed by the new colours
in things ; and the smell of myrrh and the taste of
honey would be despised, and the swan's song and the
many-toned melodies on Phoebus's strings would in like
manner be smothered and mute : for something more
excellent than all else would ever be arising. Likewise,
all things would sink back on the worse side, just as we
have told that they would rise towards the better. For,
on the other hand, something would be more loathly
too than all else to nostrils and ears and eyes, and the

As it is,

taste of the mouth. And since these things are not so,

[1] Again it is likely that some lines are lost in which Lucretius stated
the general argument that if variety of shapes in the atoms were
infinite, all extremes in our experience would be far surpassed : he
then proceeds to illustration.

but a fixed limit to things marks the extreme on either there are
side, you must needs confess that the first-matter too fixed limits.
has a limited difference in shapes. Again from fire right
on to the icy frost of winter [1] is but a limited way, and in
like manner is the way measured back again. For all
heat and cold and tepid warmths in the middle lie between
the two, filling up the sum in due order. And so they
are brought to being differing with limited degrees,
since they are marked off at either end by the twin points,
beset on this side by flames, on that by stiffening frosts.

And since I have taught this much, I will hasten to *The atoms*
link on a truth which holds to it and wins belief from it, *of any one*
that the first-beginnings of things, which are formed *shape are*
with a shape like to one another, are in number infinite. *infinite in number.*
For since the difference of forms is limited, it must needs *Otherwise,*
be that those which are alike are unlimited, or else that *the sum of matter*
the sum of matter is created limited, which I have proved *would be limited.*
not to be, showing [2] in my verses that the tiny bodies of
matter from everlasting always keep up the sum of things,
as the team of blows is harnessed on unbroken on every
side. For in that you see [n] that certain animals are more *Animals*
rare, and perceive that nature is less fruitful in them, *rare in one place are*
yet in another quarter and spot, in some distant lands, *common in another.*
there may be many in that kind, and so the tale is made up;
even as in the race of four-footed beasts we see that
elephants with their snaky hands come first of all, by
whose many thousands India is embattled with a bulwark
of ivory, so that no way can be found into its inner
parts: so great is the multitude of those beasts, whereof
we see but a very few samples. But still, let me grant *Even a*
this too, let there be, if you will, some one thing unique, *unique thing*
alone in the body of its birth, to which there is not *would*

---

[1] This is the sense, though the text is uncertain.
[2] Reading *ostendens* with Munro.

imply
infinite
atoms of
the required
kind.

If limited
in number,
they might
be tossed
about the
universe
and never
meet.

a fellow in the whole wide world; yet unless there is
an unlimited stock of matter, from which it might be
conceived and brought to birth, it will not be able to
be created, nor, after that, to grow on and be nourished.
Nay, in very truth, if I were to suppose this too, that
the bodies creative of one single thing were limited as
they tossed about the universe, whence, where, by what
force, in what manner will they meet and come together
in that vast ocean, that alien turmoil of matter? They
have not, I trow, a plan for union, but as, when many
a great shipwreck has come to pass, the great sea is wont
to cast hither and thither benches, ribs, yards, prow,
masts and swimming oars, so that along all the coasts of
the lands floating stern-pieces are seen, giving warning
to mortals, to resolve to shun the snares of the sea and its
might and guile, nor trust it at any time, when the wiles
of the windless waves smile treacherous; even so, if you
once suppose that the first-beginnings of a certain kind
are limited, then scattered through all time they must
needs be tossed hither and thither by the tides of matter,
setting towards every side, so that never can they be
driven together and come together in union, nor stay
fixed in union, nor take increase and grow; yet that
each of these things openly comes to pass, fact proves
for all to see, that things can be brought to birth and being
born can grow. It is manifest then that there are, in
any kind of things you will, infinite first-beginnings, by
which all things are supplied.

Creation
and destruc-
tion wage
equal
warfare.

And so, neither can the motions of destruction prevail
for ever, and bury life in an eternal tomb, nor yet can the
motions of creation and increase for ever bring things
to birth and preserve them. So war waged from time

everlasting is carried on by the balanced strife of the first-beginnings. Now here, now there, the vital forces of things conquer and are conquered alike. With the funeral mingles the wailing which babies raise as they come to look upon the coasts of light; nor has night ever followed on day, or dawn on night, but that it has heard mingled with the baby's sickly wailings, the lament that escorts death and the black funeral.

Herein it is right to have this truth also surely sealed and to keep it stored in your remembering mind, that there is not one of all the things, whose nature is seen before our face, which is built of one kind of first-beginnings, nor anything which is not created of well-mingled seed; and whatever possesses within it more forces and powers, it thus shows that there are in it most kinds of first-beginnings and diverse shapes. First of all the earth holds within it the first-bodies, by which the springs welling out coldness ever and anon renew the measureless sea, it holds those whence fires are born. For in many places the surface of the earth is kindled and blazes, but the outburst of Aetna rages with fire from its lowest depths. Then further, it holds those whence it can raise for the races of men the smiling crops and glad trees, whence too it can furnish to the tribe of wild beasts, which ranges the mountains, streams, leaves and glad pastures. Wherefore earth alone has been called the Great Mother of the gods,[n] and the mother of the wild beasts, and the parent of our body.

Of her in days of old the learned poets of the Greeks sang that ⟨borne on from her sacred⟩ [1] shrine in her car she

Nothing is created of one single kind of atoms.

Earth has every kind,

and is therefore called Mother.

The worship of Mother

---

[1] A line is lost, of which this must have been the general sense.

Earth as
Cybele.
The
meaning
of her
attributes:
the lions;
the mural
crown;
drove a yoke of lions, teaching thereby that the great earth
hangs in the space of air nor can earth rest on earth. To
the car they yoked wild beasts, because, however wild the
brood, it ought to be conquered and softened by the loving
care of parents. The top of her head they wreathed
with a battlemented crown, because embattled on glorious
heights she sustains towns; and dowered with this emblem
even now the image of the divine mother is carried in
awesome state through lands far and wide. On her the
diverse nations in the ancient rite of worship call as the
the
Phrygian
escort;
Mother of Ida, and they give her Phrygian bands to bear
her company, because from those lands first they say
corn began to be produced throughout the whole world.
the Galli;
The mutilated priests they assign to her, because they
wish to show forth that those who have offended the
godhead of the Mother, and have been found ungrateful
to their parents, must be thought to be unworthy to
bring offspring alive into the coasts of light. Taut
music
timbrels thunder in their hands, and hollow cymbals
all around, and horns menace with harsh-sounding bray,
and the hollow pipe goads their minds in the Phrygian
and
weapons;
mode, and they carry weapons before them, the symbols
of their dangerous frenzy, that they may be able to fill
with fear of the goddess's power the thankless minds
and unhallowed hearts of the multitude. And so as soon
as she rides on through great cities, and silently blesses
mortals with unspoken salutation, with bronze and silver
they strew all the path of her journey, enriching her with
bounteous alms, and snow rose-blossoms over her, over-
shadowing the Mother and the troops of her escort.
the
Curetes.
Then comes an armed band,[n] whom the Greeks call by
name the Curetes of Phrygia, and because now and again

they join in mock conflict of arms and leap in rhythmic movement, gladdened at the sight of blood and shaking as they nod the awesome crests upon their heads, they recall the Curetes of Dicte, who are said once in Crete to have drowned the wailing of the infant Jove, while, a band of boys around the baby boy, in hurrying dance all armed, they beat in measured rhythm brass upon brass, that Saturn might not seize and commit him to his jaws, and plant an everlasting wound deep in the Mother's heart. For this cause in arms they escort the Great Mother, or else because they show forth that the goddess preaches that they should resolve with arms and valour to defend their native land and prepare to be a guard and ornament to their parents. Yet all this, albeit well Yet all this and nobly set forth and told, is nevertheless far removed is false. from true reasoning. For it must needs be that all the The gods nature of the gods enjoys life everlasting in perfect peace, live a sundered and separated far away from our world. For placid life apart from free from all grief, free from danger, mighty in its own the world. resources, never lacking aught of us, it is not won by virtuous service nor touched by wrath. Verily, the earth is without feeling throughout all time, and 'tis because it has possession of the first-beginnings of many things, that it brings forth many in many ways into the light of the sun. Herein, if any one is resolved to call the sea Neptune and corn Ceres, and likes rather to misuse the title of Bacchus than to utter the true name of the vine-juice, let us grant that he may proclaim that the world is the Mother of the gods, if only in very truth he forbear to stain his own mind with shameful religious awe.

And so often fleecy flocks and the warrior brood of

The same
food may
nourish
different
animals

horses and horned herds, cropping the grass from one field beneath the same canopy of heaven, and slaking their thirst from one stream of water, yet live their life with different aspect, and keep the nature of their parents and imitate their ways each after his own kind. So great is the difference of matter in any kind of grass

Their flesh,
bones, &c.,
are dif-
ferent.

you will, so great in every stream. Moreover, any one living creature of them all is made of bones, blood, veins, heat, moisture, flesh and sinews: and they as well are far different, formed as they are with first-beginnings of unlike shape. Then once again, all things that are

Different
bodies
contain
the seeds
of fire.

set ablaze and burnt up by fire, store in their body, if nothing else, yet at least those particles, from which they may be able to toss fire abroad and shoot out light, and make sparks fly, and scatter cinders far and wide. Traversing all other things with the like reasoning of your mind, you will find then that they hide in their body the seeds of many things and contain diverse shapes.

The same
thing
can stir
different
senses.

Again, you see many things to which both colour and taste are given together with smell. First of all, most of the offerings ⟨burnt on the altars of the gods⟩:[1] these then must needs be made of diverse shapes; for the burning smell pierces, where the hue passes not into the limbs, even so the hue in one way, the taste in another, finds its way into our senses; so that you may know that

All things
then con-
tain atoms
of various
shapes.

they differ in the shapes of their first-bodies. So different forms come together into one mass and things are made with mingled seeds. Nay, more, everywhere in these very verses of mine you see many letters common to many words, and yet you must needs grant that verses and words are formed of different letters, one from

---

[1] A line is lost here, of which this was the probable sense.

another; not that but a few letters run through them
in common, or that no two of them are made of letters
all the same, but that they are not all alike the same
one with another. So in other things likewise since *There are*
there are first-beginnings common to many things, yet *common*
elements,
they can exist with sums different from one another: *but the*
sums are
so that the human race and corn and glad trees are *different.*
rightly said to be created of different particles.

And yet we must not think that all particles can be *But not all*
linked together in all ways, for you would see monsters [n] *combina-*
tions are
created everywhere, forms coming to being half man, *possible.*
half beast, and sometimes tall branches growing out
from a living body, and many limbs of land-beasts linked
with beasts of the sea, and nature too throughout the
lands, that are the parents of all things, feeding Chimaeras
breathing flame from their noisome mouths. But it is *Each thing*
has its
clear to see that none of these things comes to be, since *appropriate*
we see that all things are born of fixed seeds and a fixed *seeds, food,*
and move-
parent, and can, as they grow, preserve their kind. *ments.*
You may be sure that that must needs come to pass
by a fixed law. For its own proper particles separate
from every kind of food and pass within into the limbs
of everything, and are there linked on and bring about
the suitable movements. But, on the other hand, we
see nature cast out alien matter on to the ground, and
many things with bodies unseen flee from the body,
driven by blows, which could not be linked to any part
nor within feel the lively motions in harmony with the
body and imitate them. But lest by chance you should *This is*
true of
think that living things alone are bound by these laws, *inanimate*
the same condition sets a limit to all things. For even *as well as*

living
things.

as all things begotten are in their whole nature unlike one to the other, so it must needs be that each is made of first-beginnings of a different shape; not that but a few are endowed with a like form, but that they are not all alike the same one with another. Moreover, since the seeds are different, there must needs be a difference in their spaces, passages, fastenings, weights, blows, meetings, movements, which not only sunder living things, but part earth and the whole sea, and hold all the sky away from the earth.

C. The
atoms have
no colour,

Come now, listen to discourse gathered by my joyful labour, lest by chance you should think that these white things, which you perceive shining bright before your eyes are made of white first-beginnings, or that things which are black are born of black seeds; or should believe that things which are steeped in any other colour you will, bear this colour because the bodies of matter are dyed with a colour like it. For the bodies of matter have no colour at all, neither like things nor again unlike them.

though the
mind can
well con-
ceive them.

And if by chance it seems to you that the mind cannot project itself [n] into these bodies, you wander far astray. For since those born blind, who have never descried the light of the sun, yet know bodies by touch, never linked with colour for them from the outset of their life, you may know that for our mind too, bodies painted with no tint may become a clear concept.[n] Again, we ourselves feel that whatever we touch in blind darkness is not dyed with any colour. And since I convince you that this may be, I will now teach you that ⟨the first-beginnings⟩

1. Colour
changes,

are ⟨deprived of all colour⟩.[1]

For any colour, whatever it be, changes into any other;

---

[1] A line is lost, of which this must have been the sense.

but the first-beginnings ought in no wise to do this. For
it must needs be that something abides unchangeable,
that all things be not utterly brought to naught. For
whenever a thing changes and passes out of its own
limits, straightway this is the death of that which was
before. Therefore take care not to dye with colour the
seeds of things, lest you see all things altogether pass away
to naught.

but the
atoms must
be un-
changeable.

Moreover, if the nature of colour has not been granted
to the first-beginnings, and yet they are endowed with
diverse forms, out of which they beget and vary colours
of every kind, forasmuch as it is of great matter with
what others all the seeds are bound up, and in what
position, and what movements they mutually give and
receive, you can most easily at once give account, why
those things which were a little while before of black
colour, are able of a sudden to become of marble white-
ness ; as the sea, when mighty winds have stirred its
level waters, is turned into white waves of shining marble.
For you might say that when the substance of that which
we often see black has been mingled up, and the order
of its first-beginnings changed and certain things added
and taken away, straightway it comes to pass that it is
seen shining and white. But if the level waters of the
ocean were made of sky-blue seeds, they could in no
wise grow white. For in whatever way you were to
jostle together seeds which are sky-blue, never can they
pass into a marble colour. But if the seeds which make
up the single unmixed brightness of the sea are dyed
with this colour and that, even as often out of different
forms and diverse shapes some square thing is made up
with a single shape, then it were natural that, as in the
square we perceive that there are unlike forms, so we

2. If
atoms are
colourless,
their
varieties of
shape, &c.,
will account
for the
different
colours of
things.

But (a) if
they are of
the colour
of the
things they
compose,
change is
impossible,
and (b) if
they are of
all colours,
the separate
colours
would be
seen,

should perceive in the water of the ocean, or in any other single and unmixed brightness, colours far different and diverse one from another. Moreover, the unlike shapes do not a whit thwart and hinder the whole from being square in its outline; but the diverse colours in things do check and prevent the whole thing being of a single brightness. Then, further, the reason which leads us on and entices us sometimes to assign colours to the first-beginnings of things, is gone, since white things are not made of white, nor those which are seen black of black, but of diverse colours. And in very truth much more readily will white things be born and rise up out of no colour than out of black, or any other colour you will which fights with it and thwarts it.

Moreover, since colours cannot be without light nor do the first-beginnings of things come out into the light, you may know how they are not clothed with any colour. For what colour can there be in blind darkness? Nay even in the light it changes according as it shines brightly, struck with a straight or slanting beam of light; even as the plumage of doves, which is set about their throats and crowns their necks, is seen in the sunshine; for anon it comes to pass that it is red with bright garnet, sometimes in a certain view it comes to pass that it seems to mingle green emeralds among coral. And the tail of the peacock, when it is bathed in bounteous light, in like manner changes its colours as it moves round; and since these colours are begotten by a certain stroke of light, you may know that we must not think that they could come to be without it. And since the pupil of the eye receives in itself a certain kind of blow, when it is said to perceive white colour, and another again, when it perceives black

and the whole could not be uniform in colour;

further, this contradicts our reason for thinking atoms might have colour.

3. Colour needs light, with which the atoms have no relation.

4. The perception of colour is due to a

and the rest, nor does it matter with what colour things you touch may choose to be endowed, but rather with what sort of shape they are fitted, you may know that the first-beginnings have no need of colours, but by their diverse forms produce diverse kinds of touch.

Moreover, since no fixed nature of colour belongs to fixed shapes, and all conformations of first-beginnings may exist in any hue you will, why on like grounds are not those things which are made out of them steeped with every kind of colour in every kind? For it were natural that often flying crows too should throw off white colour from white wings, and that black swans should be made of black seeds or of any other colour you will, simple or diverse.

Nay again, the more each thing is pulled asunder into tiny parts, the more can you perceive colour little by little fading away and being quenched: as comes to pass when purple is plucked apart into small pieces: when it has been unravelled thread by thread, the dark purple or the scarlet, by far the brightest of colours, is utterly destroyed; so that you can know from this that the tiny shreds dissipate all their colour before they are sundered into the seeds of things.

Lastly, since you do not allow that all bodies send out sound or smell, it comes to pass, therefore, that you do not assign sound and smell to them. Even so, since we cannot with the eyes descry all things, you may know that some things are made bereft of colour, just as some are without any smell and far parted from sound, yet that the keen mind can come to know them no less than it can mark those devoid of other things.

blow on the eye: and for touch it is shape, not colour which matters.
5. Colour and shape not being connected, if atoms have colour, we should have individuals of different colours in the same species.
6. The smaller a body, the less colour it has.
7. Just as some things have not smell or sound, so the atoms are without colour

The atoms are also without heat, sound, taste or smell,

But lest by chance you think that the first-bodies abide bereft only of colour, they are also sundered altogether from warmth and cold, and fiery heat, and are carried along barren of sound and devoid of taste, nor do they give off any scent of their own from their body. Even as when you set about to make the delicious liquid of marjoram or myrrh, or scent of nard, which breathes nectar to the nostrils, first of all it is right to seek, in so far as you may and can find it, the nature of scentless oil, which may send off no breath of perfume to the nostrils, so that it may as little as possible taint and ruin with its own strong smell the scents mingled in its body and boiled along with it. Therefore after all the first-beginnings of things are bound not to bring to the begetting of things their own scent or sound, since they cannot give anything off from themselves, nor in the same way acquire any taste at all, nor cold, nor once more warm and fiery heat . . . and the rest :[1] yet since they are such as to be created mortal, the pliant of soft body, the brittle of crumbling body, the hollow of rare, they must needs all be kept apart from the first-beginnings, if we wish to place immortal foundations beneath things, on which the sum of life may rest ; lest you see all things pass away utterly into nothing.

for they cannot emit anything from their body.

Neither have atoms sense.

It must needs be [n] that you should admit that all things which we see have sense are yet made of insensible first-beginnings. The clear facts, which are known for all to see, neither refute this nor fight against it, but

[1] It is impossible to make sense of the passage as it stands, and Giussani is probably right in supposing several verses lost, in which the poet said that only such things could give anything off as contained void, and then gave a list of examples, ending up with the *cetera* of line 859.

rather themselves lead us by the hand and constrain us to believe that, as I say, living things are begotten of insensible things. Why we may see worms come forth alive from noisome dung, when the soaked earth has gotten muddiness from immeasurable rains; moreover, we may see all things in like manner change themselves. Streams, leaves, and glad pastures change themselves into cattle, cattle change their nature into our bodies, and from our bodies the strength of wild beasts often gains increase, and the bodies of birds strong of wing. And so nature changes all foods into living bodies, and out of food brings to birth all the senses of living things, in no far different way than she unfolds dry logs into flames and turns all things into fires. Do you not then see now that it is of great matter in what order all the first-beginnings of things are placed, and with what others mingled they give and receive motions?

1. We see the sensible created elsewhere from the senseless.

2. Inanimate food makes animate bodies.

Next then, what is it, that strikes on the very mind, which stirs it and constrains to utter diverse thoughts, that you may not believe that the sensible is begotten of the insensible? We may be sure it is that stones [1] and wood and earth mixed together yet cannot give out vital sense. Herein it will be right to remember this, that I do not say that sensations are begotten at once from all and every of the things which give birth to sensible things, but that it is of great matter, first of what size are these bodies, which create the sensible, and with what form they are endowed, then what they are in their motions, arrangements and positions. And

3. The fact that sensible things do not normally arise from the insensible is no objection.

All depends on the size, position, arrangements, and motions of the atoms.

---

[1] Giussani may be right in thinking that we should read *latices* (water) instead of *lapides* (stones), as it suits better with what follows.

none of these things can we perceive in logs and sods; and yet, when they are, as it were, made muddy through the rains, they give birth to little worms, because the bodies of matter stirred by the newcomer from their old arrangements are brought into union in the way in which living things are bound to be begotten. Next, those who think [n] that the sensible could be created out of sensible bodies which in turn were used to owe their sense to others, ⟨these make the seeds of their own sense mortal⟩,[1] when they make them soft. For all sensation is linked to flesh, sinews and veins, which we see are always soft in nature built up of mortal body. But still let us grant now that these can abide for ever: still doubtless they must either have [n] the sense proper to a part, or be thought to be of a sense like to that of whole living things. But it must needs be that the parts cannot have sense by themselves; for all sensation in the limbs depends on us, nor severed from us can the hand nor any part of the body at all keep sensation by itself. It remains that they are made like whole living things. Thus it must needs be that they feel likewise what we feel, so that they may be able to share with us in every place in the vital sensations. How then will they be able to be called the first-beginnings of things and to shun the paths of death, since they are living things, and living things are one and the same with mortal things? Yet grant that they can, still by their meeting and union, they will make nothing besides a crowd and mob of living things, even as, as you may

4. Sensible seeds would be soft and therefore mortal.

5. If everlasting, they must either (a) feel as a part of the whole, or (b) as an independent whole. But (a) a part does not feel by itself;

(b) (1) they could not be eternal;

(2) they would only make a confused

---

[1] A line is lost, which might have been of the form *hi proprii sensus mortalia semina reddunt.*

know, men, herds of cattle and wild beasts could not beget anything by coming together with one another. But if by chance they lose their own sense, when inside a body, and receive another, what good was it that that should be assigned to them which is taken away? Then, moreover, as we saw before. inasmuch as we perceive the eggs of birds turn into living chickens, and worms swarm out when mud has seized on the earth owing to immoderate rains, we may know that sensations can be begotten out of that which is not sensation.

mass of sentient beings; (3) if in the body they lose their sense, why give it them? But our previous examples are enough.

But if by chance any one shall say [n] that sensation can in any case arise from not-sensation by change of substance or, as it were, by a kind of birth, by which it is thrust out into being, it will be enough to make clear and prove to him that birth cannot come to be, unless when a union has been formed before, nor is anything changed except after union. First of all, no body at all can have sensation before the nature of the living thing is itself begotten, because, we may be sure, its substance is scattered abroad and is kept in the air, in streams, in earth and things sprung from earth, nor has it come together in appropriate way and combined with one another the vital motions, whereby the all-seeing senses are kindled and see to the safety of each living thing.

6. Sensation cannot arise from the insensate by change or birth; for both imply union. (a) A body cannot have sensation before the union of its substance.

Moreover, a heavier blow than its nature can endure, of a sudden fells any living creature, and hastens to stun all the sensations of its body and mind. For the positions of the first-beginnings are broken up and the vital motions are checked deep within, until the substance, after the shock throughout all the limbs, loosens the vital clusters of the soul from the body, scatters it abroad and drives it out through every pore. For what else

(b) A blow puts an end to sensation, because it dissolves unions and stops the vital motions.

are we to think that a blow can do when it meets each
thing, but shake it to pieces and break it up? It comes
to pass too, that when a blow meets us with less force,
the vital motions that remain are often wont to win,
yea, to win and to allay the vast disturbances of the
blow and summon each part back again into its proper
path, and to shake to pieces the movement of death
that now, as it were, holds sway in the body, and to kindle
the sensations almost lost. For by what other means
could living things gather their wits and turn back to life
even from the very threshold of death rather than pass on,
whither their race is already almost run, and pass away?

Recovery
means re-
union and
motion
restarted.

Moreover, since there is pain when the bodies of
matter, disturbed by some force throughout the living
flesh and limbs, tremble each in their abode within, and
when they settle back into their place, comforting
pleasure comes to pass, you may know that the first-
beginnings cannot be assailed by any pain, and can find
no pleasure in themselves: inasmuch as they are not
made of any bodies of first-beginnings, through whose
newness of movement they may be in pain or find any
enjoyment of life-giving delight. They are bound then
not to be endowed with any sensation.

7. Plea-
sure and
pain are
caused by
the internal
movements
of atoms:
atoms
cannot then
themselves
experience
them.

Again, if, in order that all living things may be able to
feel, we must after all assign sensation to their first-
beginnings, what of those whereof the race of men has its
peculiar increment? [n] You must think that they are
shaken with quivering mirth and laugh aloud and sprinkle
face and cheeks with the dew of their tears. And they
have the wit to say much about the mingling of things,
and they go on to ask what are their first-beginnings;
inasmuch as, being made like to whole mortal men, they

8. Re-
ductio ad
absurdum.
Sensible
atoms must
themselves
laugh and
cry and
think and
dispute.

too must needs be built of other particles in their turn,
and those again of others, so that you may never dare to
make a stop : nay, I will press hard on you, so that,
whatsoever you say speaks and laughs and thinks, shall
be composed of other particles which do these same
things. But if we perceive this to be but raving madness,
and a man can laugh, though he has not the increment of
laughing atoms, and can think and give reasons with
learned lore, though he be not made of seeds thoughtful
and eloquent, why should those things, which, as we see,
have feeling, any the less be able to exist, mingled of seeds
which lack sense in every way ?

And so, we are all sprung from heavenly seed ; there is
the one father of us all, from whom when live-giving
earth, the mother, has taken within her the watery drops
of moisture, teeming she brings forth the goodly crops
and the glad trees and the race of men ; she brings forth
too all the tribes of the wild beasts, when she furnishes
the food, on which all feed their bodies and pass a pleasant
life and propagate their offspring ; wherefore rightly has
she won the name of mother. Even so, what once sprung
from earth, sinks back into the earth, and what was sent
down from the coasts of the sky, returns again, and the
regions of heaven receive it. Nor does death so destroy
things as to put an end to the bodies of matter, but only
scatters their union. Then she joins anew one with
others, and brings it to pass that all things thus alter their
forms, and change their colours, and receive sensations,
and in an instant of time yield them up again, so that
you may know that it matters with what others the first-
beginnings of things are bound up and in what position
and what motions they mutually give and receive, and

Summary
Earth is the
universal
mother.

Death
is not
destruction
but re-
formation,
and com-
bination
produces
qualities
and
sensation.

may not think that what we see floating on the surface of things [n] or at times coming to birth, and on a sudden passing away, can abide in the possession of eternal first-bodies. Nay, indeed, even in my verses it is of moment with what others and in what order each letter is placed. For the same letters signify sky, sea, earth, rivers, sun, the same too crops, trees, living creatures; if not all, yet by far the greater part, are alike, but it is by position that things sound different. So in things themselves likewise when meetings, motions, order, position, shapes are changed, things too are bound to be changed.

D. Other worlds in space. Introduction. Put aside the alarm of novelty,

Now turn your mind, I pray, to a true reasoning. For a truth wondrously new is struggling to fall upon your ears, and a new face of things to reveal itself. Yet neither is anything so easy, but that at first it is more difficult to believe, and likewise nothing is so great or so marvellous but that little by little all decrease their wonder at it. First of all the bright clear colour of the sky, and all it holds within it, the stars that wander here and there, and the moon and the sheen of the sun with its brilliant light; all these, if now they had come to being for the first time for mortals, if all unforeseen they were in a moment placed before their eyes, what story could be told more marvellous than these things, or what that the nations would less dare to believe beforehand? Nothing, I trow: so worthy of wonder would this sight have been. Yet think how no one now, wearied with satiety of seeing, deigns to gaze up at the shining quarters of the sky! Wherefore cease to spew out reason from your mind, struck with terror at mere newness, but rather with eager judgement weigh things, and, if you see them true, lift your hands and yield, or, if it is false, gird yourself to battle. For our mind now seeks to reason, since the sum

of space is boundless out beyond the walls of this world, and inquire
what there is far out there, whither the spirit desires what there
always to look forward, and whither the unfettered projection of our mind[n] flies on unchecked. our world.

First of all, we find that in every direction everywhere, There are
and on either side, above and below, through all the uni- other
worlds
verse, there is no limit, as I have shown, and indeed the than ours.
truth cries out for itself and the nature of the deep shines 1. With
clear. Now in no way must we think it likely, since infinite
atoms
towards every side is infinite empty space, and seeds in meeting in
unnumbered numbers in the deep universe fly about in infinite
space,
many ways driven on in everlasting motion, that this chance will
one world and sky was brought to birth, but that beyond to time
it all those bodies of matter do naught ; above all, since produce
this world was so made by nature, as the seeds of things them.
themselves of their own accord, jostling from time to
time, were driven together in many ways, rashly, idly,
and in vain, and at last those united, which, suddenly cast
together, might become ever and anon the beginnings of
great things, of earth and sea and sky, and the race of
living things. Wherefore, again and again, you must
needs confess that there are here and there other gatherings of matter, such as is this, which the ether holds in
its greedy grip.

Moreover, when there is much matter ready to hand, 2. Matter,
when space is there, and no thing, no cause delays, things space, and
nature
must, we may be sure, be carried on and completed. As remaining
it is, if there is so great a store of seeds as the whole life the same,
necessity
of living things could not number, and if the same force must
and nature abides which could throw together the seeds produce
them.
of things, each into their place in like manner as they are
thrown together here, it must needs be that you confess

that there are other worlds in other regions, and diverse races of men and tribes of wild beasts.

3. Nothing in nature is unique.

This there is too that in the universe there is nothing single,[n] nothing born unique and growing unique and alone, but it is always of some tribe, and there are many things in the same race. First of all turn your mind to living creatures; you will find that in this wise is begotten the race of wild beasts that haunts the mountains, in this wise the stock of men, in this wise again the dumb herds of scaly fishes, and all the bodies of flying fowls. Wherefore you must confess in the same way that sky and earth and sun, moon, sea, and all else that exists, are not unique, but rather of number numberless; inasmuch as the deep-fixed boundary-stone of life awaits these as surely, and they are just as much of a body that has birth, as every race which is here on earth, abounding in things after its kind.

Nature is thus seen to work of herself, free of the control of the gods.

And if you learn this surely, and cling to it, nature is seen, free at once, and quit of her proud rulers, doing all things of her own accord alone, without control of gods. For by the holy hearts of the gods, which in their tranquil peace pass placid years, and a life of calm, who can avail to rule the whole sum of the boundless, who to hold in his guiding hand the mighty reins of the deep, who to turn round all firmaments at once, and warm all fruitful lands with heavenly fires, or to be at all times present in all places, so as to make darkness with clouds, and shake the calm tracts of heaven with thunder, and then shoot thunderbolts, and often make havoc of his own temples, or moving away into deserts rage furiously there, plying the bolt, which often passes by the guilty and does to death the innocent and undeserving?

And since the time of the world's birth, and the first birthday of sea and earth, and the rising of the sun, many bodies have been added from without, and seeds added all around, which the great universe in its tossing has brought together; that from them sea and lands might be able to increase, and from them too the mansion of the sky might gain new room and lift its high vault far away from the lands, and the air might rise up. For from all places all bodies are separated by blows each to its own kind, and they pass on to their own tribes; moisture goes to moisture, with earthy substance earth grows, fires forge fires, and sky sky, until nature, parent of all, with perfecting hand has brought all things on to the last end of growing; as it comes to pass, when there is now no whit more which is sent within the veins of life, than what flows out and passes away. Here the growth of all things must stop, here nature by her powers curbs increase. For whatsoever things you see waxing large with joyful increase, and little by little climbing the steps to full-grown years, take more into themselves than they send out from their body, so long as food is passed easily into all their veins, and so long as the things are not so widely spread that they throw off much, and cause waste greater than that on which their growth feeds. For of a surety you must throw up your hands and grant that many bodies flow away and pass from things; but more must needs be added to them, until they have reached the topmost point of increase. Then little by little age breaks their powers and their full-grown strength, and wastes away on the downhill path. For verily the huger a thing is and the wider it is, when once its bulk begins to go, the more bodies now does it scatter abroad and

The world in its period of growth was increased by constant additions from without.

So all bodies grow, so long as they take in more than they give out.

Then comes the period of decay, when they lose more than they can take in.

throw off from itself, nor is its food easily dispersed into all its veins, nor is there store enough, whence matter may arise and be supplied to equal the vast ebb which it gives out. With reason then they perish, when all things have been made rare by the ebb, and yield before the blows from without, inasmuch as at last food fails the aged life, nor do bodies from without cease to thump upon it, and wear it away, and to overcome it with hostile

So it will be with the world,

blows. Thus then even the walls of the wide world all round will be stormed and fall into decay and crumbling ruin. For it is food which must needs repair all things and renew them, food must support them, and food sustain all things; yet all is vain, since neither the veins can bear to receive what is enough, nor does nature furnish all that is needful. Yea, even now its life is broken, and the worn-out earth scarce creates tiny animals, though once it created all the tribes, and brought to birth huge bodies of wild beasts. For it was no golden rope,[n] I trow, which let down the races of living things from heaven above on to the fields, nor did the sea or the waves, that lash the rocks, create them, but the same earth conceived them, which now nourishes them of her substance. Moreover, at first by herself of her own accord she created for mortals the smiling crops and glad vine-plants, herself

which even now shows signs of decay.

brought forth sweet fruits and glad pastures; which now scarce wax great, though aided by our toil: we wear out our oxen and the strength of our husbandmen: we exhaust the iron ploughshare, though scarce supplied by the fields so much do they grudge their produce and increase our toil. And now the aged ploughman shaking his head sighs ever and again that the toil of his hands has perished all for naught, and when he matches the present days against the days of the past, he often praises the fortunes of his father. So too gloomily the planter of the worn-out, wrinkled vine rails at the trend of the times, and wearies heaven, and grumbles to think how the generations of old, rich in piety, easily supported life on a narrow plot, since aforetime the limit of land was far less to each man. Nor does he grasp that all things waste away little by little and pass to the grave [1] foredone by age and the lapse of life.

[1] Read *capulum* with Vossius.

BOOK III

Introduc-
tion :
praise of
Epicurus,
who has
revealed
the
universe
to man.

THOU, who out of deep darkness didst first avail to
raise a torch so clear, shedding light upon the true joys
of life, 'tis thee I follow, bright star of the Greek race,
and in thy deepset prints firmly now I plant my footsteps, not in eager emulation, but rather because for love
I long to copy thee ; for how could a swallow rival
swans, or what might kids with trembling limbs accomplish in a race to compare with the stout strength of
a horse ? Thou art our father, thou discoverer of truth,
thou dost vouchsafe to us a father's precepts, and from
thy pages, our hero, even as bees in flowery glades sip
every plant, we in like manner browse on all thy sayings
of gold, yea, of gold, and always most worthy of life for
evermore. For as soon as thy philosophy, springing from
thy godlike soul, begins to proclaim aloud the nature of
things, the terrors of the mind fly away, the walls of the
world part asunder, I see things moving on through all
the void. The majesty of the gods is revealed, and their
peaceful abodes, which neither the winds shake [n] nor
clouds soak with showers, nor does the snow congealed
with biting frost besmirch them with its white fall, but
an ever cloudless sky vaults them over, and smiles with
light bounteously spread abroad. Moreover, nature supplies all they need, nor does anything gnaw at their peace
of mind at any time. But on the other hand, the quarters

of Acheron are nowhere to be seen, nor yet is earth a barrier to prevent all things being descried, which are carried on underneath through the void below our feet. At these things, as it were, some godlike pleasure and a thrill of awe seizes on me, to think that thus by thy power nature is made so clear and manifest, laid bare to sight on every side.

And since I have shown of what kind are the beginnings The of all things, with what diverse shapes they differ, and the nature of the soul. how of their own accord they fly on, impelled by everlasting motion, and in what manner each several thing can be created out of them; next after this it seems that the nature of the mind and the soul must now be displayed in my verses, and the old fear of Acheron driven headlong away, which utterly confounds the life of men from the very root, clouding all things with the blackness of death, and suffering no pleasure to be pure and unalloyed. For, although men often declare that disease and a life of False professions of disgrace are more to be feared than the lower realm of philosophy. death, and that they know that the soul's nature is of blood, or else of wind,[n] if by chance their whim so wills it, and that so they have no need at all of our philosophy, you may be sure by this that all is idly vaunted to win praise, and not because the truth is itself accepted. These A crisis reveals the same men, exiled from their country and banished far old fear from the sight of men, stained with some foul crime, beset of death, with every kind of care, live on all the same, and, spite of all, to whatever place they come in their misery, they make sacrifice to the dead, and slaughter black cattle and despatch offerings to the gods of the dead, and in their bitter plight far more keenly turn their hearts to religion. Wherefore it is more fitting to watch a man in doubt and

danger, and to learn of what manner he is in adversity;
for then at last a real cry is wrung from the bottom of his
heart: the mask is torn off, and the truth remains behind.

which is
the cause
of many
vices and
crimes,

Moreover, avarice and the blind craving for honours,
which constrain wretched men to overleap the boundaries
of right, and sometimes as comrades or accomplices in
crime to struggle night and day with surpassing toil to
rise up to the height of power—these sores in life are
fostered in no small degree by the fear of death. For
most often scorned disgrace and biting poverty are seen
to be far removed from pleasant settled life, and are, as
it were, a present dallying before the gates of death;
and while men, spurred by a false fear, desire to flee far
from them, and to drive them far away, they amass substance by civil bloodshed and greedily multiply their
riches, heaping slaughter on slaughter. Hardening their
heart they revel in a brother's bitter death, and hate and
fear their kinsmen's board. In like manner, often through
the same fear, they waste with envy that he is powerful,
he is regarded, who walks clothed with bright renown;
while they complain that they themselves are wrapped in
darkness and the mire. Some of them come to ruin to
win statues and a name; and often through fear of
death so deeply does the hatred of life and the sight of
the light possess men, that with sorrowing heart they
compass their own death, forgetting that it is this fear
which is the source of their woes, which assails their
honour, which bursts the bonds of friendship, and over-
turns affection from its lofty throne.[1] For often ere
now men have betrayed country and beloved parents,

[1] The reading is uncertain, but may have been *e summa . . . sede.*

seeking to shun the realms of Acheron. For even as and must children tremble and fear everything in blinding dark- be dispelled ness, so we sometimes dread in the light things that are by science. no whit more to be feared than what children shudder at in the dark, and imagine will come to pass. This terror then, this darkness of the mind, must needs be scattered, not by the rays of the sun and the gleaming shafts of day, but by the outer view and the inner law of nature.

First I say that the mind,[n] which we often call the A. Nature understanding, in which is placed the reasoning and guid- of (*a*) the ing power of life, is a part of a man no whit the less than mind. hand and foot and eyes are created parts of the whole The mind is a part of living being. ⟨Yet many wise men have thought⟩[1] that the body, the sensation of the mind is not placed in any part deter- mined, but is a certain vital habit of the body, which the Greeks call a harmony,[n] in that it makes us live with sensa- not a tion, although in no part does an understanding exist; 'harmony'. as when often good health is said to belong to the body, and yet it is not itself any part of a healthy man. In this wise they do not set the sensation of the mind in any part determined; and in this they seem to me to wander very far astray. Thus often the body, which is clear to 1. Mind see, is sick, when, all the same we feel pleasure in some and body are in- other hidden part; and contrariwise it happens that the dependent reverse often comes to be in turn, when one wretched in pleasure in mind feels pleasure in all his body; in no other wise and pain. than if, when a sick man's foot is painful, all the while, may be, his head is in no pain. Moreover, when the limbs 2. In sleep are given up to soft sleep, and the heavy body lies slack the body is senseless, and senseless, yet there is something else in us, which but the mind at that very time is stirred in many ways, and admits active.

---

[1] A line is lost, of which this must have been the general sense.

within itself all the motions of joy and baseless cares of heart. Now that you may be able to learn that the soul too is in the limbs, and that it is not by a harmony that the body is wont to feel, first of all it comes to pass that when a great part of the body is removed yet often the life lingers on in our limbs; and then again, when a few bodies of heat are scattered abroad and some air has been driven out through the mouth, that same life of a sudden abandons the veins and leaves the bones; so that you may be able to know from this that not all kinds of bodies have an equal part to play, nor do all equally support existence, but that rather those, which are the seeds of wind and burning heat, are the cause that life lingers in the limbs. There is then heat and a life-giving wind in the very body, which abandons our dying frame. Wherefore, since the nature of mind and soul has been revealed as a part of man, give up the name of harmony, which was handed down to musicians from high Helicon: or else they themselves have dragged it forth from some other source, and brought it over to this thing, which then was without a name of its own. Whatever it is, let them keep it: do you listen to the rest of my discourse.

Now I say that mind and soul are held in union one with the other, and form of themselves a single nature, but that the head, as it were, and lord in the whole body is the reason, which we call mind or understanding, and it is firmly seated in the middle region of the breast. For here it is that fear and terror throb, around these parts are soothing joys; here then is the understanding and the mind. The rest of the soul, spread abroad throughout the body, obeys and is moved at the will and inclina-

(b) The soul is in the body, not a harmony: 1. it survives, when much of the body is lost, but 2. the loss of particles of heat and air causes death.

The notion of the vital principle as 'a harmony' must be abandoned.

Mind and soul are one nature,

but mind, in the breast, is supreme.

tion of the understanding. The mind alone by itself has *It has pain and joy by itself,* understanding for itself and rejoices for itself, when no single thing stirs either soul or body. And just as, when head or eye hurts within us at the attack of pain, we are not tortured at the same time in all our body; so the mind sometimes feels pain by itself or waxes strong with joy, when all the rest of the soul through the limbs and frame is not roused by any fresh feeling. Nevertheless, *but excessive feeling is shared by the soul and so communicated to the body.* when the understanding is stirred by some stronger fear, we see that the whole soul feels with it throughout the limbs, and then sweat and pallor break out over all the body, and the tongue is crippled and the voice is choked, the eyes grow misty, the ears ring, the limbs give way beneath us, and indeed we often see men fall down through the terror in their mind; so that any one may easily learn from this that the soul is linked in union with the mind; for when it is smitten by the force of the mind, straightway it strikes the body and pushes it on.

This same reasoning shows that the nature of mind *Mind and soul are corporeal.* and soul is bodily. For when it is seen to push on the limbs, to pluck the body from sleep, to change the *For mind acts on body by touch,* countenance, and to guide and turn the whole man— none of which things we see can come to pass without touch, nor touch in its turn without body—must we not allow that mind and soul are formed of bodily nature? Moreover, you see that our mind suffers along with the body, and shares its feelings together in the body. If the *and is affected by the body's wounds.* shuddering shock of a weapon, driven within and laying bare bones and sinews, does not reach the life, yet faintness follows, and a pleasant swooning to the ground, and a turmoil of mind which comes to pass on the ground, and from time to time, as it were, a hesitating will to rise. Therefore it must needs be that the nature of the mind is bodily, since it is distressed by the blow of bodily weapons.

Mind and soul are formed of very minute particles:

Now of what kind of body this mind is, and of what parts it is formed, I will go on to give account to you in my discourse. First of all I say that it is very fine in texture, and is made and formed of very tiny particles. That this is so, if you give attention, you may be able to learn from this. Nothing is seen to come to pass so swiftly as what the mind pictures to itself coming to pass and starts to do itself. Therefore the mind bestirs itself more quickly than any of the things whose nature is manifest for all to see. But because it is so very nimble, it is bound to be formed of exceeding round and exceeding tiny seeds, so that its particles may be able to move when smitten by a little impulse. For so water moves and oscillates at the slightest impulse, seeing it is formed of little particles, quick to roll. But, on the other hand, the nature of honey is more stable, its fluid more sluggish, and its movement more hesitating; for the whole mass of its matter clings more together, because, we may be sure, it is not formed of bodies so smooth, nor so fine and round. For a light trembling breath can constrain a high heap of poppy-seed to scatter from top to bottom before your eyes: but, on the other hand, a pile of stones or corn-ears it can by no means separate. Therefore, in proportion as bodies are tinier and smoother, so they are gifted with nimbleness. But, on the other hand, all things that are found to be of greater weight or more spiky, the more firm set they are. Now, therefore, since the nature of the mind has been found nimble beyond the rest, it

1. because they are so mobile;

must needs be formed of bodies exceeding small and smooth and round. And this truth, when known to you, will in many things, good friend, prove useful, and will be reckoned of service. This fact, too, declares the nature of the mind, of how thin a texture it is formed, and in how small a place it might be contained, could it be gathered in a mass; that as soon as the unruffled peace of death has laid hold on a man, and the nature of mind and soul has passed away, you could discern nothing there, that sight or weight can test, stolen from the entire body; death preserves all save the feeling of life, and some warm heat. And so it must needs be that the whole soul is made of very tiny seeds, and is linked on throughout veins, flesh, and sinews; inasmuch as, when it is all already gone from the whole body, yet the outer contour of the limbs is preserved unbroken, nor is a jot of weight wanting. Even so it is, when the flavour of wine has passed away or when the sweet breath of a perfume is scattered to the air, or when its savour is gone from some body; still the thing itself seems not a whit smaller to the eyes on that account, nor does anything seem withdrawn from its weight, because, we may be sure, many tiny seeds go to make flavours and scent in the whole body of things. Wherefore once and again you may know that the nature of the understanding and the soul is formed of exceeding tiny seeds, since when it flees away it carries with it no jot of weight.

2. because their departure at death makes no change in appearance or weight.

Nevertheless we must not think that this nature is simple. For it is a certain thin breath that deserts the dying, mingled with heat, and heat moreover draws air with it; nor indeed is there any heat, that has not air too mixed with it. For because its nature is rare, it

Composition of the soul: wind, heat, air;

must needs be that many first-beginnings of air move about in it. Already then we have found the nature of the soul to be triple; and yet all these things are not enough to create sensation, since the mind does not admit that any of these can create the motions that bring sensation ⟨or the thoughts of the mind⟩.[1] It must needs be then that some fourth nature [n] too be added to these. But it is altogether without name; than it there exists nothing more nimble, nothing more fine, nor made of smaller or smoother particles. It first sends abroad the motions that bring sensation among the limbs: for it is first stirred, being made up of small shapes; then heat receives the motions and the hidden power of wind, and then air; then all things are set moving, the blood receives the shock and all the flesh feels the thrill; last of all it passes to the bones and marrow, be it pleasure or the heat of opposite kind. Yet not for naught can pain pierce thus far within, nor any biting ill pass through, but that all things are so disordered that there is no more place for life, and the parts of the soul scatter abroad through all the pores of the body. But for the most part a limit is set to these motions, as it were, on the surface of the body: and by this means we avail to keep our life.

the fourth nature.

The course of sensation.

The combination of the elements in the soul.

Now, as I long to give account in what way these parts are mingled one with another, and in what manner bound together so that they can act, against my will the poverty of my country's tongue holds me back; yet, despite that, I will touch the theme, as best I can in brief. For the first-beginnings course to and fro among themselves with the motions of first-beginnings,[n] so that no single one can be put apart, nor can its powers be set in play divided

[1] The MSS. are corrupt, but this must have been the sense.

from others by empty space, but they are, as it were, the many forces of a single body. Even as in the flesh of any living creature anywhere there is smell and a certain heat and savour, and yet of all these is made up the bulk of a single body. Thus heat and air and the hidden power of wind mingled create one nature together with that nimble force, which sends among them from itself the beginning of motion, whence the motion that brings sensation first arises throughout the flesh. For right deep within this nature lies hid far below, nor is there anything further beneath than this in our bodies, and it is moreover the very soul of the whole soul. Even as in our limbs and our whole body the force of the mind and the power of the soul is secretly immingled, because it is formed of small and rare bodies. So, you see, this force without a name, made of tiny bodies, lies concealed, and is moreover, as it were, the very soul of the whole soul and holds sway in the whole body. In like manner it must needs be that wind and air and heat act mingled together throughout the limbs, and one is more above or below the rest, yet so that one single thing is seen to be composed of all; lest heat and wind apart, and apart from them the power of air, should put an end to sensation, and by their separation break it up. Moreover the mind possesses that heat, which it dons when it boils with rage, and the fire flashes more keenly from the eyes. Much cold breath too it has, which goes along with fear, and starts a shuddering in the limbs and stirs the whole frame. And it has too that condition of air lulled to rest, which comes to pass when the breast is calm and the face unruffled. But those creatures have more of heat, whose fiery heart and passionate mind easily boils up in

The hidden fourth nature.

The other elements.

Heat causes anger;

wind fear;

air calmness.

Illustrations from animals

anger. Foremost in this class is the fierce force of lions, who often as they groan break their hearts with roaring, and cannot contain in their breast the billows of their wrath. But the cold heart of deer is more full of wind, and more quickly it rouses the chilly breath in its flesh, which makes a shuddering motion start in the limbs. But the nature of oxen draws its life rather from calm air, nor ever is the smoking torch of anger set to it to rouse it overmuch, drenching it with the shadow of murky mist, nor is it pierced and frozen by the chill shafts of fear : it has its place midway between the two, the deer

and from men.

and the raging lions. So is it with the race of men. However much training gives some of them an equal culture, yet it leaves those first traces of the nature of the mind of each. Nor must we think that such maladies can be plucked out by the roots, but that one man will more swiftly fall into bitter anger, another be a little sooner assailed by fear, while a third will take some things

The power of philosophy to overcome natural habits.

more gently than is right. And in many other things it must needs be that the diverse natures of men differ, and the habits that follow thereon ; but I cannot now set forth the secret causes of these, nor discover names for all the shapes of the first atoms, whence arises this variety in things. One thing herein I see that I can affirm, that so small are the traces of these natures left, which reason could not dispel for us, that nothing hinders us from living a life worthy of the gods.

Union of soul and body is the cause of life.

This nature then of the soul [n] is protected by the whole body, and is itself the guardian of the body, and the cause of its life ; for the two cling together by common roots, and it is seen that they cannot be torn asunder without destruction. Even as it is not easy to tear out the scent from lumps of frankincense, but that its nature too passes away. So it is not easy to draw out the nature of mind and soul from the whole body, but that all alike is dissolved. With first-beginnings so closely interlaced from their very birth are they begotten, endowed with a life shared in common, nor, as is clear to see, can the power of body or mind feel apart, either for itself without the force of the other, but by the common motions of the two on this side and on that is sensation kindled and fanned throughout our flesh. Moreover, the body is never begotten by itself, nor grows alone, nor is seen to last on after death. For never, as the moisture of water often gives off the heat, which has been lent to it, and is not for that reason torn asunder itself, but remains unharmed, never, I say, in this way can the abandoned frame bear the separation of the soul, but it utterly perishes torn asunder and rots away. So from the beginning of existence body and soul, in mutual union, learn the motions that give life, yea, even when hidden in the mother's limbs and womb, so that separation cannot come to pass without hurt and ruin; so that you can see, since the cause of their life is linked together, that their natures too must be linked in one.

Each is necessary to the other,

and cannot exist without it.

For the rest, if any one is for proving that the body does not feel, and believes that it is the soul mingled with the whole body that takes up this motion, which we call sensation, he is fighting even against plain and true facts. For who will ever tell us what the feeling of the body is, if it be not what the clear fact itself has shown and taught us? 'But when the soul has passed away the body is utterly deprived of sensation.' Yes, for it loses that which was not its own in life, and many other things besides it loses, when it is driven out of life.

The body itself feels owing to its combination with soul.

Example :
the eyes
themselves
see and
are not
' doors to
the soul '.

To say, moreover, that the eyes can see nothing, but
that the mind looks out through them as when doors are
opened, is hard, seeing that the feeling in the eyes leads
us the other way ; for that feeling drags us on and forces us
to the very pupils ;[1] yea, for often we cannot see bright
things, because our sight is thwarted by the light. But
that does not happen with doors ; for the doors, through
which we see, do not suffer any pain when they are
opened. Moreover, if our eyes are as doors,[n] then
the mind, it is clear, ought to discern things better
if the eyes were taken out and removed, door-posts
and all.

Soul and
body atoms
do not
alternate.

Herein you could by no means accept the teaching,
which the judgement of the holy man, Democritus,[n] sets
before us, that the first-beginnings of soul and body alternate, set each next each, first one and then the other, and

Soul atoms
are set at
intervals.

so weave the web of our limbs. For, as the particles of
soul are far smaller than those of which our body and flesh
are composed, so too they are less in number, and only
here and there are scattered through our frame ; so that
you may warrant this : that the first-beginnings of soul
preserve distances apart as great as are the smallest bodies
which, when cast upon us, can first start the motions of

Proof from
things
which we
do not feel
when they
touch the
body.

sensation in the body. For sometimes we do not feel
the clinging of dust on the body, nor know that chalk
has been shaken on us and settled on our limbs, nor do
we feel a mist at night, nor the slender threads of the
spider that strike against us, when we are caught in its
meshes as we move, nor know that his twisted web has
fallen on our head, or the feathers of birds or the flying
down from plants, which from its exceeding lightness,

[1] i. e. forces us to conclude that it is they which see.

for the most part falls not lightly ; nor do we feel the
passage of every kind of crawling creature nor each single
footstep, which gnats and other insects plant upon our
body. Indeed, so many things must first be stirred in
us, before the seeds of soul mingled with our bodies
throughout our frame feel that the first-beginnings have
been shaken, and before they can by jostling in these
spaces set between, rush together, unite and leap back
in turn.

Now the mind is more the keeper of the fastnesses of
life, more the monarch of life than the power of the soul.
For without the mind and understanding no part of the
soul can hold out in the frame for a tiny moment of time,
but follows in its train without demur, and scatters into
air, and deserts the chill frame in the frost of death. Yet
one, whose mind and understanding have abode firm,
abides in life.   However much the trunk is mangled with
the limbs hewn all around, though the soul be rent from
him all around and wrested from his limbs, he lives and
draws in the breath of heaven to give him life. Robbed,
if not of all, yet of a great part of his soul, still he lingers
on and clings to life.   Even as, when the eye is mangled
all around, if the pupil has abode unharmed, then the
living power of sight stands firm, if only you do not
destroy the whole ball of the eye, and cut all round the
pupil, and leave it by itself : for that will not be done
without the destruction of the eyes too.   But if that tiny
part in the middle of the eye is eaten away, at once light
is gone, and darkness follows on, however much the bright
ball is in other places unharmed.   In such a compact are
soul and mind ever bound together.

Come now, that you may be able to learn that the

[margin note:] The mind is more essential for life than the soul.

[margin note:] Illustration from the pupil of the eye.

B. The
soul is
mortal.

minds and the light souls [n] of living things have birth and
death, I will hasten to set forth verses long sought out
and found with glad effort, worthy to guide your life.
Be it yours [n] to link both of these in a single name, and
when, to choose a case, I continue to speak of the soul,
proving that it is mortal, suppose that I speak of mind as
well, inasmuch as they are at one each with the other
and compose a single thing.   First of all, since I have

Proofs.
1. It is
mobile and
made of
minute
atoms :

shown that it is finely made of tiny bodies and of first-
beginnings far smaller than the liquid moisture of water
or cloud or smoke—for it far surpasses them in speed of
motion, and is more prone to move when smitten by some
slender cause ; for indeed it is moved by images of smoke
and cloud : [n] even as when slumbering in sleep we see
altars breathing steam on high, and sending up their
smoke ; for beyond all doubt these are idols that are
borne to us :—now therefore, since, when vessels are
shattered, you behold the water flowing away on every
side, and the liquid parting this way and that, and since

therefore
it cannot
be held
together in
air when
it has left
the body.

cloud and smoke part asunder into air, you must believe
that the soul too is scattered and passes away far more
swiftly, and is dissolved more quickly into its first-bodies,
when once it is withdrawn from a man's limbs, and has
departed.   For indeed, since the body, which was, as it
were, the vessel of the soul, cannot hold it together, when
by some chance it is shattered and made rare, since the
blood is withdrawn from the veins, how could you believe
that the soul could be held together by any air, which is
more rare than our body ⟨and can contain it less⟩ ? [1]

2. It is
born,

Moreover, we feel that the understanding is begotten
along with the body, and grows together with it, and

---

[1] The text is uncertain, but this was probably the meaning.

along with it comes to old age. For as children totter with feeble and tender body, so a weak judgement of mind goes with it. Then when their years are ripe and their strength hardened, greater is their sense and increased their force of mind. Afterward, when now the body is shattered by the stern strength of time, and the frame has sunk with its force dulled, then the reason is maimed, the tongue raves, the mind stumbles, all things give way and fail at once. And so it is natural that all the nature of the mind should also be dissolved, even as is smoke, into the high breezes of the air; inasmuch as we see that it is born with the body, grows with it, and, as I have shown, at the same time becomes weary and worn with age.

grows, and ages with the body:

therefore it is dissolved with it.

Then follows this that we see that, just as the body itself suffers wasting diseases and poignant pain, so the mind too has its biting cares and grief and fear; wherefore it is natural that it should also share in death. Nay more, during the diseases of the body the mind often wanders astray; for it loses its reason and speaks raving words, and sometimes in a heavy lethargy is carried off into a deep unending sleep, when eyes and head fall nodding, in which it hears not voices, nor can know the faces of those who stand round, summoning it back to life, bedewing face and cheeks with their tears. Therefore you must needs admit that the mind too is dissolved, inasmuch as the contagion of disease pierces into it. For both pain and disease are alike fashioners of death, as we have been taught ere now by many a man's decease. Again, when the stinging strength of wine has entered into a man, and its heat has spread abroad throughout his veins, why is it that there follows a heaviness in the limbs, his legs are entangled as he staggers, his tongue is sluggish,

3. The mind, like the body, has pains.

4. The diseases of the body affect the mind.

5. Intoxication affects body and mind alike.

and his mind heavy, his eyes swim, shouting, sobbing, quarrelling grows apace, and then all the other signs of this sort that go along with them ; why does this come to pass, except that the mastering might of the wine is wont to confound the soul even within the body? But whenever things can be so confounded and entangled, they testify that, if a cause a whit stronger shall have made its way within, they must needs perish, robbed of any further life. Nay more, some man, often before our very eyes, seized suddenly by violent disease, falls, as though by a lightning-stroke, and foams at the mouth ; he groans and shivers throughout his frame, he loses his wits, his muscles grow taut, he writhes, he breathes in gasps, and tossing to and fro wearies his limbs. Because, you may be sure, his soul rent asunder by the violence of disease throughout his frame,[1] is confounded, and gathers foam, as on the salt sea the waters boil beneath the stern strength of the winds. Further, the groaning is wrung from him, because his limbs are racked with pain, and more than all because the particles of voice are driven out, and are carried crowding forth from his mouth, along the way they are wont, where is their paved path. Loss of wits comes to pass, because the force of mind and soul is confounded, and, as I have shown, is torn apart and tossed to and fro, rent asunder by that same poison. Thereafter, when by now the cause of malady has ebbed, and the biting humours of the distempered body return to their hiding-places, then, as it were staggering, he first rises, and little by little returns to all his senses, and regains his soul. When mind and soul then even within the body are tossed by such great maladies, and in wretched plight

6. Still more does epilepsy, which tears and rends the soul.

---

[1] The text is uncertain, but the sense probably this.

are rent asunder and distressed, why do you believe that
without the body in the open air they can continue life
amid the warring winds? And since we perceive that the
mind is cured, just like the sick body, and we see that it
can be changed by medicine, this too forewarns us that
the mind has a mortal life. For whosoever attempts and
essays to alter the mind, or seeks to change any other
nature, must indeed add parts to it or transfer them from
their order, or take away some small whit at least from
the whole. But what is immortal does not permit its
parts to be transposed, nor that any whit should be added
or depart from it. For whenever a thing changes and
passes out of its own limits, straightway this is the death
of that which was before. And so whether the mind is
sick, it gives signs of its mortality, as I have proved, or
whether it is changed by medicine. So surely is true fact
seen to run counter to false reasoning, and to shut off
retreat from him who flees, and with double-edged refutation to prove the falsehood.

Again, we often behold a man pass away little by little
and limb by limb lose the sensation of life; first of all
the toes and nails on his feet grow livid, then the feet and
legs die, thereafter through the rest of his frame, step by
step, pass the traces of chill death. Since this nature
of the soul is severed nor does it come forth all intact at
one moment, it must be counted mortal. But if by
chance you think that it could of its own power draw
itself inwards through the frame, and contract its parts
into one place, and so withdraw sensation from all the
limbs, yet nevertheless that place, to which so great
abundance of soul is gathered together, must needs be

7. Mind, like body, can be cured by medicine.

8. In cases of mortifi-cation, the soul perishes bit by bit with the body.

It cannot contract into one place,

seen possessed of greater sensation; but since such place is nowhere found, you may be sure, as we said before, it is rent in pieces and scattered abroad, and so perishes. Nay more, if it were our wish to grant what is false, and allow that the soul could be massed together in the body of those, who as they die leave the light of day part by part, still you must needs confess that the soul is mortal, nor does it matter whether it passes away scattered through the air, or is drawn into one out of all its various parts and grows sottish, since sense more and more in every part fails the whole man, and in every part less and less of life remains.

or if it does, still it perishes.

9. The mind, like any other organ of sense, cannot exist without the body.

And since the mind is one part of man,[n] which abides rooted in a place determined, just as are ears and eyes and all the other organs of sense which guide the helm of life; and, just as hand and eye or nostrils, sundered apart from us, cannot feel nor be, but in fact are in a short time melted in corruption, so the mind cannot exist by itself without the body and the very man, who seems to be, as it were, the vessel of the mind, or aught else you like to picture more closely bound to it, inasmuch as the body clings to it with binding ties.

10. Soul and body live by their mutual union.

Again, the living powers of body and mind prevail by union, one with the other, and so enjoy life; for neither without body can the nature of mind by itself alone produce the motions of life, nor yet bereft of soul can body last on and feel sensation. We must know that just as the eye by itself, if torn out by the roots, cannot discern anything apart from the whole body, so, it is clear, soul and mind by themselves have no power. Doubtless because in close mingling throughout veins and flesh, throughout sinews and bones, their first-beginnings are held close by all the body, nor can they freely leap asunder with great spaces between; and so shut in they make those sense-giving motions, which outside the body cast out into the breezes of air after death they cannot make, because they are not in the same way held together. For indeed air will be body, yea a living thing, if the soul can hold itself together, and confine itself to those motions, which before it made in the sinews and right within the body. Wherefore, again and again, when the whole protection of the body is undone and the breath of life is driven without, you must needs admit that the sensations of the mind and the soul are dissolved, since the cause of life in soul and body is closely linked.

In the air the soul could not be held together or produce the vital motions.

Again, since the body cannot endure the severing of the soul, but that it decays with a foul stench, why do you doubt that the force of the soul has gathered together from deep down within, and has trickled out, scattering abroad like smoke, and that the body has changed and fallen crumbling in such great ruin, because its foundations have been utterly moved from their seat, as the soul trickles forth through the limbs, and through all the winding ways, which are in the body, and all the pores? So that in many ways you may learn that the nature of the soul issued through the frame sundered in parts, and that even within the body it was rent in pieces in itself, before it slipped forth and swam out into the breezes of air. Nay more, while it moves still within the limits of life, yet often from some cause the soul seems to be shaken and to move, and to wish to be released from the whole body; the face seems to grow flaccid, as at the hour of death, and all the limbs to fall limp on the bloodless trunk. Even so it is, when, as men

11. The gradual decay of the body testifies to the breaking up of the soul before departure.

12. A great shock, not resulting in death, shows the same disturbance of the soul.

say, the heart has had a shock, or the heart has failed ; [n] when all is alarm, and one and all struggle to clutch at the last link to life. For then the mind is shaken through and through, and all the power of the soul, and both fall in ruin with the body too ; so that a cause a whit stronger might bring dissolution. Why do you doubt after all this but that the soul, if driven outside the body, frail as it is, without in the open air, robbed of its shelter, would not only be unable to last on through all time, but could not hold together even for a moment ? For it is clear that no one, as he dies, feels his soul going forth whole from all his body, nor coming up first to the throat and the gullet up above, but rather failing in its place in a quarter determined ; just as he knows that the other senses are dissolved each in their own place. But if our mind were immortal, it would not at its death so much lament that it was dissolved, but rather that it went forth and left its slough, as does a snake.

For no dying man feels his soul depart all at once.

Again, why is the understanding and judgement of the mind never begotten in head or feet or hands, but is fixed for all men in one abode in a quarter determined, except that places determined are assigned to each thing for its birth, and in which each several thing can abide when it is created,[1] that so it may have its manifold parts arranged that never can the order of its limbs be seen reversed? So surely does one thing follow on another, nor is flame wont to be born of flowing streams, nor cold to be conceived in fire.

13. The mind has its fixed place, like any other perishable thing.

Moreover, if the nature of the soul is immortal and

---

[1] There may be a verse lost here, or else the construction is slightly careless.

can feel when sundered from our body, we must, I trow, suppose it endowed with five senses. Nor in any other way can we picture to ourselves [n] the souls wandering in the lower world of Acheron. And so painters and the former generations of writers have brought before us souls thus endowed with senses. Yet neither eyes nor nose nor even hand can exist for the soul apart from body, nor again tongue apart or ears ; the souls cannot therefore feel by themselves or even exist.

14. An immortal soul must have senses of its own :

but they cannot exist apart from body.

And since we feel that the sensation of life is present in the whole body, and we see that the whole is a living thing, if some force suddenly hew it in the middle with swift blow, so that it severs each half apart, beyond all doubt the force of the soul too will be cleft in twain, torn asunder and riven together with the body. But what is cleft and separates into any parts, disclaims, assuredly, that its nature is everlasting. They tell how often scythe-bearing chariots, glowing in the mellay of slaughter, so suddenly lop off limbs, that the part which falls lopped off from the frame is seen to shiver on the ground, while in spite of all the mind and spirit of the man cannot feel the pain, through the suddenness of the stroke, and at the same time, because his mind is swallowed up in the fervour of the fight; with the body that is left him he makes for the fight and the slaughter, and often knows not that his left arm with its shield is gone, carried away by the wheels among the horses and the ravening scythes ; and another sees not that his right arm has dropped, while he climbs up and presses onward. Then another struggles to rise when his leg is lost, while at his side on the ground his dying foot twitches its toes. And the head lopped off from the warm living trunk keeps on the

15. When the body is cut, bits of soul survive in the severed parts, so that it cannot be immortal. Examples : limbs hewn off in battle ;

ground the look of life and the wide-open eyes, until it
has yielded up all the last vestiges of soul.   Nay more, if

a snake
chopped
into bits;

you should choose to chop into many parts with an axe
the body [1] of a snake with quivering tongue, angry tail,
and long body, you will then perceive all the hewn parts
severally writhing under the fresh blow, and scattering the
ground with gore, and the fore part making open-mouthed
for its own hinder part, in order that, smitten by the
burning pain of the wound, it may quench it with its
bite.   Shall we say then that there is a whole soul in all
those little parts?   But by that reasoning it will follow
that one living creature had many souls in its body.   And

in each case
the soul is
divided.

so that soul which was one together with the body has
been severed; wherefore both body and soul must be
thought mortal, since each alike is cleft into many parts.

16. If the
soul is
eternal, we
ought to
remember
a previous
existence.

Moreover, if the nature of the soul is immortal, and it
enters into the body at our birth, why can we not remember also the part of our life already gone, why
do we not preserve traces of things done before?   For if
the power of the mind is so much changed that all remembrance of things past is lost to it, that state is not,
I trow, a far step from death; wherefore you must needs
admit that the soul, which was before, has passed away,
and that that which now is, has now been created.

17. If
the soul
entered the
body from
without, it
could not
be so closely
connected
with it.

Moreover, if when our body [n] is already formed the
living power of the mind is wont to be put in just when
we are born, and when we are crossing the threshold into
life, it would not then be natural that it should be seen
to grow with the body, yea, together with the limbs in
the very blood, but 'tis natural that it should live all
alone by itself as in a den, yet so that the whole body

---

[1] Reading *truncum* for *utrumque*, but the text is uncertain.

nevertheless is rich in sensation. Wherefore, again and again, we must not think that souls are without a birth, or released from the law of death. For neither can we think that they could be so closely linked to our bodies if they were grafted in them from without—but that all this is so, plain fact on the other hand declares : for the soul is so interlaced through veins, flesh, sinews, and bones that the teeth, too, have their share in sensation ; as toothache shows and the twinge of cold water, and the biting on a sharp stone if it be hid in a piece of bread—nor, when they are so interwoven, can they, it is clear, issue forth entire, and unravel themselves intact from all the sinews and bones and joints. But if by chance you think that the soul is wont to be grafted in us from without, and then permeate through our limbs, all the more will it perish as it fuses with the body. For that which permeates dissolves, and so passes away. For even as food parcelled out among all the pores of the body, when it is sent about into all the limbs and members, perishes and furnishes a new nature out of itself, so soul and mind, however whole they may pass into the fresh-made body, still are dissolved as they permeate, while through all the pores there are sent abroad into the limbs the particles, whereof this nature of the mind is formed, which now holds sway in our body, born from that which then perished, parcelled out among the limbs. Wherefore it is seen that the nature of the soul is neither without a birthday nor exempt from death.

18. If it enters and is then distributed, it must perish in the operation.

Moreover, are seeds of soul left or not in the lifeless body? For if they are left and are still there, it will follow that it cannot rightly be held immortal, since it

19. If soul atoms are left in the body, the

soul must
be broken
up : if not,
how ac-
count for
the genera-
tion of
worms in
a corpse ?
Their souls
cannot
come from
without,

has left the body maimed by the loss of some parts. But if it has been removed and fled from the limbs while still entire, so that it has left no part of itself in the body, how is it that corpses, when the flesh is now putrid, teem with worms, and how does so great a store of living creatures, boneless and bloodless, swarm over the heaving frame ? But if by chance you believe that the souls are grafted in the worms from without, and can pass severally into their bodies, and do not consider why many thousands of souls should gather together, whence one only has departed, yet there is this that seems worth asking and putting to the test, whether after all those souls go hunting for all the seeds of the little worms, and themselves build up a home to live in, or whether they are, as it were, grafted in bodies

or (*a*)
they could
not fashion
bodies for
themselves

already quite formed. But there is no ready reason why they should make the bodies themselves, why they should be at such pains. For indeed, when they are without a body, they do not flit about harassed by disease and cold and hunger. For the body is more prone to suffer by these maladies, and 'tis through contact with the body that the mind suffers many ills. But still grant that it be ever so profitable for them to fashion a body wherein to enter ; yet there seems to be no way whereby they could. Souls then do not fashion for themselves bodies and frames.

nor (*b*)
enter bodies
already
formed.
20. Races
of animals
can only
keep their
characteris-
istics be-
cause their
soul is

Nor yet can it be that they are grafted in bodies already made ; for neither will they be able to be closely inter-woven, nor will contact be made by a sharing of sensation.

Again, why does fiery passion [n] go along with the grim brood of lions and cunning with foxes ; why is the habit of flight handed on to deer from their sires, so that their father's fear spurs their limbs ? And indeed all other habits of this sort, why are they always implanted in the

limbs and temper from the first moment of life, if it be
not because a power of mind determined by its own seed
and breed grows along with the body of each animal?
But if the soul were immortal and were wont to change
its bodies, then living creatures would have characters
intermingled; the dog of Hyrcanian seed would often
flee the onset of the horned hart, and the hawk would fly
fearful through the breezes of air at the coming of the
dove; men would be witless, and wise the fierce tribes
of wild beasts. For it is argued on false reasoning, when
men say that an immortal soul is altered, when it changes
its body: for what is changed, is dissolved, and so passes
away. For the parts are transferred and shift from their
order; wherefore they must be able to be dissolved too
throughout the limbs, so that at last they may all pass
away together with the body. But if they say that the
souls of men always pass into human bodies, still I will
ask why a soul can become foolish after being wise, why
no child has reason, why the mare's foal is not as well
trained as the bold strength of a horse. We may be sure
they will be driven to say that in a weak body the mind
too is weak. But if that indeed comes to pass, you must
needs admit that the soul is mortal, since it changes so
much throughout the frame, and loses its former life and
sense. Or in what manner will the force of mind be able
along with each several body to wax strong and attain
the coveted bloom of life, unless it be partner too with
the body at its earliest birth? Or why does it desire[n] to
issue forth abroad from the aged limbs? does it fear to
remain shut up in a decaying body, lest its home, worn
out with the long spell of years, fall on it? But an
immortal thing knows no dangers.

Side notes:

determined by and grows with their body.

21. If immortal souls entered their bodies, animals would be of miscellaneous characters. For an immortal soul could not change in passing from one body to another.

22. Even if human souls only pass into men, they change from old to young.

23. The soul cannot grow with the body, unless born with it.

24. An immortal soul would not wish to leave the body in old age.

25. Think
of the im-
mortal souls
wrangling
for their
mortal
body!

Again, that the souls should be present at the wedlock of Venus and the birth of wild beasts, seems to be but laughable; that immortal souls should stand waiting for mortal limbs in numbers numberless, and should wrangle one with another in hot haste, which first before the others may find an entrance; unless by chance the souls have a compact sealed, that whichever arrives first on its wings, shall first have entrance, so that they strive not forcibly at all with one another.

26. Soul
and mind,
like all
other
things,
have their
appointed
place, apart
from which
they can-
not exist.

Again, a tree cannot exist in the sky,[n] nor clouds in the deep waters, nor can fishes live in the fields, nor blood be present in wood, nor sap in stones. It is determined and ordained where each thing can grow and have its place. So the nature of the mind cannot come to birth alone without body, nor exist far apart from sinews and blood. But if this could be, far sooner might the force of mind itself exist in head or shoulders, or right down in the heels, and be wont to be born in any part you will, but at least remain in the same man or the same vessel. But since even within our body it is determined and seen to be ordained where soul and mind can dwell apart and grow, all the more must we deny that it could continue or be begotten outside the whole body. Wherefore, when the body has perished, you must needs confess that the soul too has passed away, rent asunder in the whole body.

27. The
union of
mortal and
immortal
is absurd.

Nay, indeed, to link the mortal with the everlasting, and to think that they can feel together and act one upon the other, is but foolishness. For what can be pictured more at variance, more estranged within itself and inharmonious, than that what is mortal should be linked in union with the immortal and everlasting to brave raging storms? Moreover, if ever things abide for everlasting,[n] it must needs be either that, because they are of solid body, they beat back assaults, nor suffer anything to come within them which might unloose the close-locked parts within, such as are the bodies of matter whose nature we have declared before; or that they are able to continue throughout all time, because they are exempt from blows, as is the void, which abides untouched, nor suffers a whit from assault; or else because there is no supply of room all around, into which, as it were, things might part asunder and be broken up—even as the sum of sums is eternal— nor is there any room without into which they may scatter, nor are there bodies which might fall upon them and break them up with stout blow. But if by chance the soul is rather to be held immortal for this reason, because it is fortified and protected from things fatal to life, or because things harmful to its life come not at all, or because such as come in some way depart defeated before we can feel what harm they do us ⟨clear facts show us that this is not so⟩.[1] For besides that it falls sick along with the diseases of the body, there comes to it that which often torments it about things that are to be, and makes it ill at ease with fear, and wears it out with care; and when its evil deeds are past and gone, yet sin brings remorse. There is too the peculiar frenzy of the mind and forgetfulness of the past, yes, and it is plunged into the dark waters of lethargy.

Death, then, is naught to us,[n] nor does it concern us a whit, inasmuch as the nature of the mind is but a mortal possession. And even as in the time gone by we felt no ill, when the Poeni came from all sides to the shock of battle, when all the world, shaken by the hurrying turmoil

Marginal notes:

28. The soul does not fulfil any of the conditions of immortality.

C. Death is nothing to us. We shall not be conscious after death

---

[1] A line is lost, of which this was probably the sense.

any more
than we
were before
birth.

of war, shuddered and reeled beneath the high coasts of
heaven, in doubt to which people's sway must fall all
human power by land and sea; so, when we shall be no
more, when there shall have come the parting of body
and soul, by whose union we are made one, you may
know that nothing at all will be able to happen to us,
who then will be no more, or stir our feeling; no, not if
earth shall be mingled with sea, and sea with sky. And

Even if the
soul could
feel alone,
it would
not concern
us.
If time
should
reunite the
same atoms
that now
form us,
still it
would not
affect us.

even if the nature of mind and the power of soul has
feeling, after it has been rent asunder from our body, yet
it is naught to us, who are made one by the mating and
marriage of body and soul. Nor, if time should gather
together our substance after our decease and bring it back
again as it is now placed, if once more the light of life
should be vouchsafed to us, yet, even were that done, it
would not concern us at all, when once the remembrance
of our former selves were snapped in twain. And even
now we care not at all for the selves that we once were,
not at all are we touched by any torturing pain for them.
For when you look back over all the lapse of immeasurable
time that now is gone, and think how manifold are the
motions of matter, you could easily believe this too, that
these same seeds, whereof we now are made, have often
been placed in the same order as they are now; and yet
we cannot recall that in our mind's memory; for in between lies a break in life, and all the motions have wandered
everywhere far astray from sense. For, if by chance there

Grief
and pain
necessitate
a per-
cipient :
but death
prevents
our feeling.

is to be grief and pain for a man, he must needs himself
too exist at that time, that ill may befall him. Since
death forestalls this, and prevents the being of him, on
whom these misfortunes might crowd, we may know that
we have naught to fear in death, and that he who is no

more cannot be wretched, and that it were no whit different if he had never at any time been born, when once immortal death hath stolen away mortal life.

And so, when you see a man chafing at his lot, that after death he will either rot away with his body laid in earth, or be destroyed by flames, or the jaws of wild beasts, you may be sure that his words do not ring true, and that deep in his heart lies some secret pang, however much he deny himself that he believes that he will have any feeling in death. For he does not, I trow, grant [n] what he professes, nor the grounds of his profession, nor does he remove and cast himself root and branch out of life, but all unwitting supposes something of himself to live on. For when in life each man pictures to himself that it will come to pass that birds and wild beasts will mangle his body in death, he pities himself; for neither does he separate himself from the corpse, nor withdraw himself enough from the outcast body, but thinks that it is he, and, as he stands watching, taints it with his own feeling. Hence he chafes that he was born mortal, and sees not that in real death there will be no second self, to live and mourn to himself his own loss, or to stand there and be pained that he lies mangled or burning. For if it is an evil in death to be mauled by the jaws and teeth of wild beasts, I cannot see how it is not sharp pain to be laid upon hot flames and cremated, or to be placed in honey and stifled, and to grow stiff with cold,[n] lying on the surface on the top of an icy rock, or to be crushed and ground by a weight of earth above.

'Now no more shall thy glad home welcome thee, nor thy good wife and sweet children run up to snatch the first kisses, and touch thy heart with a silent thrill of

A professed believer in the mortality of the soul is often insincere.

He imagines a self surviving to grieve at the fate of the body.

Yet one treatment of it will hurt him no more than another.

The dead has no more desire for the joys of life,

joy. No more shalt thou have power to prosper in thy ways, or to be a sure defence to thine own. Pitiful thou art,' men say, 'and pitifully has one malignant day taken from thee all the many prizes of life.' Yet to this they add not: 'nor does there abide with thee any longer any yearning for these things.' But if they saw this clearly in mind, and followed it out in their words, they would free themselves from great anguish and fear of mind.

and the living should not grieve at his entering into rest.

'Thou, indeed, even as thou art now fallen asleep in death, shalt so be for all time to come, released from every pain and sorrow. But 'tis we who have wept with tears unquenchable for thee, as thou wert turned to ashes hard by us on the awesome place of burning, and that unending grief no day shall take from our hearts.' But of him who speaks thus we should ask, what there is so exceeding bitter, if it comes at the last to sleep and rest, that any one should waste away in never-ending lamentation.

Men say: 'Let us drink, for to-morrow we die': but in death they will have no thirst.

This too men often do, when they are lying at the board, and hold their cups in their hands, and shade their faces with garlands: they say from the heart, 'Brief is this enjoyment for us puny men: soon it will be past, nor ever thereafter will it be ours to call it back.' As though in death this were to be foremost among their ills, that thirst would burn the poor wretches and parch them with its drought, or that there would abide with

In sleep we have no desire for life, much less in death.

them a yearning for any other thing. For never does any man long for himself and life, when mind and body alike rest in slumber. For all we care sleep may then be never-ending, nor does any yearning for ourselves then beset us. And yet at that time those first-beginnings stray not at all far through our frame away from the motions that bring sense, when a man springs up from sleep and gathers himself together. Much less then should we think that death is to us, if there can be less than what we see to be nothing; for at our dying there follows a greater turmoil and scattering abroad of matter, nor does any one wake and rise again, whom the chill breach of life has once overtaken.

Again, suppose that the nature of things should of a sudden lift up her voice, and thus in these words herself rebuke some one of us : 'Why is death so great a thing to thee, mortal, that thou dost give way overmuch to sickly lamentation? why groan and weep at death? For if the life that is past and gone has been pleasant to thee, nor have all its blessings, as though heaped in a vessel full of holes,[n] run through and perished unenjoyed, why dost thou not retire like a guest sated with the banquet of life, and with calm mind embrace, thou fool, a rest that knows no care? But if all thou hast reaped hath been wasted and lost, and life is a stumbling-block, why seek to add more, all to be lost again foolishly and pass away unenjoyed; why not rather make an end of life and trouble? For there is naught more, which I can devise or discover to please thee : all things are ever as they were. If thy body is not yet wasted with years, nor thy limbs worn and decayed, yet all things remain as they were, even if thou shouldst live on to overpass all generations, nay rather, if thou shouldst never die.' What answer can we make, but that nature brings a just charge against us, and sets out in her pleading a true plaint? But if now some older man, smitten in years, should make lament, and pitifully bewail his decease more than is just, would she not rightly raise her voice and chide him in sharp tones? 'Away with tears henceforth, thou

Nature may justly rebuke us for lamenting our death.

Especially when an old man grieves to die.

rogue, set a bridle on thy laments. Thou hast enjoyed all the prizes of life and now dost waste away. But because thou yearnest ever for what is not with thee, and despisest the gifts at hand, uncompleted and unenjoyed thy life has slipped from thee, and, ere thou didst think it, death is standing by thy head, before thou hast the heart to depart filled and sated with good things. Yet now give up all these things so ill-fitted for thy years, and with calm mind, come, yield them to thy sons : [1] for so thou must.' She would be right, I trow, in her plea, right in her charge and chiding. For the old ever gives place thrust out by new things, and one thing must be restored at the expense of others : nor is any one sent down to the pit and to black Tartarus. There must needs be substance that the generations to come may grow ; yet all of them too will follow thee, when they have had their fill of life ; yea, just as thyself, these generations have passed away before, and will pass away again. So one thing shall never cease to rise up out of another, and life is granted to none for freehold, to all on lease.[n] Look back again to see how the past ages of everlasting time, before we are born, have been as naught to us. These then nature holds up to us as a mirror of the time that is to come, when we are dead and gone. Is there aught that looks terrible in this, aught that seems gloomy ? Is it not a calmer rest than any sleep ?

He should be glad to make room for future generations.

The future, after our death, will be no more to us than the past before our birth.

Yea, we may be sure, all those things, of which stories tell us in the depths of Acheron, are in our life. Neither does wretched Tantalus fear the great rock that hangs

The mythical tortures of the lower

---

[1] Bernays' suggestion *gnatis* seems the best of many proposals.

over him in the air, as the tale tells, numbed with idle terror; but rather 'tis in life that the vain fear of the gods threatens mortals; they fear the fall of the blow which chance may deal to each. Nor do birds make their way into Tityos, as he lies in Acheron, nor can they verily in all the length of time find food to grope for deep in his huge breast. However vast the mass of his outstretched limbs, though he cover not only nine acres with his sprawling limbs, but the whole circle of earth, yet he will not be able to endure everlasting pain, nor for ever to supply food from his own body. But this is our Tityos, whom as he lies smitten with love the birds mangle, yea, aching anguish devours him, or care cuts him deep through some other passion. The Sisyphus in our life too is clear to see, he who open-mouthed seeks from the people the rods and cruel axes, and evermore comes back conquered and dispirited. For to seek for a power, which is but in name, and is never truly given, and for that to endure for ever grinding toil, this is to thrust uphill with great effort a stone, which after all rolls back from the topmost peak, and headlong makes for the levels of the plain beneath. Then to feed for ever the ungrateful nature of the mind, to fill it full with good things, yet never satisfy it, as the seasons of the year do for us, when they come round again, and bring their fruits and their diverse delights, though we are never filled full with the joys of life, this, I trow, is the story of the maidens in the flower of youth, who pile the water into the vessel full of holes, which yet can in no way be filled full. Cerberus and the furies, moreover, and the lack of light, Tartarus, belching forth awful vapours from his jaws,

world are allegories of the miseries of this life. Tantalus is the man oppressed by the terrors of religion; Tityos the careworn lover;

Sisyphus the unsuccessful public man;

the Danaids the discontented.

. . . .
                                                                    1

Hell is the fear of punishment in this life. which are not anywhere, nor verily can be. But it is fear of punishment for misdeeds in life—fear notable as the deeds are notable—and the atonement for crime, the dungeon and the terrible hurling down from the rock, scourgings, executioners, the rack, pitch, the metal plate, torches; for although they are not with us, yet the conscious mind, fearing for its misdeeds, sets goads to itself, and sears itself with lashings, nor does it see meanwhile what end there can be to its ills, or what limit at last to punishment, yea, and it fears that these same things may grow worse after death. Here after all on earth the life of fools becomes a hell.

Think of those who have died before you, the kings, This too you might say to yourself from time to time: 'Even Ancus the good [n] closed his eyes on the light of day, he who was a thousand times thy better, thou knave. And since him many other kings and rulers of empires have fallen, who held sway over mighty nations. Even he himself, who once [n] paved a way over the great sea, and made a path for his legions to pass across the deep, and taught them on foot to pass over the salt pools, and made naught of the roarings of ocean, prancing upon it with his horses, yet lost the light of day, and breathed **and heroes,** out his soul from his dying body. The son of the Scipios, thunderbolt of war, terror of Carthage, gave his bones to earth, even as though he had been the meanest house- **and poets,** slave. Yes, and the inventors of sciences and delightful arts, yes and the comrades of the sisters of Helicon: among whom Homer, who sat alone, holding his sceptre, has **and philo-sophers.** fallen into the same sleep as the rest. Again, after a ripe old age warned Democritus that the mindful motions of his memory were waning, of his own will he met death

[1] Some lines are lost here.

and offered her up his head. Epicurus himself died, when he had run his course in the light of life, Epicurus, who surpassed the race of men in understanding and quenched the light of all, even as the sun rising in the sky quenches the stars. Wilt thou then hesitate and chafe to meet thy doom? thou, whose life is wellnigh dead while thou still livest and lookest on the light, who dost waste in sleep the greater part of thy years, and snore when wide awake, nor ever cease to see dream-visions, who hast a mind harassed with empty fear, nor canst discover often what is amiss with thee, when like a sot thou art beset, poor wretch, with countless cares on every side, and dost wander drifting on the shifting currents of thy mind.'

You must not hesitate to die, whose life is a waking sleep.

If only men, even as they clearly feel a weight in their mind, which wears them out with its heaviness, could learn too from what causes that comes to be, and whence so great a mass, as it were, of ill lies upon their breast, they would not pass their lives, as now for the most part we see them; knowing not each one of them what he wants, and longing ever for change of place, as though he could thus lay aside the burden. The man who is tired of staying at home, often goes out abroad from his great mansion, and of a sudden returns again, for indeed abroad he feels no better. He races to his country home, furiously driving his ponies, as though he were hurrying to bring help to a burning house; he yawns at once, when he has set foot on the threshold of the villa, or sinks into a heavy sleep and seeks forgetfulness, or even in hot haste makes for town, eager to be back. In this way each man struggles to escape himself: yet, despite his will he clings to the self, which, we may be sure, in fact

If men knew the cause of their cares, they would not lead restless lives, as they do now,

struggling to escape from self,

he cannot shun, and hates himself, because in his sickness he knows not the cause of his malady ; but if he saw it clearly, every man would leave all else, and study first to learn the nature of things, since it is his state for all eternity, and not for a single hour, that is in question, the state in which mortals must expect all their being, that is to come after their death.

but would study nature, to learn their condition after death.

Our craving for life is fruitless.

Again, what evil craving for life is this which constrains us with such force to live so restlessly in doubt and danger? Verily, a sure end of life is ordained for mortals, nor can we avoid death, but we must meet it. Moreover, we move ever, we spend our time amid the same things, nor by length of life is any new pleasure hammered out. But so long as we have not what we crave, it seems to surpass all else ; afterward, when that is ours, we crave something else, and the same thirst for life besets us ever, open-mouthed. It is uncertain too what fortune time to come may carry to us, or what chance may bring us, or what issue is at hand. Nor in truth by prolonging life do we take away a jot from the time of death, nor can we subtract anything whereby we may be perchance less long dead. Therefore you may live on to close as many generations as you will : yet no whit the less that everlasting death will await you, nor will he for a less long time be no more, who has made an end of life with to-day's light, than he who perished many months or years ago.

A longer life could give us no new pleasure,

nor could it diminish the period of death.

BOOK IV

I TRAVERSE the distant haunts [n] of the Pierides, never Intro-
trodden before by the foot of man. 'Tis my joy to duction :
Lucretius's
approach those untasted springs and drink my fill, 'tis mission.
my joy to pluck new flowers and gather a glorious coronal
for my head from spots whence before the muses have
never wreathed the forehead of any man. First because
I teach about great things, and hasten to free the mind
from the close bondage of religion, then because on
a dark theme I trace verses so full of light, touching all
with the muses' charm. For that too is seen to be not
without good reason; for even as healers, when they
essay to give loathsome wormwood to children, first touch
the rim all round the cup with the sweet golden moisture
of honey, so that the unwitting age of children may be
beguiled as far as the lips, and meanwhile may drink the
bitter draught of wormwood, and though charmed may
not be harmed, but rather by such means may be restored
and come to health; so now, since this philosophy full
often seems too bitter to those who have not tasted it,
and the multitude shrinks back away from it, I have
desired to set forth to you my reasoning in the sweet-
tongued song of the muses, and as though to touch it
with the pleasant honey of poetry, if perchance I might
avail by such means to keep your mind set upon my verses,
while you take in the whole nature of things, and are
conscious of your profit.

But since I have taught of what manner are the

A. The
Idols.

beginnings of all things, and how, differing in their diverse
forms, of their own accord they fly on, spurred by everlasting motion ; and in what way each several thing can
be created from them ; and since I have taught what was
the nature of the mind, and whereof composed it grew in
due order with the body, and in what way rent asunder

The images
which are
the cause
of vision.

it passed back into its first-beginnings : now I will begin
to tell you what exceeding nearly concerns this theme,
that there are what we call idols [n] of things ; which, like
films stripped from the outermost body of things, fly
forward and backward through the air ; and they too
when they meet us in waking hours affright our minds,
yea, and in sleep too, when we often gaze on wondrous
shapes, and the idols of those who have lost the light of
day, which in awful wise have often roused us, as we lay
languid, from our sleep ; lest by chance we should think
that souls escape from Acheron, or that shades fly abroad
among the living, or that something of us can be left
after death, when body alike and the nature of mind have
perished and parted asunder into their several first-
beginnings.

The
existence of
such images
is proved
by parallels
in the
visible
world.

I say then that likenesses of things and their shapes are
given off by things from the outermost body of things,
which may be called, as it were, films or even rind,
because the image bears an appearance and form like to
that, whatever it be, from whose body it appears to be
shed, ere it wanders abroad. That we may learn from

1. Things
throw off
films,
either loose,
like smoke,
&c., or
more com-

this, however dull be our wits. First of all, since among
things clear to see many things give off bodies, in part
scattered loosely abroad, even as wood gives off smoke
and fires heat, and in part more closely knit and packed
together, as when now and then the grasshoppers lay

aside their smooth coats in summer, and when calves at
their birth give off a caul from their outermost body, and
likewise when the slippery serpent rubs off its vesture on
the thorns; for often we see the brambles laden with
these wind-blown spoils from snakes. And since these
things come to pass, a thin image from things too must
needs be given off from the outermost body of things.
For why these films should fall and part from things any
more than films that are thin, none can breathe a word
to prove; above all, since on the surface of things[n] there
are many tiny bodies, which could be cast off in the same
order wherein they stood, and could preserve the outline
of their shape, yea, and be cast the more quickly, inasmuch
as they can be less entangled, in that they are few, and
placed in the forefront. For verily we see many things
cast off and give out bodies in abundance, not only from
deep beneath, as we said before, but often too from the
surface, such as their own colour. And commonly is this
done by awnings, yellow and red and steely-blue, when
stretched over great theatres they flap and flutter, spread
everywhere on masts and beams. For there they tinge
the assembly in the tiers beneath, and all the bravery of
the stage and the gay-clad company of the elders,[1] and
constrain them to flutter in their colours. And the more
closely are the hoardings of the theatre shut in all around,
the more does all the scene within laugh, bathed in brightness, as the light of day is straitened. Since then the
canvas gives out this hue from its outermost body, each
several thing also must needs give out thin likenesses, since
in either case they are throwing off from the surface.
There are then sure traces of forms, which fly about every-

Marginal notes:

pact like the slough of snakes, &c.

So images can be thrown off, because there are unimpeded atoms on the surface ready to part.

2. Colour is thrown off from the surface of things, as from the awnings of a theatre.

---

[1] Translating Munro's suggestion *patrum coetumque decorum.*

Nor is colour hindered like the other effluences which come from deep beneath.

where, endowed with slender bulk, nor can they be seen apart one by one. Moreover, all smell, smoke, heat, and other like things stream forth from things, scattering loosely, because while they arise and come forth from deep within, they are torn in their winding course, nor are there straight outlets to their paths, whereby they may hasten to issue all in one mass. But, on the other hand, when the thin film of surface-colour is cast off, there is nothing which can avail to rend it, since it is ready at hand, and placed in the forefront. Lastly, when-

3. Mirrors, &c., return a constant succession of images of things.

ever idols appear to us in mirrors, in water, and in every shining surface, it must needs be, seeing that they are endowed with an appearance like the things, that they are made of the images of things given off. There are then thin shapes of things and likenesses, which, although no one can see them one by one, yet thrown back with constant and ceaseless repulse, give back a picture from the surface of the mirrors, and it is seen that they cannot by any other means be so preserved that shapes so exceeding like each several thing may be given back.

**Fineness of texture of the images.
1. Think of the fineness of the atoms of which they are composed.
(a) They are much smaller than the smallest part of the smallest**

Come now and learn of how thin a nature this image is formed. And to begin with, since the first-beginnings are so far beneath the ken of our senses, and so much smaller than the things which our eyes first begin to be unable to descry, yet now that I may assure you of this too, learn in a few words how fine in texture are the beginnings of all things. First of all there are living things sometimes so small that a third part of them could by no means be seen. Of what kind must we think any one of their entrails to be? What of the round ball of their heart or eye? what of their members? what of their limbs? how small are they? still more, what of the several first-beginnings whereof their soul and the nature of their mind must needs be formed? do you not see how fine and how tiny they are? Moreover, whatever things breathe out a pungent savour from their body, panacea, sickly wormwood, and strongly-smelling abrotanum, and bitter centaury; if by chance ⟨you press⟩ any one of these lightly between two [1] ⟨fingers, the scent will for long cling to your fingers, though never will you see anything at all: so that you may know how fine is the nature of the first-beginnings, whereof the scent is formed . . .⟩ . . . and not rather learn that many idols of things wander abroad in many ways with no powers, unable to be perceived?

living thing we can see.

(b) Things can leave a strong scent on you when you touch them, and yet you can see nothing. [2.]

But that you may not by chance think that after all only those idols of things wander abroad, which come off from things, there are those too which are begotten of their own accord, and are formed of themselves in this sky which is called air; which moulded in many ways are borne along on high, and being fluid cease not to change their appearance, and to turn it into the outline of forms of every kind; even as from time to time we see clouds lightly gathering together in the deep sky, and staining the calm face of the firmament, caressing the air with their motion. For often the faces of giants are seen to fly along and to trail a shadow far and wide, and sometimes mighty mountains and rocks torn from the mountains are seen to go on ahead and to pass before the sun; and then a huge beast seems to draw on and lead forward the storm clouds.

There are other idols, too, which form in the sky, ever-changing, like the masses of clouds.

Come now, in what swift and easy ways those idols are begotten, and flow unceasingly from things and fall off

These images are

---

[1] We may fill in the sense of the immediately succeeding lines with certainty, but a long passage has been lost, probably of about 50 lines.

very swiftly formed.

1. The surface of things is ever quick to stream away.

2. The quick formation of the image in the mirror gives us an example.

3. So does the constant succession of light from the sun.

4. Clouds form in the sky in a moment; how much quicker the little images!

and part from them, ⟨I will set forth . . .⟩.[1] For ever the outermost surface is streaming away from things, that so they may cast it off. And when this reaches some things, it passes through them, as above all through glass: but when it reaches rough stones or the substance of wood, there at once it is torn, so that it cannot give back any idol. But when things that are formed bright and dense are set athwart its path, such as above all is the mirror, neither of these things comes to pass. For neither can they pass through, as through glass, nor yet be torn; for the smoothness is careful to ensure their safety. Wherefore it comes to pass that the idols stream back from it to us. And however suddenly, at any time you will, you place each several thing against the mirror, the image comes to view; so that you may know that from the outermost body there flow off unceasingly thin webs and thin shapes of things. Therefore many idols are begotten in a short moment, so that rightly is the creation of these things said to be swift. And just as the sun must needs shoot out many rays of light in a short moment, so that the whole world may unceasingly be filled, so too in like manner from things it must needs be that many idols of things are borne off in an instant of time in many ways in all directions on every side; inasmuch as to whatever side we turn the mirror to meet the surface of things, things in the mirror answer back alike in form and colour. Moreover, even when the weather in the sky has but now been most clear, exceeding suddenly it becomes foully stormy, so that on all sides you might think that all darkness has left Acheron, and filled the great vault of the sky; so terribly, when the noisome night of clouds

---

[1] At least one line is lost here.

has gathered together, do the shapes of black fear hang over us on high; yet how small a part of these is an idol, there is no one who could say or give an account of this in words.

Come now, with what swift motion the idols are carried on, and what speed is given them as they swim through the air, so that a short hour is spent on a long course, towards whatever place they each strain on with diverse impulse, I will proclaim in verses of sweet discourse rather than in many; even as the brief song of a swan is better than the clamour of cranes, which spreads abroad among the clouds of the south high in heaven. First of all very often we may see that light things made of tiny bodies are swift. In this class there is the light of the sun and his heat, because they are made of tiny first-particles, which, as it were, are knocked forward, and do not pause in passing on through the space of air between, smitten by the blow from those that follow. For in hot haste the place of light is taken by light, and as though driven in a team, one flash is goaded by another flash. Wherefore in like manner it must needs be that the idols can course through space unthinkable in an instant of time, first because it is a tiny cause,[n] far away behind which drives and carries them forward, and after that, in that they are borne on with so swift a lightness of bulk; and then because they are given off endowed with texture so rare that they can easily pass into anything you will, and as it were ooze through the intervening air. Moreover, when particles of things[n] are given out abroad from deep within, like the sun's light and heat, these are seen to fall in a moment of time and spread themselves over the whole expanse of heaven, and to fly over sea and earth and flood the sky. What then of those things which are ready at

Swiftness
of motion
of idols.

1. Proof
from
analogy.
Light
bodies of
rare texture
usually
move fast:
e. g. the
light
particles of
the sun.

2. Proof
from
theory.
Bodies
starting
from the
surface of
things move

quicker
than those
rising from
within.

3 Proof
from
experience.
The
immediate
reflection
of the
heavens
shows the
pace of
movement
of the idols.

B. These
idols are
the cause
of sight.
1. Our
other senses
are affected
by similar
effluences.

once in the forefront? When they are cast off and
nothing hinders their discharge, do you not see that they
must needs move swifter and further, and course through
many times the same expanse of space in the same time
in which the rays of the sun crowd the sky? This, too,
more than all seems to show forth truly in what swift
motion the idols of things are borne on, that as soon as
a bright surface of water is placed beneath the open sky,
when the heaven is starry, in a moment the calm beaming
stars of the firmament appear in answer in the water.
Do you not then see now in how short an instant of time
the image falls from the coasts of heaven to the coasts of
earth? Wherefore more and more you must needs confess that bodies are sent off such as strike the eyes and
awake our vision. And from certain things scents stream
off unceasingly; just as cold streams off from rivers, heat
from the sun, spray from the waves of the sea, which
gnaws away walls all around the shores. Nor do diverse
voices cease to fly abroad through the air. Again, often
moisture of a salt savour comes into our mouth, when
we walk by the sea, and on the other hand, when we watch
wormwood being diluted and mixed, a bitter taste
touches it. So surely from all things each several thing
is carried off in a stream, and is sent abroad to every
quarter on all sides, nor is any delay or respite granted in
this flux, since we feel unceasingly, and we are suffered
always to descry and smell all things, and to hear them
sound.

Moreover, since a shape felt by the hands in the darkness is known to be in some way the same as is seen in the light and the clear brightness, it must needs be that touch and sight are stirred by a like cause. If then we handle a square thing, and it stirs our touch in the darkness, what square thing can fall upon our sight in the light, except its image? Wherefore 't is clear that the cause of seeing lies in the images, nor without them can anything be seen.

2. Touch and sight give us the same information: they must be affected by similar causes.

Next those things which I call the idols of things are borne everywhere, and are cast off and meted out to every side. But because we can see them only[n] with our eyes, for that cause it comes to pass that, to whatever side we turn our sight, all things there strike against it with their shape and hue. And how far each thing is away from us, the image causes us to see and provides that we distinguish. For when it is given off,[n] straightway it pushes and drives before it all the air that has its place between it and the eyes, and thus it all glides through our eyeballs, and, as it were, brushes through the pupils, and so passes on. Therefore it comes to pass that we see how far away each thing is. And the more air is driven on in front, and the longer the breeze which brushes through our eyes, the further each thing is seen to be removed. But you must know that these things are brought to pass by means exceeding quick, so that we see what it is and at the same time how far it is away. Herein by no means must we deem[n] there is cause to wonder why the idols which strike the eyes cannot be seen one by one, but the whole things are descried. For when wind too lashes us little by little,

The idols meet our eyes wherever we turn.

They drive before them a current of air, by whose length we can judge the distance of the object.

We do not perceive the separate idols, but the whole object.

So we do
not feel
individual
particles of
wind or
cold,

and when piercing cold streams on us, we are not wont to
feel each separate particle of that wind and cold, but
rather all at once, and then we perceive blows coming to
pass on our body, just as if something were lashing us

and though
we strike
only the
surface of
a stone, we
feel the
resistance of
the whole.

and giving us the feeling of its body without. Moreover, when we strike a stone with our finger, we touch
the very outside of the rock and its colour on the
surface, yet we do not feel the colour with our touch, but
rather we feel the very hardness of the rock deep down
beneath.

Peculiarities
of the
mirror.
1. The
image
seems to
be behind
the mirror,
because, as
with things
seen
through
doors, we
receive first
a current
of air, then
the image
of the
mirror,
then
another
current,
and finally
the image
of the
object.

Come now and learn why the image is seen beyond the
mirror; for indeed it seems removed far within. It is
even as those things which in very truth are seen outside
a door, when the door affords an unhindered sight through
it, and lets many things out of doors be seen from the
house. For that vision too is brought to pass by two
twin airs. For first the air on our side of the jambs is
seen in such a case, then follow the folding doors themselves on right and left, afterwards the light outside
brushes through the eyes, and a second air, and then those
things which in very truth are seen without the doors.
So when first the image of the mirror has cast itself adrift,
while it is coming to our pupils, it pushes and drives
before it all the air which has its place between it and
our eyes, and so makes us able to perceive all this air
before the mirror. But when we have perceived the
mirror itself too, straightway the image which is borne
from us passes to the mirror, and being cast back returns
to our eyes and drives on and rolls in front of it another
air, and makes us see this before itself, and therefore seems
to be just so much distant from the mirror. Wherefore,
again and again, it is not right at all that we should wonder

⟨that this appearance comes to be both for those things
which are really seen out of doors, and also⟩[1] for those
things which send back a vision from the level surface of
the mirrors ; since in either case it is brought about by
the two airs. Next it comes to pass that the part of
our limbs which is on the right is seen in mirrors on the
left, because when the image comes to the plane of the
mirror and strikes against it, it is not turned round unchanged, but is dashed back straight ; just as if one were
to dash a plaster mask, before it is dry, against a pillar or
a beam, and it at once were to preserve its shape turned
straight to meet us, and were to mould again its own
features dashed back towards us. Thus it will come to
pass that what was before the right eye, now in turn is
the left, and the left in exchange is now the right. It
comes to pass too that the image is handed on from mirror
to mirror, so that even five or six idols are wont to be
made. For even when things are hidden far back in an
inner part of the room, yet, however far distant from the
sight along a twisting path, it may be that they will all
be brought out thence by winding passages, and, thanks
to the several mirrors, be seen to be in the house. So
surely does the image reflect from mirror to mirror, and
when a left hand is presented, it comes to pass that it is
changed to the right, and then once again it is changed
about and returns to where it was before. Moreover, all
flank-curved mirrors,[n] endowed with a curve like to our
flanks, send back to us right-handed idols, either because
the image is borne across from one part of the mirror to

Marginal notes:
2. Right hand and left are changed in the mirror, because the image is turned straight back, like a plaster mask dashed against a post.

3. Images may be reflected from mirror to mirror, changing their cheirality each time.

4. Curved horizontal mirrors return images with the right cheirality.

---

[1] A line has probably been lost, such as *hoc illis fieri, quae transpiciuntur, idemque.*

another, and then flies towards us, twice dashed back, or else because the image[n] is twisted around, when it has arrived, because the curved shape of the mirror teaches it to turn round towards us. Moreover, you would believe that idols walk step by step and place their feet as we do, and imitate our gait, just because, from whatever part of the mirror you retire, straightway the idols cannot be turned back from it, inasmuch as nature[n] constrains all things to be carried back, and leap back from things, sent back at equal angles.

5. The image in the mirror keeps step with us.

Bright things moreover the eyes avoid, and shun to look upon. The sun, too, blinds, if you try to raise your eyes to meet him, because his own power is great, and the idols from him are borne through the clear air, sinking heavily into the deep, and strike upon the eyes, disordering their texture. Moreover, any piercing brightness often burns the eyes for the reason that it contains many seeds of fire, which give birth to pain in the eyes, finding their way in. Moreover, whatever the jaundiced look upon becomes sickly-yellow, because many seeds of yellow stream off from their bodies to meet the idols of things, and many also are mixed in their eyes, which by their infection tinge all things with their pallor.

Peculiarities of vision. 1. Bright things blind and burn the eyes, because of the seeds they contain.

2. Jaundiced persons infect the images with their own yellow.

Now we see things that are in the light out of the darkness, because, when the black air of the gloom, which is nearer, first enters and seizes on the open eyes, there follows in hot haste a bright air full of light, which, as it were, cleanses the eyes and scatters abroad the dark shadows of the former air. For the latter is many times more nimble, many times finer and more potent. And as soon as it has filled the passages of the eyes with light, and opened up those which before the black air had

3. We can see things in the light out of darkness, because the light clears the eyes;

beleaguered, straightway follow the idols of the things
which are lying in the light, and excite our eyes so that
we see. But, on the other hand, we cannot do this in
the darkness out of the light, because the air of the gloom,
which is denser, comes on afterwards, and fills all the
channels and beleaguers the passages of the eyes, so that
none of the idols of things can be cast upon them and
stir them.

but not in the darkness out of light, because the darkness chokes the eyes.

And when we see from afar off [n] the square towers of
a town, it comes to pass for this cause that they often look
round, because every angle from a distance is seen flattened,
or rather it is not seen at all, and the blow from it passes
away, nor does its stroke come home to our eyes, because,
while the idols are being borne on through much air, the
air by its frequent collisions constrains it to become
blunted. When for this cause every angle alike has escaped
our sense, it comes to pass that the structures of stone are
worn away as though turned on the lathe; yet they do not
look like things which are really round to a near view, but
a little resembling them as though in shadowy shape. Likewise our shadow seems to us to move in the sunshine, and
to follow our footsteps and imitate our gait; if indeed you
believe that air bereft of light can step forward, following
the movements and gait of men. For that which we are
wont to name a shadow can be nothing else but air devoid
of light. But in very truth it is because in certain spots
in due order the ground is bereft of the light of the sun
wherever we, as we move on, cut it off, and likewise the
part of it which we have left is filled again; for this cause
it comes to pass that, what was but now the shadow of
our body, seems always to follow unaltered straight along
with us. For always new rays of light are pouring out,
and the former perish, like wool drawn into a flame.

4. Square towers look round from a distance, because the angles are worn off the images in transit.

5. Our shadow seems to follow us, because, as we move, the light is cut off from successive pieces of the ground

Therefore readily is the ground robbed of light, and is likewise filled again and washes away its own black shadows.

In all such cases sensation is not false, but the mind draws a wrong inference.

And yet we do not grant that in this the eyes are a whit deceived. For it is theirs to see in what several spots there is light and shade : but whether it is the same light or not, whether it is the same shadow which was here, that now passes there, or whether that rather comes to pass which I said a little before, this the reasoning of the mind alone must needs determine, nor can the eyes know the nature of things. Do not then be prone to fasten on the eyes this fault in the mind. The ship, in which we journey,[n] is borne along, when it seems to be standing still ; another, which remains at anchor, is thought to be passing by. The hills and plains seem to be flying towards the stern, past which we are driving on our ship with skimming sail. All the stars, fast set in the vault of the firmament, seem to be still, and yet they are all in ceaseless motion, inasmuch as they rise and return again to their distant settings, when they have traversed the heaven with their bright body. And in like manner sun and moon seem to abide in their places, yet actual fact shows that they are borne on. And mountains rising up afar off from the middle of the waters, between which there is a free wide issue for ships, yet seem united to make a single island. When children have ceased turning round themselves, so sure does it come to appear to them that the halls are turning about, and the pillars racing round, that scarcely now can they believe that the whole roof is not threatening to fall in upon them. And again, when nature begins to raise on high the sunbeam ruddy with twinkling fires, and to lift it above the mountains,

1. Stationary objects seen from a moving ship seem to move.

2. The stars seem to be at rest.

3. Passages between mountains are not seen at a distance.
4. To giddy persons their surroundings seem to spin.
5. The rising sun

those mountains above which the sun seems to you to stand, as he touches them with his own fire, all aglow close at hand, are scarce distant from us two thousand flights of an arrow, nay often scarce five hundred casts of a javelin: but between them and the sun lie the vast levels of ocean, strewn beneath the wide coasts of heaven, and many thousands of lands are set between, which diverse races inhabit, and tribes of wild beasts. And yet a pool of water not deeper than a single finger-breadth, which lies between the stones on the paved street, affords us a view beneath the earth to a depth as vast as the high gaping mouth of heaven stretches above the earth; so that you seem to descry the clouds and the heaven and bodies wise hidden beneath the earth—yet in a magic sky. Again, when our eager horse has stuck fast amid a river, and we look down into the hurrying waters of the stream, the force seems to be carrying on the body of the horse, though he stands still, athwart the current, and to be thrusting it in hot haste up the stream; and wherever we cast our eyes all things seem to be borne on and flowing forward, as we are ourselves. Though a colonnade runs on straight-set lines all the way, and stands resting on equal columns from end to end, yet when its whole length is seen from the top end, little by little it contracts to the pointed head of a narrow cone, joining roof with floor, and all the right hand with the left, until it has brought all together into the point of a cone that passes out of sight. It happens to sailors on the sea that the sun seems to rise from the waves, and again to set in the waves, and hide its light; since verily they behold

Marginal notes:

seems close to mountains in the east.

6. A tiny pool of no depth can reflect the whole sky.

7. A horse standing in a stream seems to be borne upstream.

8. Perspective.

9. Sunrise at sea.

nothing else but water and sky; so that you must not lightly think that the senses waver at every point. But to

10. Refraction.

those who know not the sea, ships in the harbour seem to press upon the water maimed, and with broken poop. For all the part of the oars which is raised up above the salt sea spray, is straight, and the rudders are straight above; but all that is sunk beneath the water, seems to be broken back and turned round, yes, and to turn upwards again and twist back so that it almost floats on the

11. Moving clouds make the stars seem to move.

water's surface. And when winds in the night season carry scattered clouds across the sky, then the shining signs seem to glide athwart the storm-clouds, and to be moving on high in a direction far different from their true

12. A finger on the eyeball makes it see double.

course. Then if by chance a hand be placed beneath one eye and press it, it comes to pass by a new kind of perception that all things which we look at seem to become double as we look, double the lights of the lamps with their flowery flames, double the furniture throughout the whole house in twin sets, and double the faces of men,

13. Dreams.

double their bodies. Again, when sleep has bound our limbs in sweet slumber, and all the body lies in complete rest, yet then we seem to ourselves to be awake and moving our limbs, and in the blind gloom of night we think to see the sun and the light of day, and, though in some walled room, we seem to pass to new sky, new sea, new streams, and mountains, and on foot to cross over plains, and to hear sounds, when the stern silence of night is set all about us, and to give answer, when we do not speak. Wondrously many other things of this sort we see, all of which would fain spoil our trust in the senses; all in vain, since the greatest part of these things deceives us on account of the opinions of the mind, which we add ourselves, so that things not seen by the senses are counted as seen. For nothing is harder than to distinguish things manifest from things uncertain, which the mind straightway adds of itself.

Again, if any one thinks[n] that nothing is known, he knows not whether that can be known either, since he admits that he knows nothing. Against him then I will refrain from joining issue, who plants himself with his head in the place of his feet. And yet were I to grant that he knows this too, yet I would ask this one question; since he has never before seen any truth in things, whence does he know what is knowing, and not knowing each in turn, what thing has begotten the concept of the true and the false,[n] what thing has proved that the doubtful differs from the certain? You will find that the concept of the true is begotten first from the senses, and that the senses cannot be gainsaid. For something must be found with a greater surety, which can of its own authority refute the false by the true. Next then, what must be held to be of greater surety than sense? Will reason, sprung from false sensation,[n] avail to speak against the senses, when it is wholly sprung from the senses? For unless they are true, all reason too becomes false. Or will the ears be able to pass judgement on the eyes, or touch on the ears? or again will the taste in the mouth refute this touch; will the nostrils disprove it, or the eyes show it false? It is not so, I trow. For each sense has its faculty set apart, each its own power, and so it must needs be that we perceive in one way what is soft or cold or hot, and in another the diverse colours of things, and see all that goes along with colour.[n] Likewise, the taste of the mouth has its power apart; in one way smells

If the sceptic denies that anything can be known, how can he know that?
Where does he get his criterion of truth?

If the senses are false, he must find a truer standard.

But (*a*) reason, resting on sensation, cannot refute the senses;
(*b*) the senses cannot refute one another;

arise, in another sounds. And so it must needs be that
one sense cannot prove another false. Nor again will

nor (c) can
the senses
convict
themselves.

they be able to pass judgement on themselves, since equal
trust must at all times be placed in them. Therefore,

Sensation
is true.
It is better
to admit
that reason
may fail
than to
impugn the
senses, the
foundation
of all
knowledge,
and the
only guide
for life.

whatever they have perceived on each occasion, is true.
And if reason is unable to unravel the cause, why those
things which close at hand were square, are seen round
from a distance, still it is better through lack of reasoning
to be at fault in accounting for the causes of either
shape, rather than to let things clear seen slip abroad
from your grasp, and to assail the grounds of belief,
and to pluck up the whole foundations on which life
and existence rest. For not only would all reasoning
fall away ; life itself too would collapse straightway, unless you chose to trust the senses, and avoid headlong
spots and all other things of this kind which must be
shunned, and to make for what is opposite to these.

To deny
the veracity
of sensation
is to build
a fabric
with faulty
instru-
ments.

Know, then, that all this is but an empty store of words,
which has been drawn up and arrayed against the senses.
Again, just as in a building, if the first ruler is awry, and
if the square is wrong and out of the straight lines, if the
level sags a whit in any place, it must needs be that the
whole structure will be made faulty and crooked, all
awry, bulging, leaning forwards or backwards, and
out of harmony, so that some parts seem already to
long to fall, or do fall, all betrayed by the first wrong
measurements ; even so then your reasoning of things
must be awry and false, which all springs from false
senses.

The other
senses.

Now it is left to explain in what manner the other

senses perceive each their own object—a path by no means
stony to tread.

First of all, every kind of sound[n] and voice is heard,
when they have found their way into the ears and struck
upon the sense with their body. For that voice too and
sound are bodily you must grant, since they can strike
on the senses. Moreover, the voice often scrapes the
throat and shouting makes the windpipe over-rough as it
issues forth ; since, indeed, the first-beginnings of voices
have risen up in greater throng through the narrow
passage, and begun to pass forth : and then, in truth,
when the passages are crammed, the door too is scraped.
There is no doubt then that voices and words are composed
of bodily elements, so that they can hurt. And likewise it
does not escape you how much body is taken away and
drawn off from men's very sinews and strength by speech
continued without pause from the glimmer of rising dawn
to the shades of dark night, above all if it is poured out
with loud shouting. And so the voice must needs be of
bodily form, since one who speaks much loses a part from
his body. Now roughness of voice comes from roughness in its first-beginnings, and likewise smoothness is begotten of their smoothness. Nor do the first-beginnings
pierce the ears with like form, when the trumpet bellows
deep with muffled tones, and when the barbarous Bere-
cyntian pipe shrieks [1] with shrill buzzing sound, and
when the swans at night from the cold marches of Helicon
lift with mournful voice their clear lament.[2]

These voices then, when we force them forth from deep

Marginal notes:

1. Hear-
ing is
produced
when
sounds
strike the
sense.
Sound is
corporeal :
(*a*) it can
strike
the
sense ;
(*b*) shout-
ing makes
the throat
sore ;
(*c*) con-
tinued
speaking
weakens
the body.

Roughness
or smooth-
ness of
sound is
due to the
form of the
component
atoms.

---

[1] Read, with I. Vossius, *et reboat raucum Berecyntia*
[2] Read, with Bernays, *et gelidis cycni nocte oris*

The voice is formed to words by tongue and lips. At close quarters it keeps its form,

within our body, and shoot them abroad straight through our mouth, the pliant tongue, artificer of words, severs apart, and the shaping of the lips in its turn gives them form. Therefore, when it is no long distance from which each single utterance starts and reaches to us, it must needs be that the very words too are clearly heard and distinguished sound by sound. For each utterance pre-

but at greater distance is dislocated and becomes indistinct.

serves its shaping and preserves its form. But if the space set between be over great, passing through much air the words must needs be jostled together, and the utterance disordered, while it flies across the breezes. And so it comes to pass that you can perceive the sound, yet not distinguish what is the meaning of the words : so confounded and entangled does the utterance come to you. Again one

One voice can travel to many ears,

single word often awakes the ears of all in an assembly, shot out from the crier's mouth. Therefore one voice flies apart immediately into many voices, since it sunders itself into all the several ears, imprinting on the words

or else it is scattered abroad.

a shape and a clear-cut sound. But that part of the voices which falls not straight upon the ears, passes by and perishes scattered in vain through the air. Some

Solid things can beat the voice back. Hence the echo,

beating upon solid spots are cast back, and give back the sound, and at times mock us with the echo of a word. And when you see this clearly, you could give account to yourself and others, in what manner among solitary places rocks give back the counterparts of words each in due order, when we seek our comrades wandering amid the dark hills, and with loud voice summon them scattered here and there. I have seen places give back even six or seven cries, when you sent forth but one : so surely did one hill beat back to another and repeat the words trained to come back again. Such places the dwellers around

fancy to be the haunt of goat-footed satyrs and nymphs, which
and they say that there are fauns, by whose clamour gives rise
spreading through the night and sportive revels they to country
declare that the dumb silence is often broken ; and that fauns, &c.
sounds of strings are awakened, and sweet sad melodies,
which the pipe pours forth, stopped by the fingers of
players; and that the race of country folk hears far and wide,
when Pan, tossing the piny covering of his half-monstrous
head, ofttimes with curling lip runs over the open reeds,
so that the pipe ceases not to pour forth woodland music.
All other marvels and prodigies of this kind they tell, lest
by chance they be thought to live in lonely places, deserted even of the gods. Therefore they boast such
wonders in discourse, or else are led on in some other way,
even as the whole race of man is over greedy of pratt-
ling tales.

For the rest, we need not wonder by what means voices We hear
come and arouse the ears through places, though which where we
the eyes cannot see things clear to view. Often too we cannot see,
see a talk carried on through closed doors, because, we (*a*) because
may be sure, voice can pass unharmed through winding voices can
pores in things, but idols refuse to pass. For they are through
torn asunder, unless they stream through straight pores, any kind
as are those in glass, through which every image can fly. the idols
Moreover, a voice is severed in every direction, since of sight
voices are begotten one from another, when once one through
voice has issued forth and sprung apart into many, even straight
as a spark of fire is often wont to scatter itself into its openings;
several fires. And so places hidden far from sight are (*b*) because
filled with voices ; they are in a ferment all around, alive in all

directions, the idols only move straight as they start.

with sound. But all idols press on in the direct line, as they have once been started; wherefore no one can see beyond the wall, but can perceive voices outside. And yet even this voice, while it passes through the walls of the house, is dulled, and enters the ear all confounded, and we seem to hear a sound rather than words.

2. Taste is produced when the savour squeezed from the food enters the pores of the palate.

Smooth elements will produce pleasant taste, rough unpleasant.

Taste is confined to the palate and does not accompany digestion.

Nor do the tongue and palate,[n] whereby we perceive taste, need longer account or give more trouble. First of all we perceive taste in our mouth, when we press it out in chewing our food, just as if one by chance begins to squeeze with the hand and dry a sponge full of water. Then what we press out is all spread abroad through the pores of the palate, and through the winding passages of the loose-meshed tongue. Therefore, when the bodies of the oozing savour are smooth, they touch pleasantly, and pleasantly stroke all around the moist sweating vault above the tongue. But, on the other hand, the more each several thing is filled with roughness, the more does it prick the sense and tear it in its onslaught. Next pleasure comes from the savour within the limit of the palate; but when it has passed headlong down through the jaws, there is no pleasure while it is all being spread abroad into the limbs. Nor does it matter a whit with what diet the body is nourished, provided only you can digest what you take, and spread it abroad in the limbs, and keep an even moistness in the stomach.

Different foods suit different creatures,

Now how for different creatures there is different food and poison I will unfold, or for what cause, what to some is noisome and bitter, can yet seem to others most sweet to eat. And there is herein a difference and disagreement so great that what is food to one, is to others biting poison ; even as there is a certain serpent,[1] which, when touched by a man's spittle, dies and puts an end to itself by gnawing its own body. Moreover, to us hellebore is biting poison, but it makes goats and quails grow fat. That you may be able to learn by what means this comes to be, first of all it is right that you remember what we have said ere now, that the seeds contained in things are mingled in many ways. Besides all living creatures which take food, just as they are unlike to outer view and a diverse outward contour of the limbs encloses them each after their kind, so also are they fashioned of seeds of varying shape. And further, since the seeds are unlike, so must the spaces and passages, which we call the openings, be different in all their limbs, and in the mouth and palate too. Some of these then must needs be smaller, some greater, they must be three-cornered for some creatures, square for others, many again round, and some of many angles in many ways. For according as the arrangement of shapes and the motions demand, so the shapes of the openings must needs differ, and the passages vary according to the texture which shuts them in. Therefore, when what is sweet to some becomes bitter to others, for the man to whom it is sweet, the smoothest bodies must needs enter the pores of the palate caressingly, but, on the other hand, for those to whom the same thing is sour within, we can be sure it is the rough and hooked bodies which penetrate the passages. Now from these facts it is easy to learn of each case : thus when fever has attacked a man, and

Marginal notes:

and what is sweet to one is bitter to another.

This is caused (*a*) because many different seeds are mingled in things ; (*b*) because the formation of the palate and its pores differs in different animals.

For similar causes a

---

[1] The text is uncertain, but this must be the general sense.

man's taste
may change
when he
is ill

his bile rises high, or the violence of disease is aroused in some other way, then his whole body is disordered, and then all the positions of the first-beginnings are changed about; it comes to pass that the bodies which before suited his taste, suit it no longer, and others are better fitted, which can win their way in and beget a sour taste. For both kinds are mingled in the savour of honey; as I have often shown you above ere now.

3. Similarly
smell
streams off
things to
the nostrils,

Come now, I will tell n in what manner the impact of smell touches the nostrils. First there must needs be many things whence the varying stream of scents flows and rolls on, and we must think that it is always streaming off and being cast and scattered everywhere abroad; but

and dif-
ferent scents
attract
or repel
different
creatures.

one smell is better fitted to some living things, another to others, on account of the unlike shapes of the elements. And so through the breezes bees are drawn on however far by the scent of honey, and vultures by corpses. Then the strength of dogs sent on before leads on the hunters whithersoever the cloven hoof of the wild beasts has turned its steps, and the white goose, saviour of the citadel of Romulus's sons, scents far ahead the smell of man. So diverse scents assigned to diverse creatures lead on each to its own food, and constrain them to recoil from noisome poison, and in that way are preserved the races of wild beasts.

Smell never
travels
as far as
sound,

This very smell then, whenever it stirs the nostrils, may in one case be thrown further than in another. But yet no smell at all is carried as far as sound, as voice, I forebear to say as the bodies which strike the pupil of the eyes and stir the sight. For it strays abroad and comes but slowly, and dies away too soon, its frail nature scattered little by little among the breezes of air. Firstly, because coming from deep within [n] it is not readily set loose from the thing : for that smells stream off and depart from things far beneath the surface is shown because all things seem to smell more when broken, when crushed, when melted in the fire.   Again, one may see that it is fashioned of larger first-beginnings than voice, since it does not find a path through stone walls, where voice and sound commonly pass.   Wherefore too you will see that it is not so easy to trace in what spot that which smells has its place.   For the blow grows cool as it dallies through the air, nor do tidings of things rush hot to the sense. And so dogs often go astray, and have to look for the footprints.

(a) because it starts from deep within things;

(b) because it is made of larger atoms.

Consequently it is less easy to trace to its source.

[1] Yet this does not happen only among smells and in the class of savours, but likewise the forms and colours of things are not all so well fitted to the senses of all, but that certain of them are too pungent to the sight of some creatures.   Nay, indeed, ravening lions [n] can by no means face and gaze upon the cock, whose wont it is with clapping wings to drive out the night, and with shrill cry to summon dawn ; so surely do they at once bethink themselves of flight, because, we may be sure, there are in the body of cocks certain seeds, which, when they are cast into the eyes of lions, stab into the pupils, and cause sharp pain, so that they cannot bear up against them in fierce confidence ; and yet these things cannot in any way hurt our eyes, either because they do not pierce them or because, although they do, a free outlet from the eyes is afforded them, so that they cannot by staying there hurt the eyes in any part.

The same thing occurs with sight : certain things hurt the eyes of certain creatures : e.g. lions cannot look at cocks ;

because there are certain seeds in cocks which hurt their eyes, but not ours.

[1] This section seems misplaced, and should possibly come before the preceding paragraph.

The cause
of thought.

Idols,
wandering
every-
where,
may unite,

Come now, let me tell you [n] what things stir the mind, and learn in a few words whence come the things which come into the understanding. First of all I say this, that many idols of things wander about in many ways in all directions on every side, fine idols, which easily become linked with one another in the air, when they come across one another's path, like spider's web and gold leaf. For indeed these idols are far finer in their texture than those

and piercing
through to
the mind,
make us
think of
monstrous
forms.

which fill the eyes and arouse sight, since these pierce through the pores of the body and awake the fine nature of the mind within, and arouse its sensation. And so we see Centaurs and the limbs of Scyllas, and the dog-faces of Cerberus and idols of those who have met death, and whose bones are held in the embrace of earth ; since idols of every kind are borne everywhere, some which are created of their own accord even in the air, some which depart in each case from diverse things, and those again which are made and put together from the shapes of these. For in truth the image of the Centaur comes not from a living thing, since there never was the nature of such a living creature, but when by chance the images of man and horse have met, they cling together readily at once, as we have said ere now, because of their subtle nature and fine fabric. All other things of this kind are fashioned in the same way. And when they move nimbly with exceeding lightness, as I have shown ere now, any one such subtle image stirs their mind ; for the mind is fine and of itself wondrous nimble.

The mind
sees as the
eyes do :

That these things come to pass as I tell, you may easily learn from this. Inasmuch as the one is like the other, what we see with the mind, and what we see with the eyes, they must needs be created in like manner. Now, therefore, since I have shown that I see a lion maybe, by means of idols, which severally stir the eyes, we may know that the mind is moved in like manner, in that it sees a lion and all else neither more nor less than the eyes, except that it sees finer idols. And when sleep has relaxed the limbs, the understanding of the mind is for no other cause awake, but that these same idols stir our minds then, as when we are awake, insomuch that we seem surely to behold even one who has quitted life, and is holden by death and the earth. This nature constrains to come to pass just because all the senses of the body are checked and at rest throughout the limbs, nor can they refute the falsehood by true facts. Moreover, the memory lies at rest, and is torpid in slumber, nor does it argue against us that he, whom the understanding believes that it beholds alive, has long ago won to death and doom. For the rest, it is not wonderful that the idols should move and toss their arms and their other limbs in rhythmic time. For it comes to pass that the image in sleep seems to do this; inasmuch as when the first image passes away and then another comes to birth in a different posture, the former seems then to have changed its gesture. And indeed we must suppose that this comes to pass in quick process: so great is the speed, so great the store of things, so great, in any one instant that we can perceive, the abundance of the little parts of images, whereby the supply may be continued.

And in these matters [n] many questions are asked, and there are many things we must make clear, if we wish to set forth the truth plainly. First of all it is asked why, whatever the whim may come to each of us to think of,

Marginal notes:

therefore the process is the same.

So too the visions of sleep are caused by images visiting the mind,

and memory is not awake to check their veracity.

The movement of the dream-visions is due to the constant flux of ever-different images.

Problems of thought and dreams.

1. How can we

think at
once of
anything
we want?

straightway his mind thinks of that very thing. Do the idols keep watch on our will, and does the image rise up before us, as soon as we desire, whether it pleases us to think of sea or land or sky either? Gatherings of men, a procession, banquets, battles, does nature create all things at a word, and make them ready for us? And that when in the same place and spot the mind of others is

2. How in
sleep do we
see moving
images?

thinking of things all far different. What, again, when in sleep we behold idols dancing forward in rhythmic measure, and moving their supple limbs, when alternately they shoot out swiftly their supple arms, and repeat to the eyes a gesture made by the feet in harmony? Idols in sooth are steeped in art and wander about trained to be able to tread their dance in the night-

Because
at every
instant
there is an
infinite
succession
of images;

time. Or will this be nearer truth? Because within a single time, which we perceive, that is, when a single word is uttered, many times lie unnoted, which reasoning discovers, therefore it comes to pass that in any time however small the several idols are there ready at hand in all the several spots. So great is the speed, so great the store of things. Therefore when the first image passes away and then another comes to birth in a different posture, the former seems then to have changed its

and the
mind only
sees sharply
those to
which it
attends.

gesture. Again, because they are fine, the mind cannot discern them sharply, save those which it strains to see; therefore all that there are besides these pass away, save those for which it has made itself ready. Moreover, the mind makes itself ready, and hopes it will come to pass that it will see what follows upon each

The same
is really the
case with
waking
sight.

several thing; therefore it comes to be. Do you not see the eyes too, when they begin to perceive things which are fine, strain themselves and make themselves ready, and that without that it cannot come to pass that we see things sharply? And yet even in things plain to see you might notice that, if you do not turn your mind to them, it is just as if the thing were sundered from you all the time, and very far away. How then is it strange, if the mind loses all else, save only the things to which it is itself given up? Then too on small signs we base wide opinions, and involve ourselves in the snare of self-deceit.

It happens too that from time to time an image of different kind rises before us, and what was before a woman, seems now to have become a man before our very eyes, or else one face or age follows after another. But that we should not think this strange, sleep and its forget-fulness secure.

Herein you must eagerly[n] desire to shun this fault, and with foresighted fear to avoid this error; do not think that the bright light of the eyes was created in order that we may be able to look before us, or that, in order that we may have power to plant long paces, therefore the tops of shanks and thighs, based upon the feet, are able to bend; or again, that the forearms are jointed to the strong upper arms and hands given us to serve us on either side, in order that we might be able to do what was needful for life. All other ideas of this sort, which men proclaim, by distorted reasoning set effect for cause, since nothing at all was born in the body that we might be able to use it, but what is born creates its own use. Nor did sight exist before the light of the eyes was born, nor plead-ing in words before the tongue was created, but rather the birth of the tongue came long before discourse, and the ears were created much before sound was heard, and in short all the limbs, I trow, existed before their use came about: they cannot then have grown for the pu[r]

Marginal notes:
The in-coherence of dreams is not noticed in sleep.

C. The limbs and senses were not created for the purpose of their use,

but being created evolved their use.

Art may create things for a purpose,

pose of using them. But, on the other side, to join hands in the strife of battle, to mangle limbs and befoul the body with gore; these things were known long before gleaming darts flew abroad, and nature constrained men to avoid a wounding blow, before the left arm, trained by art, held up the defence of a shield. And of a surety to trust the tired body to rest was a habit far older than the soft-spread bed, and the slaking of the thirst was born before cups. These things, then, which are invented to suit the needs of life, might well be thought to have been discovered for the purpose of using them. But all

but nature has no design.

those other things lie apart, which were first born themselves, and thereafter revealed the concept of their usefulness. In this class first of all we see the senses and the limbs; wherefore, again and again, it cannot be that you should believe that they could have been created for the purpose of useful service.

The desire for food is caused by the waste of the body's tissue, which food in turn repairs.

This, likewise, is no cause for wonder, that the nature of the body of every living thing of itself seeks food. For verily I have shown [n] that many bodies ebb and pass away from things in many ways, but most are bound to pass from living creatures. For because they are sorely tried by motion and many bodies by sweating are squeezed and pass out from deep beneath, many are breathed out through their mouths, when they pant in weariness; by these means then the body grows rare, and all the nature is undermined; and on this follows pain. Therefore food is taken to support the limbs and renew strength when it passes within, and to muzzle the gaping desire for eating through all the limbs and veins. Likewise, mois-

Drink quenches

ture spreads into all the spots which demand moisture;

and the many gathered bodies of heat, which furnish the the excessive
the fires to our stomach, are scattered by the incoming dryness and
moisture, and quenched like a flame, that the dry heat heat in
may no longer be able to burn our body. Thus then the the body.
panting thirst is washed away from our body, thus the
hungry yearning is satisfied.

Next, how it comes to pass that we are able to plant Causes of
our steps forward, when we wish, how it is granted us to our move-
move our limbs in diverse ways, and what force is wont ments.
to thrust forward this great bulk of our body, I will tell :
do you hearken to my words. I say that first of all idols 1. The
of walking fall upon our mind, and strike the mind, as we image of
have said before. Then comes the will ;[n] for indeed no moving is
one begins to do anything, ere the mind has seen before- presented
hand what it will do, and inasmuch as it sees this before- to the
hand, an image of the thing is formed. And so, when the mind: then
mind stirs itself so that it wishes to start and step forward, act of will.
it straightway strikes the force of soul which is spread The mind
abroad in the whole body throughout limbs and frame. the soul-
And that is easy to do, since it is held in union with it. atoms,
Then the soul goes on and strikes the body, and so little and the
by little the whole mass is thrust forward and set in soul-atoms
movement. Moreover, at such times the body too be- body.
comes rarefied, and air (as indeed it needs must do, since 2. Exercise
it is always quick to move), comes through the opened body, and
spaces, and pierces through the passages in abundance, its spaces
and so it is scattered to all the tiny parts of the body. with air,
Here then it is brought about by two causes acting in motion.
severally, that the body, like a ship,[1] is borne on by sails
and wind.[n] Nor yet herein is this cause for wonder, that There are
such tiny bodies can twist about a body so great, and turn parallels for

---

[1] This must be the sense, though the text is uncertain.

the moving of a great mass by tiny causes: e. g. a ship in a wind or a crane.

round the whole mass of us. For in very truth the wind that is finely wrought of a subtle body drives and pushes on a great ship of great bulk, and a single hand steers it, with whatever speed it be moving, and twists a single helm whithersoever it will; and by means of pulleys and tread-wheels a crane can move many things of great weight, and lift them up with light poise.

The cause of sleep.

Now in what ways this sleep floods repose over the limbs, and lets loose the cares of the mind from the breast, I will proclaim in verses of sweet discourse, rather than in many; even as the brief song of the swan is better than the clamour of cranes, which spreads abroad among the clouds of the south high in heaven. Do you lend me a fine ear and an eager mind, lest you should deny that what I say can be, and with a breast that utterly rejects the words of truth part company with me,

It comes when the soul is scattered in the limbs, or driven out, or hidden deep within. For sense is due to the soul: and its cessation shows that the soul has gone: but not utterly, for that would mean death.

when you are yourself in error and cannot discern. First of all sleep comes to pass [n] when the strength of the soul is scattered about among the limbs, and in part has been cast out abroad and gone its way, and in part has been pushed back and passed inward deeper within the body. For then indeed the limbs are loosened and droop. For there is no doubt that this sense exists in us, thanks to the soul; and when sleep hinders it from being, then we must suppose that the soul is disturbed and cast out abroad: yet not all of it; for then the body would lie bathed in the eternal chill of death. For indeed, when no part of the soul stayed behind hidden in the limbs, as fire is hidden when choked beneath much ashes, whence could sense on a sudden be kindled again throughout the limbs, as flame can rise again from a secret fire?

But by what means this new state of things is brought about, and whence the soul can be disturbed and the body grow slack, I will unfold : be it your care that I do not scatter my words to the winds. First of all it must needs be that the body on the outer side, since it is touched close at hand by the breezes of air, is thumped and buffeted by its oft-repeated blows, and for this cause it is that wellnigh all things are covered either by a hide, or else by shells, or by a hard skin, or by bark. Further, as creatures breathe, the air at the same time smites on the inner side, when it is drawn in and breathed out again. Wherefore, since the body is buffeted on both sides alike, and since the blows pass on through the tiny pores to the first parts and first particles of our body, little by little there comes to be, as it were, a falling asunder throughout our limbs. For the positions of the first-beginnings of body and mind are disordered. Then it comes to pass that a portion of the soul is cast out abroad, and part retreats and hides within ; part too, torn asunder through the limbs, cannot be united in itself, nor by motion act and react ; for nature bars its meetings and chokes the ways ; and so, when the motions are changed, sense withdraws deep within. And since there is nothing which can, as it were, support the limbs, the body grows feeble, and all the limbs are slackened ; arms and eyelids droop, and the hams, even as you lie down, often give way, and relax their strength. Again, sleep follows after food, because food brings about just what air does, while it is being spread into all the veins, and the slumber which you take when full or weary, is much heavier because then more bodies than ever are disordered, bruised with the great effort. In the same manner the soul comes to

(marginal notes:) This is brought about because the body is constantly buffeted by air outside, and inside, as we breathe. The blows spread and cause disruption ; and so the soul is driven out or sinks within or is distracted, and the unsupported body sinks in slackness. Food acts in just the same way as air.

be in part thrust deeper within ; it is also more abundantly driven out abroad, and is more divided and torn asunder in itself within.

Dreams repeat the actions which we pursue in waking life.

And for the most part to whatever pursuit each man clings and cleaves, or on whatever things we have before spent much time, so that the mind was more strained in the task than is its wont, in our sleep we seem mostly to traffic in the same things ; lawyers think that they plead their cases and confront law with law, generals that they fight and engage in battles, sailors that they pass a life of conflict waged with winds, and we that we pursue our task and seek for the nature of things for ever, and set it forth, when it is found, in writings in our country's tongue. Thus for the most part all other pursuits and arts seem to hold the minds of men in delusion during their sleep.

For instance, the games.

And if ever men have for many days in succession given interest unflagging to the games, we see for the most part, that even when they have ceased to apprehend them with their senses, yet there remain open passages in their minds, whereby the same images of things may enter in. And so for many days the same sights pass before their eyes, so that even wide awake they think they see men dancing and moving their supple limbs, and drink in with their ears the clear-toned chant of the lyre, and its speaking strings, and behold the same assembly and at the same time the diverse glories of the stage all

This is true even of animals :

bright before them. So exceeding great is the import of zeal and pleasure, and the tasks wherein not only men are wont to spend their efforts, but even every living animal.

horses,

In truth you will see strong horses, when their limbs are lain to rest, yet sweat in their sleep, and pant for ever, and strain every nerve as though for victory, or else as

though the barriers were opened ⟨struggle to start⟩.[1]
And hunters' dogs often in their soft sleep yet suddenly **hunting**
toss their legs, and all at once give tongue, and again and **dogs,**
again snuff the air with their nostrils, as if they had found
and were following the tracks of wild beasts; yea, roused
from slumber they often pursue empty images of stags,
as though they saw them in eager flight, until they shake
off the delusion and return to themselves. But the fawn- **house-dogs,**
ing brood of pups brought up in the house, in a moment
shake their body and lift it from the ground, just as if
they beheld unknown forms and faces. And the wilder
any breed may be, the more must it needs rage in its
sleep. But the diverse tribes of birds fly off, and on **birds,**
a sudden in the night time trouble the peace of the
groves of the gods, if in their gentle sleep they have seen
hawks, flying in pursuit, offer fight and battle. More- **and so of**
over, the minds of men, which with mighty movement **men in diverse**
perform mighty tasks, often in sleep do and dare just the **ways.**
same; kings storm towns, are captured, join battle, raise
a loud cry, as though being murdered—all without moving. Many men fight hard, and utter groans through
their pain, and, as though they were bitten by the teeth
of a panther or savage lion, fill all around them with their
loud cries. Many in their sleep discourse of high affairs,
and very often have been witness to their own guilt.
Many meet death; many, as though they were falling **They may**
headlong with all their body from high mountains to **dream even of their**
the earth, are beside themselves with fear, and, as **death,**
though bereft of reason, scarcely recover themselves
from sleep, quivering with the turmoil of their body.

---

[1] The end of the line has been ousted by an intrusion from the
next: the sense was probably this, as Munro suggests.

or of trivial needs.

Likewise a man sits down thirsty beside a stream or a pleasant spring, and gulps almost the whole river down his throat. Innocent children often, if bound fast in slumber they think they are lifting their dress at a latrine or a roadside vessel, pour forth the filtered liquid from their whole body, and the Babylonian coverlets of rich beauty are soaked   Later on to those, into the seething waters of whose life the vital seed is passing for the first time, when the ripeness of time has created it in their limbs, there come from without idols from every body, heralding a glorious face or beautiful colouring, which stir and rouse their passion to bursting.

The nature of love and desire.

There is stirred in us that seed, whereof we spoke before, when first the age of manhood strengthens our limbs. For one cause moves and rouses one thing, a different cause another; from man only the influence of man stirs human seed. And as soon as it has been aroused, bursting forth it makes its way from out the whole body through the limbs and frame, coming together into fixed places, and straightway rouses at last the natural

It makes us seek union with the object by which we are smitten.

parts of the body; and there arises the desire to seek that body, by which the mind is smitten with love. For as a rule all men fall towards the wound, and the blood spirts out in that direction, whence we are struck by the blow, and, if it is near at hand, the red stream reaches our foe. Thus, then, he who receives a blow from the darts of Venus, whoso'er it be who wounds him, inclines to that whereby he is smitten; for an unspoken desire foretells the pleasure to come.

D. Shun Venus and her cares and desires.

This pleasure is Venus for us; from it comes Cupid, our name for love, from it first of all that drop of Venus's sweetness has trickled into our heart and chilly care has followed after. For if the object of your love is away, yet images of her are at hand, her loved name is present to your ears. But it is best to flee those images,[n] and scare away from you what feeds your love, and to turn your mind some other way, and vent your passion on other objects, and not to keep it, set once for all on the love of one, and thereby store up for yourself care and certain pain. For the sore gains strength and festers For the pain only grows with indulgence. by feeding, and day by day the madness grows, and the misery becomes heavier, unless you dissipate the first wounds by new blows, and heal them while still fresh, wandering after some wanton, or else can turn the movements of the mind elsewhere.

Nor is he who shuns love bereft of the fruits of Venus, The lover's pleasure involves pain, but rather he chooses those joys which bring no pain. For surely the pleasure from these things is more untainted for the heart-whole than for the love-sick; for in the very moment of possession the passion of lovers ebbs and flows with undetermined current, nor are they sure what first to enjoy with eyes or hands. What they have grasped, they closely press and cause pain to the body, and often fasten their teeth in the lips, and dash mouth against mouth in kissing, because their pleasure is not unalloyed, and there are secret stings which spur them to hurt even the very thing, be it what it may, whence arise those germs of madness. But Venus lightly breaks the force of these pains in love, and fond pleasure mingled with them sets a curb upon their teeth. For therein there is hope that from the same body, whence comes the source of their flame, the fire may in turn be quenched. Yet and satiety never comes. nature protests that all this happens just the other way; and this is the one thing, whereof the more and more we have, the more does our heart burn with the cursed desire. For meat and drink are taken within the limbs ; and since they are able to take up their abode in certain parts, thereby the desire for water and bread is easily sated. But from the face and beauteous bloom of man nothing passes into the body to be enjoyed save delicate images ; and often this love-sick hope is scattered to the winds. Just as when in a dream a thirsty man seeks to drink and no liquid is granted him, which could allay the fire in his limbs, but he seeks after images of water, and struggles in vain, and is still thirsty, though he drinks amid the torrent stream, even so in love Venus mocks the lovers with images, nor can the body sate them, though they gaze on it with all their eyes, nor can they with their hands tear off aught from the tender limbs, as they wander aimless over all the body. Even at last when the lovers embrace and taste the flower of their years, eagerly they clasp and kiss, and pressing lip on lip breathe deeply ; yet all for naught, since they cannot tear off aught thence, nor enter in and pass away, merging the whole body in the other's frame ; for at times they seem to strive and struggle to do it. And at length when the gathering desire is sated, then for a while comes a little respite in their furious passion. Then the same madness returns, the old frenzy is back upon them, when they yearn to find out what in truth they desire to attain, nor can they discover what device may conquer their disease ; in such deep doubt they waste beneath their secret wound.

Satisfaction only begets new desire.

Love saps strength

Remember too that they waste their strength and are worn away with effort, remember that their life is passed beneath another's sway. Meanwhile their substance slips *and in-* *dependence,* away, and is turned to Babylonian coverlets, their duties *and duty* grow slack, and their fair name totters and sickens : while *and honour* on the mistress's feet laugh . . . . . . [1] and lovely *Patrimony* *is squan-* Sicyonian slippers ; yes, and huge emeralds with their *dered in* green flash are set in gold, and the sea-dark dress is for *lavish* *present* ever being frayed, and roughly used it drinks in sweat. *and enter-* The well-gotten wealth of their fathers becomes hair- *tainment,* ribbons and diadems ; sometimes it is turned to Greek robes and stuffs of Elis and Ceos. With gorgeous napery and viands feasts are set out, and games and countless cups, perfumes, and wreaths and garlands ; all in vain, *and all is* *ruined by* since from the heart of this fountain of delights wells up *some bitter* some bitter taste to choke them even amid the flowers— *thought of* *remorse or* either when the conscience-stricken mind feels the bite *jealousy.* of remorse that life is being spent in sloth, and is passing to ruin in wantonness, or because she has thrown out some idle word and left its sense in doubt, and it is planted deep in the passionate heart, and becomes alive like a flame, or because he thinks she casts her eyes around too freely, and looks upon some other, or sees in her face some trace of laughter.

And these ills are found in love that is true and fully *Crossed* *love is still* prosperous ; but when love is crossed and hopeless there *worse.* are ills, which you might detect even with closed eyes, ills without number ; so that it is better to be on the watch *Avoid love* *then, before* beforehand, even as I have taught you, and to beware *you are* that you be not entrapped. For to avoid being drawn *caught,* into the meshes of love, is not so hard a task as when caught amid the toils to issue out and break through the strong bonds of Venus. And yet even when trammelled

[1] It is impossible to replace with certainty the mutilated word.

or if caught and fettered you might escape the snare, unless you still
do not
shut your
eyes to
defects,

and cover
them with
endearing
glosses.

stand in your own way, and at the first o'erlook all the
blemishes of mind and body in her, whom you seek and
woo. For for the most part men act blinded by passion,
and assign to women excellencies which are not truly theirs.
And so we see those in many ways deformed and ugly
dearly loved, yea, prospering in high favour. And one
man laughs at another, and urges him to appease Venus,
since he is wallowing in a base passion, yet often, poor
wretch, he cannot see his own ills, far greater than the
rest. A black love is called 'honey-dark', the foul and
filthy 'unadorned', the green-eyed 'Athena's image', the
wiry and wooden 'a gazelle', the squat and dwarfish
'one of the graces', 'all pure delight', the lumpy and
ungainly 'a wonder', and 'full of majesty'. She stammers
and cannot speak, 'she has a lisp'; the dumb is 'modest';
the fiery, spiteful gossip is 'a burning torch'. One becomes a 'slender darling', when she can scarce live from
decline ; another half dead with cough is 'frail'. Then
the fat and full-bosomed is 'Ceres' self with Bacchus at
breast'; the snub-nosed is 'sister to Silenus, or a Satyr';
the thick-lipped is 'a living kiss'. More of this sort it

Even the
fairest is
not in-
dispensable,
and is
not really
different
from others.

A lover,
when he
finds this
out, is often
offended.

were tedious for me to try to tell. But yet let her be
fair of face as you will, and from her every limb let the
power of Venus issue forth : yet surely there are others
too : surely we have lived without her before, surely she
does just the same in all things, and we know it, as the
ugly, and of herself, poor wretch, reeks of noisome smells,
and her maids flee far from her and giggle in secret. But
the tearful lover, denied entry, often smothers the threshold with flowers and garlands, and anoints the haughty
door-posts with marjoram, and plants his kisses, poor

wretch, upon the doors; yet if, admitted at last, one single breath should meet him as he comes, he would seek some honest pretext to be gone, and the deep-drawn lament long-planned would fall idle, and then and there he would curse his folly, because he sees that he has assigned more to her than it is right to grant to any mortal. Nor is this unknown to our queens of love; nay the more are they at pains to hide all behind the scenes from those whom they wish to keep fettered in love; all for naught, since you can even so by thought bring it all to light and seek the cause of all this laughter, and if she is of a fair mind, and not spiteful, o'erlook faults in your turn, and pardon human weaknesses. *It is better to realize it and make allowance.*

Nor does the woman sigh always with feigned love, when clasping her lover she holds him fast, showering her kisses. For often she does it from the heart, and yearning for mutual joys she woos him to reach the goal of love. And in no other way would birds, cattle, wild beasts, the flocks, and mares be able to submit to the males, except because their nature too is afire, and is burning to overflow. Do you not see too how those whom mutual pleasure has bound, are often tortured in their common chains? Wherefore, again and again, as I say, the pleasure is common. *The female feels pleasure as well as the male.*

And often when in the mingling of sex the woman by sudden force has mastered the man's might and seized on it with her own, then children are borne like the mother, thanks to the mother's seed, just as the father's seed may make them like the father. But those whom you see with the form of both, mingling side by side the features of both parents, spring alike from the father's body and the mother's blood. It comes to pass too some- *The causes of likeness to either parent,*

or to
ancestors,

times that they can be created like their grandparents, and often recall the form of their grandparents' parents, for the reason that many first-beginnings in many ways are often mingled and concealed in the body of their parents, which, starting from the stock of the race, father hands on to father; therefrom Venus unfolds forms with varying chance, and recalls the look, the voice, the hair of ancestors; since indeed these things are none the more created from a seed determined than are our faces and bodies and limbs. Again the female sex may spring from the father's seed, and males come forth formed from the mother's body. For every offspring is fashioned of the two seeds, and whichever of the two that which is created more resembles, of that parent it has more than an equal share; as you can yourself discern, whether it be a male offspring or a female birth.

and its
connexion
with the
child's sex.

Causes of
sterility.

Nor do powers divine deny to any man a fruitful sowing of seed, that he may never be called father by sweet children, but must live out his years in barren wedlock; as men believe for the most part, and sorrowing sprinkle the altars with streams of blood and fire the high places with their gifts, that they may make their wives pregnant with bounteous seed. Yet all in vain they weary the majesty of the gods and their sacred lots. For the couplings in wedlock are seen to be very diverse. And many women have been barren in several wedlocks before, yet at length have found a mate from whom they might conceive children, and grow rich with sweet offspring. And often even for those, for whom wives fruitful ere now in the house had been unable to bear, a well-matched nature has been found, so that they might fortify their old age with children.

Sometimes 'tis by no divine act or through the shafts A woman of Venus that a woman of form less fair is loved. For at without times a woman may bring it about by her own doing, by beauty may her unselfish ways, and the neat adornment of her body, character, that she accustoms you easily to live your life with her. or dress, or Nay more, habit alone can win love; for that which is mere habit. struck ever and again by a blow, however light, is yet mastered in long lapse of time, and gives way. Do you not see too how drops of water falling upon rocks in long lapse of time drill through the rocks?

BOOK V

Intro-
duction.
Epicurus,
who dis-
covered our
philosophy,
is a god.

Wᴏ can avail by might of mind to build a poem worthy
to match the majesty of truth and these discoveries? Or
who has such skill in speech, that he can fashion praises
to match his deserts, who has left us such prizes, conceived and sought out by his own mind? There will be
no one, I trow, born of mortal body. For if we must
speak as befits the majesty of the truth now known to us,
then he was a god, yea a god, noble Memmius, who first
found out that principle of life, which now is called
wisdom, and who by his skill saved our life from high
seas and thick darkness, and enclosed it in calm waters

His services
to men are
far greater
than those
of the gods
and heroes
of old :

and bright light. For set against this the heaven-sent
discoveries of others in the days of old. Ceres is fabled to
have taught to men the growing of corn, and Liber the
liquid of the vine-born juice; and yet life could have
gone on without these things, as tales tell us that some
races live even now. But a good life could not be without
a clean heart; wherefore more rightly is he counted a god
by us, thanks to whom now sweet solaces for life soothe
the mind, spread even far and wide among great peoples.

even ot
Hercules.

But if you think that the deeds of Hercules [n] excel this,
you will be carried still further adrift from true reasoning.
For what harm to us now were the great gaping jaws of
the old Nemean lion and the bristling boar of Arcadia?
Or what could the bull of Crete do, or the curse of
Lerna, the hydra with its pallisade of poisonous snakes?
what the triple-breasted might of threefold Geryon?

⟨How could those birds⟩ have done us such great hurt, who dwelt in the Stymphalian ⟨fen⟩,[1] or the horses of Diomede the Thracian, breathing fire from their nostrils near the coasts of the Bistones and Ismara? Or the guardian of the glowing golden apples of Hesperus's daughters, the dragon, fierce, with fiery glance, with his vast body twined around the tree-trunk, yea, what harm could he have done beside the Atlantic shore and the grim tracts of ocean, where none of us draws near nor barbarian dares to venture? And all other monsters of this sort which were destroyed, had they not been vanquished, what hurt, pray, could they have done alive? Not a jot, I trow: the earth even now teems in such abundance with wild beasts, and is filled with trembling terrors throughout forests and mighty mountains and deep woods; but for the most part we have power to shun those spots. But unless the heart is cleansed, what battles and perils must we then enter into despite our will? What sharp pangs of passion then rend the troubled man, yea and what fears besides? what of pride, filthiness and wantonness? what havoc they work? what of luxury and sloth? He then who has subdued all these and driven them from the mind by speech, not arms, shall this man not rightly be found worthy to rank among the gods? Above all, since 'twas his wont to speak many sayings in good and godlike words about the immortal gods themselves, and in his discourse to reveal the whole nature of things. *For he gave us a clean heart,*

and taught us about the gods and nature.

In his footsteps I tread, and while I follow his reasonings and set out in my discourse, by what law all things are created, and how they must needs abide by it, nor *Now that I have shown the laws of nature,*

[1] A line is lost, of which the words in brackets give the general sense.

can they break through the firm ordinances of their being,
even as first of all the nature of the mind has been found
to be formed and created above other things with a body
that has birth, and to be unable to endure unharmed
through the long ages, but it is images that are wont in
sleep to deceive the mind, when we seem to behold one
whom life has left ; for what remains, the train of my
reasoning has now brought me to this point, that I must
give account how the world is made of mortal body and
also came to birth ; and in what ways that gathering of
matter established earth, sky, sea, stars, sun, and the ball
of the moon ; then what living creatures sprang from the
earth, and which have never been born at any time ;
and in what manner the race of men began to use ever-
varying speech one to another by naming things ; and
in what ways that fear of the gods found its way into
their breasts, which throughout the circle of the world
keeps revered shrines, lakes, groves, altars, and images of
the gods.   Moreover, I will unfold by what power nature,
the helmsman, steers the courses of the sun and the
wanderings of the moon ; lest by chance we should think
that they of their own will 'twixt earth and sky fulfil
their courses from year to year, with kindly favour to the
increase of earth's fruits and living creatures, or should
suppose that they roll on by any forethought of the gods.
For those who have learnt aright that the gods lead a life
free from care, yet if from time to time they wonder by
what means all things can be carried on, above all among
those things which are descried above our heads in the
coasts of heaven, are borne back again into the old beliefs
of religion, and adopt stern overlords, whom in their
misery they believe have all power, knowing not what

and the
mortality
of the soul,

I must
prove that
the world
is mortal,
and how
it came to
be made.

I must
treat of the
creation of
animals,
of the
growth of
speech, of
the origin
of the fear
of the gods,
and of the
courses
of the
heavenly
bodies.

All these
things come
to pass
without the
interference
of the gods.

can be and what cannot, yea and in what way each thing has its power limited, and its deep-set boundary-stone.

For the rest, that I may delay you no more with promises, first of all look upon seas, and lands, and sky; their threefold nature, their three bodies, Memmius, their three forms so diverse, their three textures so vast, one single day shall hurl to ruin; and the massive form and fabric of the world, held up for many years, shall fall headlong. Nor does it escape me in my mind, how strangely and wonderfully this strikes upon the understanding, the destruction of heaven and earth that is to be, and how hard it is for me to prove it surely in my discourse; even as it always happens, when you bring to men's ears something unknown before, and yet you cannot place it before the sight of their eyes, nor lay hands upon it; for by this way the paved path of belief leads straightest into the heart of man and the quarters of his mind. Yet still I will speak out. Maybe that the very fact will give credence to my words, that earthquakes will arise and within a little while you will behold all things shaken in mighty shock. But may fortune at the helm steer this far away from us, and may reasoning rather than the very fact make us believe that all things can fall in with a hideous rending crash.

The world will be destroyed.

This sounds strange, and is hard to prove.

Perhaps events will give sensible proof:

but reasoning must be tried.

Yet before I essay on this point to declare destiny in more holy wise, and with reasoning far more sure than the Pythian priestess, who speaks out from the tripod and laurel of Phoebus, I will unfold many a solace for you in my learned discourse; lest by chance restrained by religion you should think that earth and sun, and sky, sea, stars, and moon must needs abide for everlasting, because of their divine body, and therefore should suppose it right

It is no sacrilege to deny that the world and the heavenly bodies are divine.

that after the manner of the giants [n] all should pay penalty for their monstrous crime, who by their reasoning shake the walls of the world, and would fain quench the glorious sun in heaven, branding things immortal with mortal names; yet these are things so far sundered from divine power, and are so unworthy to be reckoned among gods, that they are thought rather to be able to afford us the concept of what is far removed from vital motion and sense. For verily it cannot be that we should suppose that the nature of mind and understanding can be linked with every body: even as a tree cannot exist in the sky, nor clouds in the salt waters, nor can fishes live in the fields, nor blood be present in wood nor sap in stones. It is determined and ordained where each thing can grow and have its place. So the nature of mind cannot come to birth alone without body, nor exist far apart from sinews and blood. But if this could be, far sooner might the force of mind itself exist in head or shoulders, or right down in the heels, and be wont to be born in any part you will, but at least remain in the same man or the same vessel. But since even within our body it is determined and seen to be ordained where soul and mind can dwell apart and grow, all the more must we deny that outside the whole body and the living creature's form, it could last on in the crumbling sods of earth or in the fire of the sun or in water or in the high coasts of heaven. They are not then created endowed with divine feeling, inasmuch as they cannot be quickened with the sense of life.

This, too, it cannot be that you should believe, that there are holy abodes of the gods in any parts of the world. For the fine nature of the gods, far sundered

Marginal notes:

They are not even sentient.

Soul and mind, like all other things, have their appointed place, apart from which they cannot exist.

They cannot be in earth or the heavenly bodies.

The gods have no dwellings in the world:

from our senses, is scarcely seen by the understanding of
the mind ; and since it lies far beneath all touch or blow
from our hands, it cannot indeed touch anything which
can be touched by us. For nothing can touch which
may not itself be touched. Therefore even their abodes
too must needs be unlike our abodes, fine even as are
their bodies ; all which I will hereafter prove to you [n]
with plenteous argument. Further, to say that for man's
sake they were willing to fashion the glorious nature of
the world, and for that cause 'tis fitting to praise the
work of the gods, which is worthy to be praised, and to
believe that it will be everlasting and immortal, and that
it is sin ever to stir from its seats by any force what was
established for the races of men for all time by the ancient
wisdom of the gods, or to assail it with argument, and to
overthrow it from top to bottom ; to imagine and to add
all else of this sort, Memmius, is but foolishness. For
what profit could our thanks bestow on the immortal and
blessed ones, that they should essay to do anything for
our sakes ? Or what new thing could have enticed them
so long after, when they were aforetime at rest, to desire
to change their former life? For it is clear that he must
take joy in new things, to whom the old are painful ; but
for him, whom no sorrow has befallen in the time gone
by, when he led a life of happiness, for such an one what
could have kindled a passion for new things ? Or what
ill had it been to us never to have been made ? Did
our life, forsooth, lie wallowing in darkness and grief,
until the first creation of things dawned upon us ? For
whosoever has been born must needs wish to abide in
life, so long as enticing pleasure shall hold him. But for
him, who has never tasted the love of life, and was never

nor did
they make
the world
for the sake
of man.

Our thanks
could not
benefit
them,

nor could
they have
had a desire
for novelty:

nor would
it have
hurt us if
we had
never been
created.

in the ranks of the living, what harm is it never to have been made? Further, how was there first implanted in the gods a pattern for the begetting of things, yea, and the concept of man,[n] so that they might know and see in their mind what they wished to do, or in what way was the power of the first-beginnings ever learnt, or what they could do when they shifted their order one with the other, if nature did not herself give a model of creation? For so many first-beginnings of things in many ways, driven on by blows from time everlasting until now, and moved by their own weight, have been wont to be borne on, and to unite in every way, and essay everything that they might create, meeting one with another, that it is no wonder if they have fallen also into such arrangements, and have passed into such movements, as those whereby this present sum of things is carried on, ever and again replenished.

But even if I knew not[n] what are the first-beginnings of things, yet this I would dare to affirm from the very workings of heaven, and to prove from many other things as well, that by no means has the nature of things been fashioned for us by divine grace : so great are the flaws with which it stands beset. First, of all that the huge expanse of heaven covers, half thereof mountains and forests of wild beasts have greedily seized ; rocks possess it, and waste pools and the sea, which holds far apart the shores of the lands. Besides, two thirds almost burning heat and the ceaseless fall of frost steal from mortals. Of all the field-land that remains, yet nature would by her force cover it up with thorns, were it not that the force of man resisted her, ever wont for his livelihood to groan over the strong mattock and to furrow the earth with the

Marginal notes:

How, again, could the gods have had a pattern or an idea to work on?

No; the world was made by the chance arrangement of atoms.

That the world is not divinely made for man, may be proved by its imperfections. I. Vast tracts of the earth are useless for man,

deep-pressed plough. But that by turning the fertile and only his toil can turn them to profit. clods with the share, and subduing the soil of the earth we summon them to birth, of their own accord the crops could not spring up into the liquid air; and even now sometimes, when won by great toil things grow leafy throughout the land, and are all in flower, either the sun in heaven burns them with too much heat, or sudden rains destroy them and chill frosts, and the blasts of the winds harry them with headstrong hurricane. Moreover, why does nature foster and increase the awe- 2. He is harassed by wild beasts, disease, and death. some tribe of wild beasts to do harm to the race of man by land and sea? Why do the seasons of the year bring maladies? Why does death stalk abroad before her time? Then again, the child, like a sailor tossed ashore by the 3. The human baby is helpless and defenceless. cruel waves, lies naked on the ground, dumb, lacking all help for life, when first nature has cast him forth by travail from his mother's womb into the coasts of light, and he fills the place with woful wailing, as is but right for one for whom it remains in life to pass through so much trouble. But the diverse flocks and herds grow up and the wild beasts, nor have they need of rattles, nor must there be spoken to any of them the fond and broken prattle of the fostering nurse, nor do they seek diverse garments to suit the season of heaven, nay, and they have no need of weapons or lofty walls, whereby to protect their own, since for all of them the earth itself brings forth all things bounteously, and nature, the quaint artificer of things.

First of all,[n] since the body of earth and moisture, and A. The world is mortal (a) because its component the light breath of the winds and burning heat, of which this sum of things is seen to be made up, are all created of a body that has birth and death, of such, too, must we

parts are mortal.

think that the whole nature of the world is fashioned. For verily things whose parts and limbs we see to be of a body that has birth and of mortal shapes, themselves too we perceive always to have death and birth likewise. Wherefore, when we see the mighty members and parts of the world consumed away and brought to birth again, we may know that sky too likewise and earth had some time of first-beginning, and will suffer destruction.

To prove this of the separate elements: 1. Earth is mortal. It flies away in clouds of dust,

Herein, lest you should think that I have snatched at this proof for myself, because I have assumed that earth and fire are mortal things, nor have hesitated to say that moisture and breezes perish, and have maintained that they too are born again and increase, first of all, some part of earth, when baked by ceaseless suns, trodden by the force of many feet, gives off a mist and flying clouds of dust, which stormy winds scatter through all the air.

or is destroyed by moisture. Earth is the universal mother and the universal tomb.

Part too of its sods is summoned back to swamp by the rains, and streams graze and gnaw their banks. Moreover, whatever the earth nourishes and increases, is, in its own proportion, restored ; and since without doubt the parent of all is seen herself to be the universal tomb of things, therefore you may see that the earth is eaten away, and again increases and grows.

2. Water is mortal :

For the rest, that sea, streams, and springs are ever filling with new moisture, and that waters are ceaselessly oozing forth, there is no need of words to prove : the great downrush of waters on every side shows this forth.

it is drawn up from the sea by wind and sun,

But the water which is foremost is ever taken away, and so it comes to pass that there is never overmuch moisture in the sum, partly because the strong winds as they sweep the seas, diminish them, and so does the sun in heaven, as he unravels their fabric with his rays, partly because

it is sent hither and thither under every land. For the and passes
brine is strained through, and the substance of the moisture beneath the
oozes back, and all streams together at the fountain-head reappear
of rivers, and thence comes back over the lands with in springs.
freshened current, where the channel once cleft has
brought down the waters in their liquid march.

Next then I will speak of air, which changes in its whole 3. Air is
body in countless ways each single hour. For always, mortal :
whatever flows off from things, is all carried into the stantly
great sea of air ; and unless in turn it were to give back being
bodies to things, and replenish them as they flow away, the efflux
all things would by now have been dissolved and turned from things,
into air. Air then ceases not to be created from things, ing them
and to pass back into things, since it is sure that all things by its
are constantly flowing away. restoration.

Likewise that bounteous source[n] of liquid light, the 4. Fire is
sun in heaven, ceaselessly floods the sky with fresh bright- mortal
ness, and at once supplies the place of light with new always
light. For that which is foremost of its brightness, ever sending out
perishes, on whatever spot it falls. That you may learn plies, and
from this : that as soon as clouds have begun for an instant his rays
to pass beneath the sun, and, as it were, to break off the they fall.
rays of light, straightway all the part of the rays beneath the beams
perishes, and the earth is overshadowed, wherever the cut off
clouds are carried ; so that you may learn that things by clouds.
ever have need of fresh brilliance, and that the foremost
shaft of light ever perishes, nor in any other way can
things be seen in the sunlight, except that the very
fountain-head of light gives supply for ever. Nay more, So even
lights at night, which are on the earth, hanging lamps lights on
and oily torches, bright with their flashing fires and to keep up
thick smoke, in like manner hasten by aid of their heat a constant

supply of
flame.

to supply new light; they are quick to flicker with their fires, yea quick, nor is the light, as it were, broken off, nor does it quit the spot. In such eager haste is its destruction hidden by the quick birth of flame from all the fires. So then we must think that sun, moon, and stars throw out their light from new supplies, rising again and again, and lose ever what is foremost of their flames; lest you should by chance believe that they are strong with a strength inviolable.

We con-
stantly see
examples
of the
mortality
of the
strongest
things.

Again, do you not behold stones too vanquished by time, high towers falling in ruins, and rocks crumbling away, shrines and images of the gods growing weary and worn, while the sacred presence cannot prolong the boundaries of fate nor struggle against the laws of nature? Again, do we not see the monuments of men fallen to bits, and inquiring moreover whether you believe that they grow old?[1] And stones torn up from high mountains rushing headlong, unable to brook or bear the stern strength of a limited time? For indeed they would not be suddenly torn up and fall headlong, if from time everlasting they had held out against all the siege of age without breaking.

If the sky
is the
universal
parent, it
is mortal:
for it is
constantly
diminished
and in-
creased.

Now once again gaze on this sky, which above and all around holds the whole earth in its embrace: if it begets all things out of itself, as some tell,[n] and receives them again when they perish, it is made altogether of a body that has birth and death. For whatsoever increases and nourishes other things out of itself, must needs be lessened, and replenished when it receives things back.

(b) There
are many

Moreover, if there was no birth and beginning of the earth and sky, and they were always from everlasting,

---

[1] The line is corrupt, and I have translated Munro's correction: *quaerere proporro sibi sene senescere credas.*

why beyond the Theban war and the doom of Troy have
not other poets sung of other happenings as well? whither
have so many deeds of men so often passed away? why
are they nowhere enshrined in glory in the everlasting
memorials of fame? But indeed, I trow, our whole
world is in its youth, and quite new is the nature of the
firmament, nor long ago did it receive its first-beginnings.
Wherefore even now certain arts are being perfected,
even now are growing; much now has been added to
ships, but a while ago musicians gave birth to tuneful
harmonies. Again, this nature of things, this philosophy, is but lately discovered, and I myself was found
the very first of all who could turn it into the speech of
my country. But if by chance you think that all these
same things were aforetime, but that the generations of
men perished in burning heat, or that cities have fallen
in some great upheaval of the world, or that from ceaseless rains ravening rivers have issued over the lands and
swallowed up cities, all the more must you be vanquished
and confess that there will come to pass a perishing of
earth and sky as well. For when things were assailed by
such great maladies and dangers, then if a more fatal cause
had pressed upon them, far and wide would they have
spread their destruction and mighty ruin. Nor in any
other way do we see one another to be mortal; except
that we fall sick of the same diseases as those whom
nature has sundered from life.

Moreover, if ever things abide [n] for everlasting, it must
needs be either that, because they are of solid body, they
beat back assaults, nor suffer anything to come within
them, which might unloose the close-locked parts within,
such as are the bodies of matter, whose nature we have

Margin notes:
proofs that the world is still in its youth.

If you think former civiliza-tions have passed away in some world-calamity, that would prove that the world is mortal.

(c) The world does not fulfil any of the conditions of immor-tality.

declared before; or that they are able to continue through all time, because they are exempt from blows, as is the void, which abides untouched nor suffers a whit from assault; or else because there is no supply of room all around, into which things might part asunder and be broken up—even as the sum of sums is eternal—nor is there any room without into which they may leap apart, nor are there bodies which might fall upon them and break them up with stout blow. But neither, as I have shown, is the nature of the world endowed with solid body, since there is void mingled in things; nor yet is it as the void, nor indeed are bodies lacking, which might by chance gather together out of infinite space and over-whelm this sum of things with headstrong hurricane, or bear down on it some other form of dangerous destruc-tion; nor again is there nature of room or space in the deep wanting, into which the walls of the world might be scattered forth; or else they may be pounded and

It must then be subject to death,

perish by any other force you will. The gate of death then is not shut on sky or sun or earth or the deep waters of the sea, but it stands open facing them with huge

and have had a birth.

vast gaping maw. Wherefore, again, you must needs con-fess that these same things have a birth; for indeed, things that are of mortal body could not from limitless time up till now have been able to set at defiance the stern strength of immeasurable age.

(d) The great con-test of the elements may one day be brought to

Again, since the mighty members of the world so furiously fight one against the other, stirred up in most unhallowed warfare, do you not see that some end may be set to their long contest? Either when the sun and every kind of heat have drunk up all the moisture and won the day: which they are struggling to do, but as an end by the victory of one or the other. yet they have not accomplished their effort: so great a supply do the rivers bring and threaten to go beyond their bounds, and deluge all things from out the deep abyss of ocean; all in vain, since the winds as they sweep the seas, diminish them, and so does the sun in heaven, as he unravels their fabric with his rays, and they boast that they can dry up all things, ere moisture can reach the end of its task. So vast a war Story tells that both fire and water have for a time held the upper hand. do they breathe out in equal contest, as they struggle and strive one with another for mighty issues; yet once in this fight fire gained the upper hand, and once, as the story goes, moisture reigned supreme on the plains. For fire won its way and burnt up many things, all-devouring, when the resistless might of the horses of the sun went astray and carried Phaethon amain through the whole heavens and over all lands. But, thereupon, the almighty The myth of Phaethon father, thrilled with keen anger, with sudden stroke of his thunder dashed high-souled Phaethon from his chariot to earth, and the sun, meeting him as he fell, caught the everlasting lamp of the world, and tamed the scattered steeds, and yoked them trembling, and so guiding them along their own path, replenished all things; so forsooth sang the old poets of the Greeks: but it is exceeding far removed from true reasoning. For fire can only prevail represents the excess of fire-atoms. when more bodies of its substance have risen up out of infinite space; and then its strength fails, vanquished in some way, or else things perish, burnt up by its fiery breath. Moisture likewise,[n] once gathered together and The story of the Deluge. began to prevail, as the story goes, when it overwhelmed living men with its waves. Thereafter, when its force was by some means turned aside and went its way, even all that had gathered together from infinite space, the rains ceased, and the strength of the rivers was brought low.

B. The Birth of the World. It was not made by design, but by the chance concourse of atoms after ages.

But by what means that gathering together of matter established earth and sky and the depths of ocean, and the courses of sun and moon, I will set forth in order. For in very truth not by design did the first-beginnings of things place themselves each in their order with fore-seeing mind, nor indeed did they make compact what movements each should start; but because many first-beginnings of things in many ways, driven on by blows from time everlasting until now, and moved by their own weight, have been wont to be borne on, and to unite in every way and essay everything that they might create, meeting one with another, therefore it comes to pass that scattered abroad through a great age, as they try meet-ings and motions of every kind, at last those come together, which, suddenly cast together, become often the begin-nings of great things, of earth, sea and sky, and the race of living things.

First atoms gathered together in a wild discordant storm.

Then, when things were so, neither could the sun's orb be seen, flying on high with its bounteous light, nor the stars of the great world, nor sea nor sky, nay nor earth nor air, nor anything at all like to the things we know, but only a sort of fresh-formed storm, a mass gathered together of first-beginnings of every kind, whose discord was waging war and confounding interspaces, paths, inter-lacings, weights, blows, meetings, and motions, because owing to their unlike forms and diverse shapes, all things were unable to remain in union, as they do now, and to give and receive harmonious motions. From this mass [n]

Then the various

parts began to fly off hither and thither, and like things

to unite with like, and so to unfold a world, and to sunder
its members and dispose its great parts, that is, to
mark off the high heaven from the earth, and the sea by
itself, so that it might spread out with its moisture kept
apart, and likewise the fires of the sky by themselves, unmixed and kept apart.

Yea, verily, first of all the several bodies of earth,
because they were heavy and interlaced, met together
in the middle, and all took up the lowest places ; and the
more they met and interlaced, the more did they squeeze
out those which were to make sea, stars, sun, and moon,
and the walls of the great world. For all these are of
smoother and rounder seeds, and of much smaller particles than earth. And so, bursting out from the quarter
of the earth through its loose-knit openings, first of all
the fiery ether rose up and, being so light, carried off with
it many fires, in not far different wise than often we see
now, when first the golden morning light of the radiant
sun reddens over the grass bejewelled with dew, and the
pools and ever-running streams give off a mist, yea, even
as the earth from time to time is seen to steam : and
when all these are gathered together as they move upwards, clouds with body now formed weave a web beneath
the sky on high. Thus then at that time the light and
spreading ether, with body now formed, was set all around
and curved on every side, and spreading wide towards
every part on all sides, thus fenced in all else in its greedy
embrace. There followed then the beginnings of sun and
moon, whose spheres turn in air midway betwixt earth
and ether ; for neither earth nor the great ether claimed
them for itself, because they were neither heavy enough
to sink and settle down, nor light enough to be able to

glide along the topmost coasts, yet they are so set between
the two that they can move along their living bodies, and
are parts of the whole world; even as in our bodies some
limbs may abide in their place, while yet there are others

Then earth
sank in
the middle
and formed
the sea,
moving. So when these things were withdrawn, at once
the earth sank down, where now the vast blue belt of
ocean stretches, and flooded the furrows with salt surge.
And day by day, the more the tide of ether and the
rays of the sun with constant blows along its outer edges
constrained the earth into closer texture, so that thus
smitten it condensed and drew together round its centre,
the more did the salt sweat, squeezed out from its body,
go to increase the sea and the swimming plains, as it
trickled forth; yea, and the more did those many bodies
of heat and air slip forth and fly abroad, and far away from
earth condense the high glowing quarters of the sky.

while
mountains
were left
standing.
Plains sank down, lofty mountains grew in height; for
indeed the rocks could not settle down, nor could all parts
subside equally in the same degree.

Summary:
earth sank
with sea,
air, and
ether
unmixed
above it.
So then the weight of earth, with body now formed,
sank to its place, and, as it were, all the slime of the world
slid heavily to the bottom, and sank right down like dregs;
then the sea and then the air and then the fiery ether
itself were all left unmixed with their liquid bodies; they

Highest of
all the
ether moves
on in its
constant
untroubled
course.
are lighter each than the next beneath, and ether, most
liquid and lightest of all, floats above the breezes of air,
nor does it mingle its liquid body with the boisterous
breezes of air; it suffers all our air below to be churned
by headstrong hurricanes, it suffers it to brawl with shifting storms, but itself bears on its fires as it glides in changeless advance. For that the ether can follow on quietly
and with one constant effort, the Pontos proves, the sea

which flows on with changeless tide, preserving ever the one constant rhythm of its gliding.

[1] Now let us sing what is the cause of the motions of the stars. First of all, if the great globe of the sky turns round,[n] we must say that the air presses on the pole at either end, and holds it outside and closes it in at both ends; and that then another current of air flows above, straining on to the same goal, towards which the twinkling stars of the everlasting world roll on; or else that there is another current beneath, to drive up the sphere reversely, as we see streams moving round wheels with their scoops. It may be also that the whole sky can abide in its place, while yet the shining signs are carried on; either because swift currents of ether are shut within them, and seeking a way out are turned round and round, and so roll on the fires this way and that through the nightly quarters of the sky; or else an air streaming from some other quarter without turns and drives the fires; or else they can themselves creep on, whither its own food invites and summons each as they move on, feeding their flaming bodies everywhere throughout the sky. For it is hard to declare for certain which of these causes it is in this world; but what can happen and does happen through the universe in the diverse worlds, fashioned on diverse plans, that is what I teach, and go on to set forth many causes for the motions of the stars, which may exist throughout the universe; and of these it must needs be one which in our world too

C. The motions of the stars.
1. If the whole sky moves round, it must be driven either by a current above or by a current below.
2. If the sky remains firm, the stars are moved either (a) by fire inside them or (b) by exterior currents, or (c) by desire to reach their proper fuel. All these causes act somewhere in the universe.

---

[1] This paragraph seems misplaced: but it is not clear where it should come in (possibly after the next paragraph), and it may be a subsequent addition, which the poet did not properly work into its context.

gives strength to the motions of the heavenly signs ; but to affirm which of them it is, is in no wise the task of one treading forward step by step.

Now that the earth may rest quiet in the mid region of the world, it is natural that its mass should [n] gradually thin out and grow less, and that it should have another nature underneath from the beginning of its being, linked and closely bound in one with those airy parts of the world amid which it has its place and life. For this cause it is no burden, nor does it weigh down the air ; even as for every man his own limbs are no weight, nor is the head a burden to the neck, nay nor do we feel that the whole weight of the body is resting on the feet ; but all weights which come from without and are laid upon us, hurt us, though often they are many times smaller. Of such great matter is it, what is the power of each thing. So then the earth is not suddenly brought in as some alien body, nor cast from elsewhere on alien air, but it has been begotten along with it from the first beginning of the world, a determined part of it, as our limbs are seen to be of us. Moreover, the earth, when shaken suddenly by violent thunder, shakes with its motion all that is above it ; which it could not by any means do, were it not bound up with the airy parts of the world and with the sky. For they cling one to the other with common roots, linked and closely bound in one from the beginning of their being. Do you not see too how great is the weight of our body, which the force of the soul, though exceeding fine, supports, just because it is so nearly linked and closely bound in one with it ? And again, what can lift the body in a nimble leap save the force of the soul, which steers the limbs ? Do you not see now

The earth is supported by a 'second nature' beneath it, which is closely connected with the air. Similarly 1. our limbs are no weight to us because of their close connexion;

2. the earth shows its connexion with air above by communicating to it its own shocks ; 3. the soul, thanks to its close connexion, can lift the body.

how great can be the power of a fine nature, when it is linked with a heavy body, even as the air is linked with earth, and the force of the mind with us?

Nor can the sun's blazing wheel [n] be much greater or less, than it is seen to be by our senses. For from whatsoever distances fires can throw us their light and breathe their warm heat upon our limbs, they lose nothing of the body of their flames because of the interspaces, their fire is no whit shrunken to the sight. Even so, since the heat of the sun and the light he sheds, arrive at our senses and cheer the spots on which they fall, the form and bulk of the sun as well must needs be seen truly from earth, so that you could alter it almost nothing to greater or less. The moon, too, whether she illumines places with a borrowed light as she moves along, or throws out her own rays from her own body, however that may be, moves on with a shape no whit greater than seems that shape, with which we perceive her with our eyes. For all things which we behold far sundered from us through much air, are seen to grow confused in shape, ere their outline is lessened. Wherefore it must needs be that the moon, inasmuch as she shows a clear-marked shape and an outline well defined, is seen by us from earth in the heights, just as she is, clear-cut all along her outer edges, and just the size she is. Lastly, all the fires of heaven that you see from earth; inasmuch as all fires that we see on earth, so long as their twinkling light is clear, so long as their blaze is perceived, are seen to change their size only in some very small degree from time to time to greater or less, the further they are away: so we may know that the heavenly fires can only be a very minute degree smaller or larger by a little tiny piece.

The sun is not much larger or smaller than we see it. For fires, so long as seen and felt, do not look smaller.

The moon is just the size we see it.

For as long as things are clear in outline, they do not look smaller.

The stars may be slightly smaller or larger than we see them.

The great
light and
heat of this
small sun
may be
caused

(*a*) because
it is the one
fountain-
head of all
the world's
light;

(*b*) because
it kindles
the sur-
rounding
air;

(*c*) because
it has
hidden
heat all
around it.

The orbits
of sun,
moon, and
stars may
be caused

(*a*) because
the nearer
a heavenly
body is to
earth, the
more slowly

This, too, is not wonderful,[n] how the sun, small as it is, can send out so great light, to fill seas and all lands and sky with its flood, and to bathe all things in its warm heat. For it may be that from this spot[n] the one well of light for the whole world is opened up and teems with bounteous stream, and shoots out its rays, because the particles of heat from all the world gather together on every side, and their meeting mass flows together in such wise, that here from a single fountain-head their blazing light streams forth. Do you not see too how widely a tiny spring of water sometimes moistens the fields, and floods out over the plains? Or again, it may be that from the sun's fire, though it be not great, blazing light seizes on the air with its burning heat, if by chance there is air ready to hand and rightly suited to be kindled when smitten by tiny rays of heat; even as sometimes we see crops or straw caught in widespread fire from one single spark. Perhaps, too, the sun, shining on high with its rosy torch, has at his command much fire with hidden heat all around him, fire which is never marked by any radiance, so that it is only laden with heat and increases the stroke of the sun's rays.

Nor is there any single and straightforward account[n] of the sun, to show how from the summer regions he draws near the winter turning-point of Capricorn, and how turning back thence, he betakes himself to the solstice-goal of Cancer; and how the moon is seen in single months to traverse that course, on which the sun spends the period of a year as he runs. There is not, I say, any single cause assigned for these things. For, first and foremost, it is clear that it may come to pass, as the judgement of the holy man, Democritus, sets before us, that the nearer the

several stars are to earth, the less can they be borne on
with the whirl of heaven. For its swift keen strength
passes away and is lessened beneath, and so little by little
the sun is left behind with the hindmost signs, because
it is much lower than the burning signs. And even more
the moon: the lower her course, the further it is from the
sky and nearer to earth, the less can she strain on her course
level with the signs. Moreover the weaker the whirl
with which she is borne along, being lower than the sun,
the more do all the signs catch her up all around and pass
her. Therefore, it comes to pass that she seems to turn
back more speedily to each several sign, because the signs
come back to her. It may be too that from quarters of
the world athwart his path two airs may stream alternately, each at a fixed season, one such as to push the sun
away from the summer signs right to the winter turning-
places and their icy frost, and the other to hurl him back
from the icy shades of cold right to the heat-laden quarters
and the burning signs. And in like manner must we
think that the moon and those stars which roll through [n]
the great years in great orbits, can be moved by airs
from the opposite quarters in turn. Do you not see
how by contrary winds the lower clouds too are moved
in directions contrary to those above? Why should
those stars be less able to be borne on by currents contrary one to the other through the great orbits in the
heaven?

But night shrouds the earth in thick darkness, either
when after his long journey[n] the sun has trodden the
farthest parts of heaven, and fainting has breathed out
his fires shaken by the journey and made weak by much
air, or because the same force, which carried on his orb

[marginal notes:] is it moved by the whirl of heaven. The sun then moves less swiftly than the stars, the moon than the sun, Therefore the moon seems to move quickest in the opposite direction: (b) because there are transverse currents which blow the sun from one tropic to the other: and so with moon and stars.

Night is caused either (a) because the sun's light is extinguished or (b) because he travels under the earth. Dawn is caused either (a) because the returning sun sends his rays in advance or (b) because the fires which compose the new sun gradually collect. Such regular recurrence is not wonderful. It has many parallels in nature.

above the earth, constrains him to turn his course back beneath the earth.

Likewise at a fixed time Matuta[n] sends abroad the rosy dawn through the coasts of heaven, and spreads the light, either because the same sun, returning again beneath the earth, seizes the sky in advance with his rays, fain to kindle it, or because the fires come together and many seeds of heat are wont to stream together at a fixed time, which each day cause the light of a new sun to come to birth. Even so story tells that from the high mountains of Ida scattered fires are seen as the light rises, and then they gather as if into a single ball, and make up the orb. Nor again ought this to be cause of wonder herein, that these seeds of fire can stream together at so fixed a time and renew the brightness of the sun. For we see many events, which come to pass at a fixed time in all things. Trees blossom at a fixed time, and at a fixed time lose their flower. Even so at a fixed time age bids the teeth fall, and the hairless youth grow hairy with soft down and let a soft beard flow alike from either cheek. Lastly, thunder, snow, rains, clouds, winds come to pass at seasons of the year more or less fixed. For since the first-beginnings of causes were ever thus and things have so fallen out from the first outset of the world, one after the other they come round even now in fixed order.

Where causes are original, effects come in due sequence. The disproportion of night and day, except at the equinox, may be caused either (a) because

And likewise it may be that days grow longer and nights wane, and again daylight grows less, when nights take increase ; either because the same sun,[n] as he fulfils his course in unequal arcs below the earth and above, parts the coasts of heaven, and divides his circuit into unequal portions ; and whatever he has taken away from the one part, so much the more he replaces, as he goes round, in the part opposite it, until he arrives at that sign in the sky, where the node of the year makes the shades of night equal to the daylight. For in the mid-course of the blast of the north wind and of the south wind, the sky holds his turning-points apart at a distance then made equal, on account of the position of the whole starry orbit, in which the sun covers the space of a year in his winding course, as he lights earth and heaven with his slanting rays: as is shown by the plans of those who have marked out all the quarters of the sky, adorned with their signs in due order. Or else, because[n] the air is thicker in certain regions, and therefore the trembling ray of his fire is delayed beneath the earth, nor can it easily pierce through and burst out to its rising. Therefore in winter time the long nights lag on, until the radiant ensign of day comes forth. Or else again, because in the same way in alternate parts of the year the fires, which cause the sun to rise from a fixed quarter, are wont to stream together now more slowly, now more quickly, therefore it is that those seem to speak the truth ⟨who say that a new sun is born every day⟩.[1]

at that time the arcs of day and night into which the sun divides his daily revolution are necessarily equalized;

or (b) because, at some seasons, the sun is delayed by dense air; or (c) because his fires gather together more slowly.

The moon may shine[n] when struck by the sun's rays, and day by day turn that light more straightly to our sight, the more she retires from the sun's orb, until opposite him she has glowed with quite full light and, as she rises, towering on high, has seen his setting; then little by little she must needs retire back again, and, as it were, hide her light, the nearer she glides now to the sun's fire from the opposite quarter through the orbit of the signs; as those have it, who picture that the moon is like a ball, and keeps to the path of her course below the

The phases of the moon may be caused, (a) if the moon shines by reflected light, by her gradual movement to and from a position opposite the sun.

---

[1] A line is lost, of which this was possibly the sense.

(*b*) If she
shines by
her own
light:
1. by
another
opaque
body which
accom-
panies and
hides her;
2. because
she has
one light
side, which
she turns
towards us
and away
again.

sun. There is also a way by which she can roll on with her own light, and yet show changing phases of brightness. For there may be another body, which is borne on and glides together with her, in every way obstructing and obscuring her; yet it cannot be seen, because it is borne on without light. Or she may turn round, just like, if it so chance, the sphere of a ball, tinged over half its surface with gleaming light, and so by turning round the sphere produce changing phases, until she turns to our sight and open eyes that side, whichever it be, that is endowed with fires; and then little by little she twists back again and carries away from us the light-giving part of the round mass of the ball; as the Babylonian teaching of the Chaldaeans.[n] denying the science of the astronomers, essays to prove in opposition; just as if what each of them fights for may not be the truth, or there were any cause why you should venture to adopt the one less than

(*c*) If a
fresh moon
is created
daily, by a
regular
succession
of forms,
like the
succession
of the
seasons.

the other. Or again, why a fresh moon could not be created every day with fixed succession of phases and fixed shapes, so that each several day the moon created would pass away, and another be supplied in its room and place, it is difficult to teach by reasoning or prove by words, since so many things can be created in fixed order. Spring goes on her way[n] and Venus, and before them treads Venus's winged harbinger; and following close on the steps of Zephyrus, mother Flora strews and fills all the way before them with glorious colours and scents. Next after follows parching heat, and as com-panion at her side dusty Ceres and the etesian blasts of the north winds. Then autumn advances, and step by step with her Euhius Euan. Then follow the other seasons and their winds, Volturnus, thundering on high, and the south wind, whose strength is the lightning. Last of all the year's end brings snow, and winter renews numbing frost; it is followed by cold, with chattering teeth. Wherefore it is less wonderful if the moon is born at a fixed time, and again at a fixed time is blotted out, since so many things can come to pass at fixed times.

Likewise also the eclipses of the sun [n] and the hidings of the moon, you must think may be brought about by several causes. For why should the moon be able to shut out the earth from the sun's light, and thrust her head high before him in the line of earth, throwing her dark orb before his glorious rays; and at the same time it should not be thought that another body could do this, which glides on ever without light. And besides, why should not the sun be able at a fixed time to faint and lose his fires, and again renew his light, when, in his journey through the air, he has passed by places hostile to his flames, which cause his fires to be put out and perish? And why should the earth be able in turn to rob the moon of light, and herself on high to keep the sun hidden beneath, while the moon in her monthly journey glides through the sharp-drawn shadows of the cone; and at the same time another body be unable to run beneath the moon or glide above the sun's orb, to break off his rays and streaming light? And indeed, if the moon shines with her own light, why should she not be able to grow faint in a certain region of the world, while she passes out through spots unfriendly to her own light?

Eclipses of the sun may be caused (a) by the moon; (b) by some other opaque body; (c) when he passes through regions which choke his light. Eclipses of the moon may be caused (a) when earth gets between sun and moon; (b) and (c) as in the case of the sun.

For the rest, since I have unfolded in what manner each thing could take place throughout the blue vault of the great world, so that we might learn what force and what cause started the diverse courses of the sun, and the

D. We must return to the early days of the earth.

journeyings of the moon, and in what way they might go hiding with their light obscured, and shroud the unexpecting earth in darkness, when, as it were, they wink and once again open their eye and look upon all places shining with their clear rays ; now I return to the youth of the world, and the soft fields of earth, and what first with new power of creation they resolved to raise into the coasts of light and entrust to the gusty winds.

The earth brought forth first vegetable life,

First of all the earth gave birth to the tribes of herbage and bright verdure all around the hills and over all the plains, the flowering fields gleamed in their green hue, and thereafter the diverse trees were started with loose rein on their great race of growing through the air. Even as down and hair and bristles are first formed on the limbs of four-footed beasts and the body of fowls strong of wing, so then the newborn earth raised up herbage and

then living creatures :

shrubs first, and thereafter produced the races of mortal things, many races born in many ways by diverse means. For neither can living animals have fallen from the sky nor the beasts of earth have issued forth from the salt pools. It remains that rightly has the earth won the name of mother, since out of earth all things are produced. And even now many animals spring forth from the earth, formed by the rains and the warm heat of the sun ; wherefore we may wonder the less, if then more animals and greater were born, reaching their full growth when earth and air were fresh.

first birds, springing from eggs ;

First of all the tribe of winged fowls and the diverse birds left their eggs, hatched out in the spring season, as now in the summer the grasshoppers of their own will leave their smooth shells, seeking life and livelihood.

then animals,

Then it was that the earth first gave birth to the race of mortal things. For much heat and moisture abounded then in the fields ; thereby, wherever a suitable spot or place was afforded, there grew up wombs, clinging to the earth by their roots ; and when in the fullness of time the age of the little ones, fleeing moisture and eager for air, had opened them, nature would turn to that place the pores in the earth and constrain them to give forth from their opened veins a sap, most like to milk ; even as now every woman, when she has brought forth, is filled with sweet milk, because all the current of her nourishment is turned towards her paps.   The earth furnished food for the young, the warmth raiment, the grass a couch rich in much soft down.   But the youth of the world called not into being hard frosts nor exceeding heat nor winds of mighty violence : for all things grow and come to their strength in like degrees. *[margin: springing from wombs rooted in the earth. Nature fed and clothed them : nor was there excessive cold, heat, or wind.]*

Wherefore, again and again, rightly has the earth won, rightly does she keep the name of mother, since she herself formed the race of men, and almost at a fixed time brought forth every animal which ranges madly everywhere on the mighty mountains, and with them the fowls of the air with their diverse forms.   But because she must needs come to some end of child-bearing, she ceased, like a woman worn with the lapse of age.   For time changes the nature of the whole world, and one state after another must needs overtake all things, nor does anything abide like itself : all things change their abode, nature alters all things and constrains them to turn.   For one thing rots away and grows faint and feeble with age, thereon another grows up and issues from its place of scorn.   So then time changes the nature of the whole world, and one state after another overtakes the earth, so that it cannot bear what it did, but can bear what it did not of old. *[margin: Earth was thus the mother of all things ; but in time she ceased to bear in accordance with the universal law of change and succession.]*

Nature first
created
many
deformities,

And many monsters too earth [n] then essayed to create,
born with strange faces and strange limbs, the man-
woman, between the two, yet not either, sundered from
both sexes, some things bereft of feet, or in turn robbed
of hands, things too found dumb without mouths, or
blind without eyes, or locked through the whole body
by the clinging of the limbs, so that they could not do
anything or move towards any side or avoid calamity or
take what they needed.   All other monsters and prodigies

but they
could not
survive or
propagate
their kind.

of this sort she would create ; all in vain, since nature
forbade their increase, nor could they reach the coveted
bloom of age nor find food nor join in the work of Venus.
For we see that many happenings must be united for
things, that they may be able to beget and propagate
their races ; first that they may have food, and then a way
whereby birth-giving seeds may pass through their
frames, and issue from their slackened limbs ; and that
woman may be joined with man, they must needs each
have means whereby they can interchange mutual joys.

Many races
perished
which could
not protect
themselves

And it must needs be that many races of living things
then perished and could not beget and propagate their
offspring.   For whatever animals you see feeding on the
breath of life, either their craft or bravery, aye or their
swiftness has protected and preserved their kind from the

or claim
man's
protection
as a return
for their
services.

beginning of their being.   And many there are, which
by their usefulness are commended to us, and so abide,
trusted to our tutelage.   First of all the fierce race of
lions, that savage stock, their bravery has protected, foxes
their cunning, and deer their fleet foot.   But the lightly-
sleeping minds of dogs with their loyal heart, and all the
race which is born of the seed of beasts of burden, and
withal the fleecy flocks and the horned herds, are all trusted

to the tutelage of men, Memmius. For eagerly did they flee the wild beasts and ensue peace and bounteous fodder gained without toil of theirs, which we grant them as a reward because of their usefulness. But those to whom nature granted none of these things, neither that they might live on by themselves of their own might, nor do us any useful service, for which we might suffer their kind to feed and be kept safe under our defence, you may know that these fell a prey and spoil to others, all entangled in the fateful trammels of their own being, until nature brought their kind to destruction.

But neither were there Centaurs,[n] nor at any time can there be animals of twofold nature and double body, put together of limbs of alien birth, so that the power and strength of each,[1] derived from this parent and that, could be equal. That we may learn, however dull be our understanding, from this. First of all, when three years have come round, the horse is in the prime of vigour, but the child by no means so; for often even now in his sleep he will clutch for the milky paps of his mother's breasts. Afterwards, when the stout strength and limbs of horses fail through old age and droop, as life flees from them, then at last youth sets in in the prime of boyish years, and clothes the cheeks with soft down; that you may not by chance believe that Centaurs can be created or exist, formed of a man and the load-laden breed of horses, or Scyllas either, with bodies half of sea-monsters, girt about with ravening dogs, or any other beasts of their kind, whose limbs we see cannot agree one with another; for they neither reach their prime together nor gain the full strength of their bodies nor let it fall

Monsters compounded of animals of different species never could have existed, for the growths of the various animals are not parallel,

---

[1] The text is uncertain, but this must have been the general sense.

nor their
tastes and
habits alike.

away in old age, nor are they fired with a like love, nor do they agree in a single character, nor are the same things pleasant to them throughout their frame. Indeed, we may see the bearded goats often grow fat on hemlock, which to man is rank poison. Since moreover flame is wont to scorch and burn the tawny bodies of lions just as much as every kind of flesh and blood that exists on the earth, how could it have come to pass that the Chimaera, one in her threefold body, in front a lion, in the rear a dragon, in the middle, as her name shows, a goat, should breathe out at her mouth fierce flame from her body?

The notion
of the
youth of
the world
has led
to many
similar
absurdities.

Wherefore again, he who feigns that when the earth was young and the sky new-born, such animals could have been begotten, trusting only in this one empty plea of the world's youth, may blurt out many things in like manner from his lips; he may say that then streams of gold flowed everywhere over the lands, and that trees were wont to blossom with jewels, or that a man was born with such expanse of limbs, that he could plant his footsteps right across the deep seas, and with his hands twist

Such com-
binations
were no
more
possible
then than
now.

the whole sky about him. For because there were in the earth many seeds of things at the time when first the land brought forth animals, yet that is no proof that beasts of mingled breed could have been born, or the limbs of living creatures put together in one; because the races of herbage and the crops and fruitful trees, which even now spring forth abundantly from the earth, yet cannot be created intertwined one with another, but each of these things comes forth after its own manner, and all preserve their separate marks by a fixed law of nature.

But the race of man [n] was much hardier then in the

fields, as was seemly for a race born of the hard earth : Primitive
it was built up on larger and more solid bones within, man : he was
fastened with strong sinews traversing the flesh ; not hardy
easily to be harmed by heat or cold or strange food or
any taint of the body.   And during many lustres of the
sun rolling through the sky they prolonged their lives and long- lived.
after the roving manner of wild beasts.   Nor was there He did
any sturdy steerer of the bent plough, nor knew any one not till,
how to work the fields with iron, or to plant young shoots
in the earth, or cut down the old branches off high trees
with knives.   What sun and rains had brought to birth, but lived
what earth had created unasked, such gift was enough on the fruits of
to appease their hearts.   Among oaks laden with acorns the trees,
they would refresh their bodies for the most part ; and
the arbute-berries, which now you see ripening in winter-
time with scarlet hue, the earth bore then in abundance,
yea and larger.   And besides these the flowering youth
of the world then bare much other rough sustenance,
enough and to spare for miserable mortals.   But to slake and drank
their thirst streams and springs summoned them, even from streams.
as now the downrush of water from the great mountains
calls clear far and wide to the thirsting tribes of wild
beasts.   Or again they dwelt in the woodland haunts
of the nymphs, which they had learnt in their wanderings, from which they knew that gliding streams of water
washed the wet rocks with bounteous flood, yea washed
the wet rocks, as they dripped down over the green moss,
and here and there welled up and burst forth over the
level plain.   Nor as yet did they know how to serve their He had no clothing
purposes with fire, nor to use skins and clothe their body or house,
in the spoils of wild beasts, but dwelt in woods and the but lived in

caves and
forests.
caves on mountains and forests, and amid brushwood
would hide their rough limbs, when constrained to shun
There was
no common
life,
the shock of winds and the rain-showers. Nor could
they look to the common weal, nor had they knowledge
to make mutual use of any customs or laws. Whatever
booty chance had offered to each, he bore it off; for
each was taught at his own will to live and thrive for
and love
was pro-
miscuous.
himself alone. And Venus would unite lovers in the
woods; for each woman was wooed either by mutual
passion, or by the man's fierce force and reckless lust, or
by a price, acorns and arbute-berries or choice pears.
Some beasts
he hunted,
some he
avoided.
And trusting in their strange strength of hand and foot
they would hunt the woodland tribes of wild beasts with
stones to hurl or clubs of huge weight; many they would
At night
he lay on
the ground,
vanquish, a few they would avoid in hiding; and like
bristly boars these woodland men would lay their limbs
naked on the ground, when overtaken by night time,
wrapping themselves up around with leaves and foliage.
and did
not fear the
darkness
Nor did they look for daylight and the sun with loud
wailing, wandering fearful through the fields in the darkness of night, but silent and buried in sleep waited mindful, until the sun with rosy torch should bring the light
into the sky. For, because they had been wont ever
from childhood to behold darkness and light begotten,
turn by turn, it could not come to pass that they should
ever wonder, or feel mistrust lest the light of the sun
should be withdrawn for ever, and never-ending night
so much as
the attacks
of wild
beasts.
possess the earth. But much greater was another care,
inasmuch as the tribes of wild beasts often made rest
dangerous for wretched men. Driven from their home
they would flee from their rocky roof at the coming of a
foaming boar or a mighty lion, and in the dead of night in

terror they would yield their couches spread with leaves
to their cruel guests.

Nor then much more than now would the races of
men leave the sweet light of life with lamentation. For
then more often would some one of them be caught and
furnish living food to the wild beasts, devoured by their
teeth, and would fill woods and mountains and forests
with his groaning, as he looked on his living flesh being
buried in a living tomb. And those whom flight had
saved with mangled body, thereafter, holding trembling
hands over their noisome sores, would summon Orcus
with terrible cries, until savage griping pains had robbed
them of life, all helpless and knowing not what wounds
wanted. Yet never were many thousands of men led
beneath the standards and done to death in a single day,
nor did the stormy waters of ocean dash ships and men
upon the rocks. Then rashly, idly, in vain would the sea
often arise and rage, and lightly lay aside its empty
threatenings, nor could the treacherous wiles of the windless waves lure any man to destruction with smiling
waters; then the wanton art of sailing lay as yet unknown. Then, too, want of food would give over their
drooping limbs to death, now on the other hand 'tis
surfeit of good things brings them low. They all unwitting would often pour out poison for themselves, now
with more skill they give it to others.

Then after they got themselves huts and skins and fire,
and woman yoked with man retired to a single ⟨home,
and the laws of marriage⟩[1] were learnt, and they saw
children sprung from them, then first the race of man
began to soften. For fire brought it about that their

[1] A line is lost, of which this was probably the sense.

Marginal notes:

Then more men fell a prey to wild beasts than now,

but thou-sands were not killed in battle,

nor drowned at sea.

They died of hunger, not surfeit; they poisoned themselves, not others.

E. Beginning of civilization. Fire, clothing and shelter led to home life,

chilly limbs could not now so well bear cold under the roof of heaven, and Venus lessened their strength, and children, by their winning ways, easily broke down the haughty will of their parents. Then, too, neighbours began eagerly to form friendship one with another, not to hurt or be harmed,[n] and they commended to mercy children and the race of women, when with cries and gestures they taught by broken words that 'tis right for all men to have pity on the weak. Yet not in all ways could unity be begotten, but a good part, the larger part, would keep their compacts loyally; or else the human race would even then have been all destroyed, nor could breeding have prolonged the generations until now.

But the diverse sounds of the tongue[n] nature constrained men to utter, and use shaped the names of things, in a manner not far other than the very speechlessness of their tongue is seen to lead children on to gesture, when it makes them point out with the finger the things that are before their eyes. For every one feels to what purpose he can use his own powers. Before the horns of a calf appear and sprout from his forehead, he butts with them when angry, and pushes passionately. But the whelps of panthers and lion-cubs already fight with claws and feet and biting, when their teeth and claws are scarce yet formed. Further, we see all the tribe of winged fowls trusting to their wings, and seeking an unsteady aid from their pinions. Again, to think that any one then parcelled out names to things, and that from him men learnt their first words, is mere folly. For why should he be able to mark off all things by words, and to utter the diverse sounds of the tongue, and at the same time others be thought unable to do this? Moreover, if

Marginal notes:

and friendship with neighbours.

Compacts were for the most part observed.

Origin of language. Words grew up naturally by experiment, just as children and animals try their various powers.

Language cannot have been deliberately invented by any man. Why should one

others too had not used words to one another, whence **man be able to do it and not others?** was implanted in him the concept of their use; [n] whence was he given the first power to know and see in his mind what he wanted to do? Likewise one man could not **How could he have the con- ception of language? or make others accept it?** avail to constrain many, and vanquish them to his will, that they should be willing to learn all his names for things; nor indeed is it easy in any way to teach and persuade the deaf what it is needful to do; for they would not endure it, nor in any way suffer the sounds of words unheard before to batter on their ears any more to no purpose. Lastly, what is there so marvellous in this, **It is not wonderful that man evolved language, for even animals express different feelings by different sounds, e. g. the dog,** if the human race, with strong voice and tongue, should mark off things with diverse sounds for diverse feelings? When the dumb cattle, yea and the races of wild beasts are wont to give forth diverse unlike sounds, when they are in fear or pain, or again when their joys grow strong. Yea verily, this we may learn from things clear to see. When the large loose lips of Molossian dogs start to snarl in anger, baring their hard teeth, thus drawn back in rage, they threaten with a noise far other than when they bark and fill all around with their clamour. Yet when they essay fondly to lick their cubs with their tongue, or when they toss them with their feet, and making for them with open mouth, feign gently to swallow them, checking their closing teeth, they fondle them with growling voice in a way far other than when left alone in the house they bay, or when whining they shrink from a beating with cringing body. Again, is not neighing seen to differ **the horse,** likewise, when a young stallion in the flower of his years rages among the mares, pricked by the spur of winged love. and from spreading nostrils snorts for the fray, and when, it may be, at other times he whinnies with

and even
birds.

trembling limbs? Lastly, the tribe of winged fowls and the diverse birds, hawks and ospreys and gulls amid the sea-waves, seeking in the salt waters for life and livelihood, utter at other times cries far other than when they are struggling for their food and fighting for their prey. And some of them change their harsh notes with the weather, as the long-lived tribes of crows and flocks of rooks, when they are said to cry for water and rains, and anon to summon the winds and breezes. And so, if diverse feelings constrain animals, though they are dumb, to utter diverse sounds, how much more likely is it that mortals should then have been able to mark off things unlike with one sound and another.

Lightning
brought
men fire;

[1] Herein, lest by chance you should ask a silent question, it was the lightning that first of all brought fire to earth for mortals, and from it all the heat of flames is spread abroad. For we see many things flare up, kindled with flames from heaven, when a stroke from the sky has

or else the
ignition
of trees by
friction.

brought the gift of heat. Yet again, when a branching tree is lashed by the winds and sways to and fro, reeling and pressing on the branches of another tree, fire is struck out by the strong force of the rubbing, anon the fiery heat of flame sparkles out, while branches and trunks rub each against the other. Either of these happenings may have

The action
of the
sun's rays
taught
them
cooking.

given fire to mortals. And then the sun taught them to cook food and soften it by the heat of flame, since they saw many things among the fields grow mellow, van-quished by the lashing of his rays and by the heat.

And day by day those who excelled in understanding

---

[1] This and the next two paragraphs seem rather out of place here: possibly they should be placed before the preceding paragraph, or else they may be a later addition by the poet.

and were strong in mind showed them more and more how to change their former life and livelihood for new habits and for fire. Kings began to build cities and to found a citadel, to be for themselves a stronghold and a refuge; and they parcelled out and gave flocks and fields to each man for his beauty or his strength or understanding; for beauty was then of much avail, and strength stood high. Thereafter property was invented and gold found, which easily robbed the strong and beautiful of honour; for, for the most part, however strong men are born, however beautiful their body, they follow the lead of the richer man. Yet if a man would steer his life by true reasoning, it is great riches to a man to live thriftily with calm mind; for never can he lack for a little. But men wished to be famous and powerful, that their fortune might rest on a sure foundation, and they might in wealth lead a peaceful life; all in vain, since struggling to rise to the heights of honour, they made the path of their journey beset with danger, and yet from the top, like lightning, envy smites them and casts them down anon in scorn to a noisome Hell; since by envy, as by lightning, the topmost heights are most often set ablaze, and all places that rise high above others; so that it is far better to obey in peace than to long to rule the world with kingly power and to sway kingdoms. Wherefore let them sweat out their life-blood, worn away to no purpose, battling their way along the narrow path of ambition; inasmuch as their wisdom is but from the lips of others, and they seek things rather through hearsay than from their own feelings, and that is of no more avail now nor shall be hereafter than it was of old.

Marginal notes:

Then came a change.

Kings built cities,

and assigned lands, at first for personal merit.

Then came the discovery of gold, which altered everything.

It prompts ambition,

which goes before a fall.

Such a life is but built on hearsay.

Monarchy
was over-
thrown,

And so the kings were put to death and the ancient majesty of thrones and proud sceptres was overthrown and lay in ruins, and the glorious emblem on the head of kings was stained with blood, and beneath the feet of the mob mourned the loss of its high honour; for once

and anarchy
prevailed:

dreaded overmuch, eagerly now it is trampled. And so things would pass to the utmost dregs of disorder, when every man sought for himself the power and the head-

then magis-
trates and
laws were
made,

ship. Then some of them taught men to appoint magistrates and establish laws that they might consent to obey ordinances. For the race of men, worn out with leading a life of violence, lay faint from its feuds; wherefore the more easily of its own will it gave in to ordinances and

and crime
restrained
by punish-
ment.

the close mesh of laws. For since each man set out to avenge himself more fiercely in his passion than is now suffered by equal laws, for this cause men were weary of

Thence
arose the
fear of
punish-
ment,

leading a life of violence. Thence fear of punishment taints the prizes of life. For violence and hurt tangle every man in their toils, and for the most part fall on the head of him, from whom they had their rise, nor is it easy for one who by his act breaks the common pact of

which
makes a
quiet life
impossible.

peace to lead a calm and quiet life. For though he be unnoticed of the race of gods and men, yet he must needs mistrust that his secret will be kept for ever; nay indeed, many by speaking in their sleep or raving in fever have often, so 'tis said, betrayed themselves, and brought to light misdeeds long hidden.

Origin of
the belief
in the gods.

Next, what cause spread abroad the divine powers of the gods among great nations, and filled cities with altars, and taught men to undertake sacred rites at yearly festivals, rites which are honoured to-day in great empires and at great places; whence even now there is implanted

in mortals a shuddering dread, which raises new shrines
of the gods over all the world, and constrains men to
throng them on the holy days; of all this it is not hard
to give account in words. For indeed already the races
of mortals[n] used to perceive the glorious shapes of the gods
with waking mind, and all the more in sleep with wondrous bulk of body. To these then they would assign
sense because they were seen to move their limbs, and to
utter haughty sounds befitting their noble mien and
ample strength. And they gave them everlasting life
because their images came in constant stream and the
form remained unchanged, and indeed above all because
they thought that those endowed with such strength
could not readily be vanquished by any force. They
thought that they far excelled in happiness, because the
fear of death never harassed any of them, and at the same
time because in sleep they saw them accomplish many
marvels, yet themselves not undergo any toil. Moreover,
they beheld the workings of the sky in due order, and the
diverse seasons of the year come round, nor could they
learn by what causes that was brought about. And so
they made it their refuge to lay all to the charge of the
gods, and to suppose that all was guided by their will.
And they placed the abodes and quarters of the gods in the
sky, because through the sky night and the moon are seen
to roll on their way, moon, day and night, and the stern
signs of night, and the torches of heaven that rove through
the night, and the flying flames, clouds, sunlight, rain,
snow, winds, lightning, hail, and the rapid roar and
mighty murmurings of heaven's threats.

Ah! unhappy race of men, when it has assigned such
acts to the gods and joined therewith bitter anger! what

1. Men
were visited
by great
and beauti-
ful images:
they
believed
them to
have sense,
to be
immortal,

and to be
happy.

2. They
could not
understand
celestial
phenomena,
and attri-
buted them
to divine
beings,
whom they
believed to
dwell in
the sky.

What
misery this

belief
causes.
True piety
consists not
in worship,
but the
peaceful
mind.

groaning did they then beget for themselves, what sores for us, what tears for our children to come! Nor is it piety at all to be seen often with veiled head turning towards a stone,[n] and to draw near to every altar, no, nor to lie prostrate on the ground with outstretched palms before the shrines of the gods, nor to sprinkle the altars with the streaming blood of beasts, nor to link vow to vow, but rather to be able to contemplate all things with

Yet the
wonders of
heaven
may well
wake a
belief in
divine
power.

a mind at rest. For indeed when we look up at the heavenly quarters of the great world, and the firm-set ether above the twinkling stars, and it comes to our mind to think of the journeyings of sun and moon, then into our hearts weighed down with other ills, this misgiving too begins to raise up its wakened head, that there may be perchance some immeasurable power of the gods over us, which whirls on the bright stars in their diverse motions. For lack of reasoning assails our mind with doubt, whether there was any creation and beginning of the world, and again whether there is an end, until which the walls of the world may be able to endure this weariness of restless motion, or whether gifted by the gods' will with an ever-lasting being they may be able to glide on down the ever-lasting groove of time, and set at naught the mighty

So too
may a
thunder-
storm,

strength of measureless time. Moreover, whose heart does not shrink with terror of the gods, whose limbs do not crouch in fear, when the parched earth trembles beneath the awful stroke of lightning and rumblings run across the great sky? Do not the peoples and nations tremble, and proud kings shrink in every limb, thrilled with the fear of the gods, lest for some foul crime or

or a storm
at sea,

haughty word the heavy time of retribution be ripe? Or again, when the fiercest force of furious wind at sea sweeps

the commander of a fleet over the waters with his strong
legions and his elephants, all in like case, does he not seek
with vows the peace of the gods, and fearfully crave in
prayer a calm from wind and favouring breezes; all in
vain, since often when caught in the headstrong hurricane
he is borne for all his prayers to the shallow waters of
death? So greatly does some secret force grind beneath
its heel the greatness of men, and it is seen to tread down
and make sport for itself of the glorious rods and relentless axes.[n] Again, when the whole earth rocks beneath or an
men's feet, and cities are shaken to their fall or threaten earthquake.
doubtful of their doom, what wonder if the races of
mortal men despise themselves and leave room in the
world for the mighty power and marvellous strength of
the gods, to guide all things?

For the rest, copper and gold and iron were discovered, Metals were
and with them the weight of silver and the usefulness of revealed by
lead, when a fire had burnt down vast forests with its a great forest fire,
heat on mighty mountains, either when heaven's light- however
ning was hurled upon it, or because waging a forest-war caused.
with one another men had carried fire among the foe to
rouse panic, or else because allured by the richness of the
land they desired to clear the fat fields, and make the
countryside into pasture, or else to put the wild beasts
to death, and enrich themselves with prey. For hunting
with pit and fire arose first before fencing the grove with
nets and scaring the beasts with dogs. However that
may be, for whatever cause the flaming heat had eaten
up the forests from their deep roots with terrible crackling,
and had baked the earth with fire, the streams of silver and The chance
gold, and likewise of copper and lead, gathered together masses
and trickled from the boiling veins into hollow places in cooled on

the ground. And when they saw them afterwards hardened and shining on the ground with brilliant hue, they picked them up, charmed by their smooth bright beauty, and saw that they were shaped with outline like that of the several prints of the hollows. Then it came home to them that these metals might be melted by heat, and would run into the form and figure of anything, and indeed might be hammered out and shaped into points and tips, however sharp and fine, so that they might fashion weapons for themselves, and be able to cut down forests and hew timber and plane beams smooth, yea, and to bore and punch and drill holes. And, first of all, they set forth to do this no less with silver and gold than with the resistless strength of stout copper; all in vain, since their power was vanquished and yielded, nor could they like the others endure the cruel strain. For copper was of more value, and gold was despised for its uselessness, so soon blunted with its dull edge. Now copper is despised, gold has risen to the height of honour. So rolling time changes the seasons of things. What was of value, becomes in turn of no worth; and then another thing rises up and leaves its place of scorn, and is sought more and more each day, and when found blossoms into fame, and is of wondrous honour among men.

Now, in what manner the nature of iron was found, it is easy for you to learn of yourself, Memmius. Their arms of old were hands, nails, and teeth, and stones, and likewise branches torn from the forests, and flame and fires, when once they were known. Thereafter the strength of iron and bronze was discovered. And the use of bronze was learnt before that of iron, inasmuch as its nature is more tractable, and it is found in greater stores. With

the ground suggested the working of metals with fire,

and the forging of weapons and instruments.

Gold was then despised and copper valuable: now this is reversed.

The uses of iron and bronze were then discovered.

Bronze was used first,

bronze they would work the soil of the earth, and with
bronze mingle in billowy warfare, and deal wasting wounds
and seize upon flocks and fields. For all things naked
and unarmed would readily give in to them equipped
with arms. Then, little by little, the iron sword made *and then*
its way, and the form of the bronze sickle [n] was made *discarded*
a thing of scorn, and with iron they began to plough up *for iron.*
the soil of earth ; and the contests of war, now hovering
in doubt, were made equal. It was their way to climb *Horses*
armed on to the flanks of a horse, to guide it with reins, *were ridden*
and do doughty deeds with the right hand, before they *in war*
learnt to essay the dangers of war in a two-horsed chariot. *chariots*
And the yoking of two horses came before yoking four, *invented.*
and climbing up armed into chariots set with scythes.
Then it was the Poeni who taught the Lucanian kine, [n] *The Car-*
with towered body, grim beasts with snaky hands, to bear *thaginians*
the wounds of warfare, and work havoc among the hosts *elephants*
of Mars. So did gloomy discord beget one thing after *to battle.*
another, to bring panic into the races of men in warfare,
and day by day gave increase to the terrors of war.

They tried bulls, too, in the service of war, and essayed *Other*
to send savage boars against the foe. And some sent on *animals*
before them mighty lions with armed trainers and cruel *too in*
masters, who might be able to control them, and hold *warfare,*
them in chains ; all in vain, since in the heat of the mellay *more harm*
of slaughter they grew savage, and made havoc of the *to their*
hosts, both sides alike, tossing everywhere the fearful *Lions ;*
manes upon their heads, nor could the horsemen soothe
the hearts of their horses, alarmed at the roaring, and
turn them with their bridles against the foe. The lionesses
launched their furious bodies in a leap on every side, and
made for the faces of those that came against them, or

tore them down in the rear when off their guard, and
twining round them hurled them to the ground foredone
with the wound, fastening on them with their strong bite

bulls;   and crooked claws. The bulls tossed their own friends
and trampled them with their feet, and with their horns
gashed the flanks and bellies of the horses underneath,
and ploughed up the ground with threatening purpose.

boars.   And the boars gored their masters with their strong
tusks, savagely splashing with their own blood the weapons
broken in them, and threw to the ground horsemen and
footmen in one heap.   For the horses would swerve aside
to avoid the fierce onset of a tusk, or rear and beat the
air with their feet ; all in vain, since you would see them
tumble with tendons severed, and strew the ground in
their heavy fall. If ever they thought they had been
tamed enough at home before the fight, they saw them
burst into fury, when it came to conflict, maddened by
the wounds, shouting, flying, panic, and confusion, nor
could they rally any part of them ; for all the diverse
kinds of wild beasts would scatter hither and thither ;
even as now often the Lucanian kine cruelly mangled by
the steel, scatter abroad, when they have dealt many
deadly deeds to their own friends. ⟨If indeed they
ever acted thus. But scarce can I be brought to believe
that, before this dire disaster befell both sides alike, they
could not foresee and perceive in mind what would come
to pass. And you could more readily maintain [n] that this
was done somewhere in the universe, in the diverse worlds
fashioned in diverse fashion, than on any one determined
earth.⟩[1]   But indeed they wished to do it not so much in

---

[1] These six lines were probably written by the poet as a later
addition.

the hope of victory, as to give the foemen cause to moan, It was only
resolved to perish themselves, since they mistrusted their a desperate
numbers and lacked arms. expedient.

A garment tied together came before woven raiment. After iron
Woven fabric comes after iron, for by iron the loom is came woven
clothes.
fashioned, nor in any other way can such smooth treadles
be made, or spindles or shuttles and ringing rods. And Men first
worked the
nature constrained men to work wool before the race of loom, but
women ; for all the race of men far excels in skill and is afterwards
left it to
much more cunning ; until the sturdy husbandman made women and
scorn of it, so that they were glad to leave it to women's worked in
the fields.
hands, and themselves share in enduring hard toil, and
in hard work to harden limbs and hands.

But nature herself, creatress of things, was first a pattern Nature
for sowing and the beginning of grafting, since berries and taught men
sowing and
acorns fallen from the trees in due time put forth swarms grafting.
of shoots beneath ; from nature, too, they learnt to insert
grafts into branches, and to plant young saplings in the
ground over the fields. Then one after another they New kinds
essayed ways of tilling their smiling plot, and saw the earth of cultivation were
tame wild fruits with tender care and fond tilling. And tried and
day by day they would constrain the woods more and the woods
driven
more to retire up the mountains, and to give up the land further up
beneath to tilth, that on hills and plains they might have the hills.
The plain
meadows, pools, streams, crops, and glad vineyards, and was bright
the grey belt of olives might run between with its clear with every
sort of
line, spreading over hillocks and hollows and plains ; even cultivation.
as now you see all the land clear marked with diverse
beauties, where men make it bright by planting it here
and there with sweet fruit-trees, and fence it by planting
it all round with fruitful shrubs.

But imitating with the mouth the liquid notes of birds

Music arose
by the
imitation
of the
notes of
birds and
wind in
the reeds.

came long before men were able to sing in melody right through smooth songs and please the ear. And the whistling of the zephyr through the hollows of reeds first taught the men of the countryside to breathe into hollowed hemlock-stalks. Then little by little they learned the sweet lament, which the pipe pours forth, stopped by the players' fingers, the pipe invented amid the pathless woods and forests and glades, among the desolate haunts of shepherds, and the divine places of their rest. These tunes would soothe their minds and please them when

Their
rough songs
delighted
them after
meals in the
open air,

sated with food; for then all things win the heart. And so often, lying in friendly groups on the soft grass near some stream of water under the branches of a tall tree, at no great cost they would give pleasure to their bodies, above all when the weather smiled and the season of the year painted the green grass with flowers. Then were there wont to be jests, and talk, and merry laughter. For then the rustic muse was at its best; then glad mirth would prompt to wreathe head and shoulders with garlands twined of flowers and foliage, and to dance all out

with rough
dances to
match.

of step, moving their limbs heavily, and with heavy foot to strike mother earth; whence arose smiles and merry laughter, for all these things then were strong in freshness and wonder. And hence came to the wakeful a solace for lost sleep, to guide their voices through many notes, and follow the windings of a song, and to run over the reeds with curling lip; whence even now the watch-

Modern
improve-
ments
have not
increased
the pleasure.

men preserve these traditions, and have learnt to keep to the rhythm of the song, nor yet for all that do they gain a whit greater enjoyment from the pleasure, than the woodland race of earthborn men of old. For what is here at hand, unless we have learnt anything sweeter before, pleases us above all, and is thought to excel, but for the most part the better thing found later on destroys or changes our feeling for all the old things. So hatred for their acorns set in, and the old couches strewn with grass and piled with leaves were deserted. Likewise the garment of wild beasts' skin fell into contempt; yet I suppose that of old it was so envied when found, that he who first wore it was waylaid and put to death, though after all it was torn to pieces among them, and was spoiled with much blood, and could be turned to no profit. It was skins then in those days, and now gold and purple that vex men's life with cares and weary them out with war; and for this, I think, the greater fault lies with us. For cold used to torture the earth-born, as they lay naked without skins; but it does us no hurt to go without our purple robes, set with gold and massy figures, if only there be some common garment to protect us. And so the race of men toils fruitlessly and in vain for ever, and wastes its life in idle cares, because, we may be sure, it has not learned what are the limits of possession, nor at all how far true pleasure can increase. And this, little by little, has advanced life to its high plane, and has stirred up from the lowest depths the great seething tide of war.

The old food and dress were despised,

but now we fight for gold and purple, as they fought for skins.

This brings civilization and warfare.

But sun and moon, like watchmen, traversing with their light all round the great turning vault of the world, taught men that the seasons of the year come round, and that the work goes on after a sure plan and a sure order.

From sun and moon men learnt the regularity of the seasons.

Now fenced in with strong towers they would live their life, and the land was parcelled out and marked off: then

Then came walled

towns, sea-
faring, and
treaties, and
poets told
of great
events.

the sea was gay with the flying sails of ships : [1] now treaties were drawn up, and they had auxiliaries and allies, when poets first began to hand down men's deeds in songs ; yet not much before that were letters discovered. Therefore our age cannot look back to see what was done before, unless in any way reason points out traces.

Gradually
all the
sciences and
fine arts
developed.

Ships and the tilling of the land, walls, laws, weapons, roads, dress, and all things of this kind, all the prizes, and the luxuries of life, one and all, songs and pictures, and the polishing of quaintly-wrought statues, practice and therewith the experience of the eager mind taught them little by little, as they went forward step by step. So, little by little, time brings out each several thing into view, and reason raises it up into the coasts of light. For they saw one thing after another grow clear in their mind, until by their arts they reached the topmost pinnacle.

[1] Two words at the end of the line are corrupt : *puppibus* or *navibus* must have been the first.

BOOK VI

In time gone by Athens, of glorious name, first spread Introduction. among struggling mortals the fruits that bear corn, and It is the fashioned life afresh, and enacted laws; she, too, first glory of gave sweet solace for life, when she gave birth to the man Athens to have gifted with the great mind, who once poured forth all produced wisdom from his truthful lips; yea, even when his light Epicurus. was quenched, thanks to his divine discoveries his glory, noised abroad of old, is now lifted to the sky. For when He saw he saw that mortals had by now attained wellnigh all that men, in spite of things which their needs crave for subsistence, and that, all outward as far as they could, their life was established in safety, advantages, were that men abounded in power through wealth and honours miserable, and renown, and were haughty in the good name of their children, and yet not one of them for all that had at home a heart less anguished, but with torture of mind lived a fretful life without any respite, and was constrained to rage with savage complaining, he then did understand and realized that it was the vessel itself which wrought the disease, and that the that by its disease all things were corrupted within, what- fault lay in the heart. soever came into it gathered from without, yea even blessings; in part because he saw that it was leaking[n] and full of holes, so that by no means could it ever be filled; in part because he perceived that it tainted as with a foul savour all things within it, which it had taken in. And so with his discourse of truthful words he He purged purged the heart and set a limit to its desire and fear, the heart and set forth what is the highest good, towards which we and taught

it the path
to the
highest
good,

and the
means of
meeting the
ills of life.

all strive, and pointed out the path, whereby along a
narrow track we may strain on towards it in a straight
course; he showed what there is of ill in the affairs of
mortals everywhere, coming to being and flying abroad
in diverse forms, be it by the chance or the force of
nature,[n] because nature had so brought it to pass; he
showed from what gates it is meet to sally out against
each ill, and he proved that 'tis in vain for the most part
that the race of men set tossing in their hearts the gloomy

The dark-
ness of the
mind must
be dispelled
by know-
ledge.

billows of care. For even as children tremble and fear
everything in blinding darkness, so we sometimes dread
in the light things that are no whit more to be feared than
what children shudder at in the dark and imagine will
come to pass. This terror then, this darkness of the
mind, must needs be scattered not by the rays and the
gleaming shafts of day, but by the outer view and the
inner law of nature. Wherefore I will hasten the more
to weave the thread of my task in my discourse.

I must
now speak
of the
phenomena
of the sky;

And now that I have shown that the quarters of the
firmament are mortal, and that the heaven is fashioned
of a body that has birth, and have unravelled wellnigh
all that happens therein, and must needs happen, listen
still to what remains; forasmuch as once ⟨I have made
bold⟩ to climb the glorious car . . . .[1]

which men
falsely
believe
to be the
work of
gods,

⟨I will tell how the tempests⟩ of the winds arise,[2] and
are appeased, and all that once was raging is changed
again, when its fury is appeased; and all else which
mortals see coming to pass on earth and in the sky,
when often they are in suspense with panic-stricken
mind—things which bring their hearts low through dread

---

[1] Two or more lines must here be lost.

[2] Read *exsistant, placentur et omnia rursum quae furerent.*

of the gods, and bow them down grovelling to earth,
because their ignorance of true causes constrains them to
assign things to the ordinance of the gods, and to admit
their domination. For those who have learnt aright that
the gods lead a life free from care, yet if from time to
time they wonder by what means all things can be carried
on, above all among those things which are descried
above our heads in the coasts of heaven, are borne back
again into the old beliefs of religion, and adopt stern
overlords, whom in their misery they believe have all
power, knowing not what can be and what cannot, yea, *through*
and in what way each thing has its power limited, and *ignorance*
its deepset boundary-stone : wherefore all the more they *laws.*
stray, borne on by a blind reasoning. And unless you *Such belief*
spew out all this from your mind and banish far away *is a degra-*
thoughts unworthy of the gods and alien to their peace, *the gods*
the holy powers of the gods, degraded by thy thought, *and will*
will often do thee harm ; not that the high majesty of *your own*
the gods [n] can be polluted by thee, so that in wrath they *peace in*
should yearn to seek sharp retribution, but because you *worship.*
yourself will imagine that those tranquil beings in their
placid peace set tossing the great billows of wrath, nor
with quiet breast will you approach the shrines of the
gods, nor have strength to drink in with tranquil peace of
mind the images which are borne from their holy body
to herald their divine form to the minds of men. And
therefore what manner of life will follow, you may perceive. And in order that truest reasoning may drive
this far from us, although much has already gone forth
from me, yet much remains to be adorned with polished
verse ; we must grasp the outer view and inner law of the *We must*
sky, we must sing of storms and flashing lightnings, of *find out*

the laws of
storms and
lightnings.

how they act and by what cause they are severally carried
along; that you may not mark out the quarters of the
sky, and ask in frenzied anxiety, whence came this winged
flash, or to what quarter it departed hence, in what
manner it won its way through walled places, and how
after tyrant deeds it brought itself forth again: the causes
of these workings they can by no means see, and think that
a divine power brings them about. Do thou, as I speed
towards the white line of the final goal, mark out the track
before me, Calliope, muse of knowledge, thou who art rest
to men and pleasure to the gods, that with thee to guide
I may win the wreath with praise conspicuous.

A. Celestial
pheno-
mena.
1. Thunder
may be
caused
(a) when
clouds clash
together
face to face;
(being of
a texture
neither
close nor
rare);

First of all the blue of the sky is shaken by thunder
because the clouds in high heaven, scudding aloft, clash
together when the winds are fighting in combat. For
the sound comes not from a clear quarter of the sky, but
wherever the clouds are massed in denser host, from there
more often comes the roar and its loud rumbling. Moreover, the clouds cannot be of so dense a body as are
stocks and stones, nor yet so thin as are mists and flying
smoke. For either they were bound to fall dragged down
by their dead weight, as do stones, or like smoke they
could not hold together or keep within them chill snow

(b) when
they scrape
along one
another's
sides, and
make a
noise like
wind in a
flapping
awning or
paper;

and showers of hail. Again, they give forth a sound over
the levels of the spreading firmament, as often an awning
stretched over a great theatre gives a crack, as it tosses
among the posts and beams; sometimes, too, it rages
madly, rent by the boisterous breezes, and imitates the
rending noise of sheets of paper—for that kind of sound
too you may recognize in the thunder—or else a sound
as when the winds buffet with their blows and beat
through the air a hanging garment or flying papers. For

indeed it also comes to pass at times that the clouds cannot so much clash together face to face, but rather pass along the flank, moving from diverse quarters, and slowly grazing body against body; and then the dry sound brushes upon the ears, and is drawn out long, until they have issued from their close quarters.

In this way, too, all things seem often to tremble with heavy thunder, and the great walls of the containing world to be torn apart suddenly and leap asunder, when all at once a gathered storm of mighty wind has twisted its way into the clouds, and, shut up there with its whirling eddy, constrains the cloud more and more on all sides to hollow itself out with body thickening all around; and then, when the force and fierce onslaught of the wind have weakened it, it splits and makes a rending crash with a frightful cracking sound. Nor is that strange, when a little bladder full of air often likewise gives forth a little noise, if suddenly burst. *(c)* when wind is caught in a cloud and suddenly bursts it;

There is also another way, when winds blow through clouds, whereby they may make a noise. For often we see clouds borne along, branching in many ways, and rough-edged; even as, we may be sure, when the blasts of the north-west blow through a dense forest, the leaves give out a noise and the branches a rending crash. It comes to pass, too, sometimes, that the force of a mighty wind rushing on tears through the cloud and breaks it asunder with a front attack. For what the blast can do there is shown by things clear to see here on earth, where the wind is gentler and yet it tears out and sucks up tall trees from their lowest roots. There are, too, waves moving through the clouds, which as it were make a heavy roar in breaking; just as it comes to pass in deep *(d)* when wind blows through the clouds, like a forest; *(e)* when the wind bursts a cloud open; *(f)* when the rain-waves in the clouds

break ;
(*g*) when lightning, falling from one cloud into another, hisses or

(*h*) burns the cloud up ;

(*i*) when the ice and hail in the clouds crash.

2. Lightning may be caused (*a*) when two clouds colliding strike fire. (We see it before we hear the thunder, because light travels faster than sound.)

rivers and the great sea, when the tide breaks. This happens too, when the fiery force of the thunderbolt falls from cloud to cloud ; if by chance the cloud has received the flame in deep moisture, it straightway slays it with a great noise ; just as often iron white-hot from the fiery furnaces hisses, when we have plunged it quickly into cold water. Or again, if a drier cloud receives the flame, it is at once fired, and burns with a vast noise ; just as if among the laurel-leafed mountains flame were to roam abroad beneath the eddying of the winds, burning them up in its mighty onset ; nor is there any other thing which is burnt up by the crackling flame with sound so terrible as the Delphic laurel of Phoebus. Again, often the great cracking of ice and the falling of hail makes a noise in the mighty clouds on high. For when the wind packs them tight, the mountains of storm-clouds, frozen close and mingled with hail, break up.

It lightens likewise, when the clouds at their clashing have struck out many seeds of fire ; just as if stone should strike on stone or on iron ; for then, too, a flash leaps out and scatters abroad bright sparks of fire. But it comes to pass that we receive the thunder in our ears after our eyes perceive the lightning, because things always move more slowly [n] to the ears than things which stir the eyes. That you may learn from this too ; if you see some one far off cutting down a giant tree with double-edged axe, it comes to pass that you see the stroke before the blow resounds in your ear ; even so we see the lightning too before we hear the thunder, which is sent abroad at the same moment with the flash, from a like cause, yea, born indeed from the same collision.

In this manner, too, the clouds colour places with leap-

ing light, and the storm lightens with quivering dart. (*b*) when wind shut in a cloud whirls itself round till it ignites.
When wind has come within a cloud, and moving there has,
as I have shown before, made the hollow cloud grow thick,
it grows hot with its own swift movement ; even as you
see all things become hot and catch fire through motion,
yea, even a ball of lead too, whirling in a long course, will
melt. And so when this heated wind has torn through
the black cloud, it scatters abroad seeds of fire, as though
struck out all at once by force, and they make the pulsing
flashes of flame ; thereafter follows the sound, which
reaches our ears more slowly than things which come to
the light of our eyes. This, we must know, comes to This happens in high-piled masses of clouds :
pass in thick clouds, which are also piled up high one on
the other in wondrous slope ; lest you be deceived because
we below see how broad they are rather than to what
a height they stand piled up. For do but look, when
next the winds carry athwart the air clouds in the sem-
blance of mountains, or when you see them heaped along
a mighty mountain-range one above the other, pressing
down from above, at rest in their appointed place, when
the winds on all sides are in their graves. Then you will
be able to mark their mighty mass, and to see their
caverns built up, as it were, of hanging rocks : and when
the storm has risen and the winds have filled them, with the wind collects all the seeds of fire in one and then bursts through the cloud ;
loud roar they chafe prisoned in the clouds, and threaten
like wild beasts in cages ; now from this side, now from
that they send forth their roaring through the clouds,
and seeking an outlet they move round and round, and
roll together the seeds of fire from out the clouds, and
so drive many into a mass and set the flame whirling
within the hollow furnaces, until they have rent asunder
the cloud and flashed blazing out.

(c) when
the fire in
the clouds
themselves
is driven
out as they
collide,

For this cause, too, it comes to pass that this swift
golden tinge of liquid fire flies down to earth, because it
must needs be that the clouds have in themselves very
many seeds of fire; for indeed when they are without
any moisture, they have for the most part a bright and
flaming colour. For verily it must needs be that they
catch many such from the sun's light, so that with reason
they are red, and pour forth their fires. When then the
wind as it drives them has pushed and packed and com-
pelled them into one spot, they squeeze out and pour
forth the seeds which make the colours of flame to flash.

(d) or falls
naturally
as they
break:
this causes
sheet
lightning.

It lightens likewise, also when the clouds of heaven grow
thin. For when the wind lightly draws them asunder as
they move, and breaks them up, it must needs be that
those seeds, which make the flash, fall out unbidden.
Then it lightens without hideous alarm, without noise,
and with no uproar.

3. Thunder-
bolts are of
fiery nature,

For the rest, with what kind of nature the thunderbolts
are endowed, is shown by the blows and the burned mark-
ings of their heat and the brands which breathe out noisome
vapours of sulphur. For these are marks of fire, not of
wind nor rain. Moreover, often too they set the roofs of
dwellings on fire, and with swiftly-moving flame play the
tyrant even within the houses. This fire, you must know,

and formed
of exceed-
ingly subtle
fire, as we
may see
from their
effects.

nature has fashioned most subtle of all subtle fires, of tiny
swift-moving bodies—a flame to which nothing at all can
be a barrier. For the strong thunderbolt can pass through
the walls of houses, even as shouts and cries, can pass
through rocks, through things of bronze, and in a moment
of time can melt bronze and gold; likewise it causes wine
in an instant to flee away, though the vessels be untouched,
because, we may be sure, its heat as it comes easily loosens

all around and makes rarefied the porcelain of the vessel, and finding its way right into the wine, with quick motion dissolves and scatters the first-beginnings of the wine. Yet this the heat of the sun is seen to be unable to bring about in a long age, though it has such exceeding strength in its flashing blaze. So much swifter and more masterful is this force of the thunderbolt.

Now in what manner they are fashioned and made with such force that they can with their blow burst open towers, overthrow houses, pluck up beams and joists, and upset and ⟨destroy⟩ [1] the monuments of men, take the life from men, lay low the flocks on every side; by what force they are able to do all other things of this sort, I will set forth, nor keep thee longer waiting on my promise.

We must suppose that thunderbolts are produced from thick clouds, piled up on high; for none are ever hurled abroad from the clear sky or from clouds of slight thickness. For without doubt clear-seen facts show that this comes to pass; at such times clouds grow into a mass throughout all the air, so that on all sides we might think that all darkness has left Acheron and filled the great vault of the sky; so terribly, when the noisome night of clouds has gathered together, do the shapes of black fear hang over us on high, when the storm begins to forge its thunderbolts. Moreover, very often a black storm-cloud too, over the sea, like a stream of pitch shot from the sky, falls upon the waters, laden with darkness afar off, and draws on a black storm big with thunderbolts and hurricanes, itself more than all filled full with fires and winds in such wise that even on land men shudder and seek for shelter. Thus then above our head must we suppose the

We must explain their power and action.

They are created only when clouds are densely piled on high,

as we see them sometimes over the sea.

[1] The last word of the line is uncertain.

storm is raised high. For indeed they would not shroud
the earth in such thick gloom, unless there were many
clouds built up aloft on many others, shutting out all
sunlight; nor when they come could they drown it in
such heavy rain, as to make the rivers overflow and the
fields swim, unless the ether were filled with clouds piled

Such clouds are full of wind and fire.

up on high. Here, then, all is full of winds and fires; for
this cause all around come crashings and lightnings. For
verily I have shown ere now that the hollow clouds
possess very many seeds of heat, and many they must

The wind with the fire forms an eddy,

needs catch from the sun's rays and their blaze. Therefore, when the same wind, which drives them together, as
it chances, into some one place, has squeezed out many
seeds of heat, and at the same time has mingled itself
with this fire, an eddy finds its way in there and whirls
round in a narrow space and sharpens the thunderbolt in
the hot furnaces within. For it is kindled in two ways,
both when it grows hot with its own swift motion, and

which bursts the cloud and comes out as a thunder-bolt,

from contact with the fire. Next, when the force of the
wind has grown exceeding hot, and the fierce onset of
the fire has entered in, then the thunderbolt, full-forged,
as it were, suddenly rends through the cloud, and shot
out is borne on flooding all places with its blazing light.

bringing with it thunder, lightning, storm, and rain.

In its train follows a heavy crash, so that the quarters of
the sky above seem to be burst asunder on a sudden and
crush us. Then a trembling thrills violently through the
earth, and rumblings race over the high heaven; for then
all the storm is shaken into trembling and roarings move
abroad. And from this shock follows rain, heavy and
abundant, so that all the air seems to be turned into rain,
and thus falling headlong to summon earth back to

deluge : so great a shower is shot forth with the rending
of the cloud and the hurricane of wind, when the thunder-
clap flies forth with its burning blow. At times, too, the Sometimes the cloud is burst by an external wind.
rushing force of wind falls from without upon the cloud
hot with its new-forged thunderbolt ; and when it has
rent the cloud, straightway there falls out that fiery eddy
which we call by the name our fathers gave it, the thunderbolt. The same thing happens in other directions,
wherever its force has carried it. It comes to pass, too, Sometimes the wind itself ignites in its course,
sometimes that the force of the wind, starting without
fire, yet catches fire on its course and its long wandering,
as it loses in its journey, while it is approaching, certain
large bodies, which cannot like the others make their way
through the air ; and gathering other small bodies from
the air itself it carries them along, and they mingling with
it make fire in their flight ; in no other way than often like a flying ball of lead.
a ball of lead grows hot in its course, when dropping many
bodies of stiff cold it has taken in fire in the air. It comes Or the blow of wind on cloud may create fire,
to pass, too, that the force of the very blow rouses fire,
when the force of the wind, starting cold without fire,
has struck its stroke ; because, we may be sure, when it
has hit with violent blow, particles of heat can stream
together out of the wind itself, and at the same time from
the thing which then receives the blow ; just as, when we like iron striking on stone ;
strike a stone with iron, fire flies out, nor do the seeds
of blazing heat rush together any more slowly at its blow,
because the force of the iron is cold. Thus then a thing
is bound to be kindled by the thunderbolt too, if by
chance it is made fit and suitable for flame. Nor must we for the wind itself is not wholly cold.
rashly think that the force of the wind can be wholly and
utterly cold, when it has been discharged with such force

on high ; rather, **if it is not** beforehand **on its journey**
kindled with fire, yet **it arrives** warmed and mingled
with heat.

But the great speed of the thunderbolt and its heavy
blow comes to pass, yea, the thunderbolts always run
their course with swift descent, because their force un-
aided is first of all set in motion in each case, and gathers
itself within the clouds, and conceives a great effort for
starting ; and then, when the cloud has not been able
to contain the growing strength of its onset, its force is
squeezed out, and so flies with wondrous impulse even
as the missiles which are borne on, when shot from engines
of war. Remember, too, that it is made of small and
smooth particles, nor is it easy for anything to withstand
such a nature : for it flies in between and pierces through
the hollow passages, and so it is not clogged and delayed
by many obstacles, and therefore it flies on falling with
swift impulse. Again, because all weights by nature
always press downwards, but when a blow is given as well,
their swiftness is doubled and the impulse grows stronger,
so that the more violently and quickly does it scatter with
its blows all that impedes it, and continues on its journey.
Once again, because it comes with long-lasting impulse,[n]
it is bound to gather speed ever more and more, which
grows as it moves, and increases its strong might and
strengthens its stroke. For it brings it about that the
seeds of the thunderbolt are one and all carried in a
straight line, as it were towards one spot, driving them
all as they fly into the same course. It may chance too
that as it goes it picks up certain bodies even from the
air, which kindle its swiftness by their blows. And it
passes through things without harming them, and goes

*The
velocity of
the thunder-
bolt is
caused
(a) by the
impulse
with which
it is shot
from the
cloud ;*

*(b) because
it is made
of small
smooth
particles;*

*(c) because
gravitation
is aug-
mented by
a blow ;*

*(d) because
in its long
course it
overcomes
internal
vibration.*

*(e) perhaps
because it
is helped
by particles*

right through many things, and leaves them whole, be- gathered from the air.
cause the liquid fire flies through the pores. And it
pierces through many things, since the very bodies of the It can penetrate
thunderbolt have fallen on the bodies of things just where and dissolve things,
they are interlaced and held together. Moreover, it
easily melts bronze and in an instant makes gold to boil, because it impinges on them just
because its force is fashioned delicately of tiny bodies where their
and of smooth particles, which easily force a way within, atoms are joined.
and being there at once loose all the knots and slacken
the bonds. And most in autumn is the house of heaven, Thunder-
set with shining stars, shaken on all sides and all the earth, bolts occur
and again when the flowery season of spring spreads itself mostly in
abroad. For in the cold fires are lacking, and in the heat spring and autumn,
winds fail, nor are clouds of so dense a body. And so because then
when the seasons of heaven stand midway between the the various
two, then all the diverse causes of the thunderbolt meet elements needful for
together. For the narrow channel [n] of the year of itself their com-
mingles cold and heat—of both of which the cloud has position most
need for the forging of thunderbolts—so that there is coincide.
a wrangling among things, and with great uproar the air
rages and tosses with fires and winds. For the first part
of the heat is the last of the stiff cold, that is the spring
season : wherefore it must needs be that different elements, mingled with one another, make battle and turmoil. And again, when the last heat rolls on mingled
with the first cold—the season which is called by the
name of autumn—then, too, keen winters do battle with
summers. For this cause these seasons must be called
the narrow channels of the year, nor is it strange, if at
that time thunderbolts come most often, and a turbulent
tempest is gathered in the sky, since from either side is

roused the turmoil of doubtful battle, on the one side with flames, on the other with mingled wind and wet.

The thunderbolt is no sign of divine wrath.

This is the way to see into the true nature of the thunderbolt, and to perceive by what force it does each thing, and not by unrolling vainly the Tyrrhenian prophecies [n] and seeking out tokens of the hidden purpose of the gods, marking whence came the winged flash, or to what quarter it departed hence, in what manner it won its way through walled places, and how after tyrant deeds it brought itself forth again, or what harm the stroke of

If so, why do the gods hit the innocent and leave the guilty?

the thunderbolt from heaven can do. But if Jupiter [n] and the other gods shake the shining quarters of heaven with awe-inspiring crash and hurl the fire to whatever point each may will, why do they not bring it about that those who have not guarded against some sin from which men hide their face, are struck and reek of the flames of lightning, with their breast pierced through, a sharp lesson to mortals? why rather is one conscious of no foul guilt wrapt and entangled, all innocent, in the flames, caught

Why waste their strokes on deserts?

up in a moment in the fiery whirlwind of heaven? why again do they aim at waste places and spend their strength for naught? are they then practising their arms and strengthening their muscles? and why do they suffer the father's weapon to be blunted on the earth? why does he himself endure it and not spare it for his foes?

Why not hurl them from the clear sky?

Again, why does Jupiter never hurl his thunderbolt to earth and pour forth his thunders when the heaven is clear on all sides? Or, as soon as the clouds have come up, does he himself then come down into them, so that from them he may direct the blow of his weapon from close at hand?

Why at the sea?

Again, with what purpose does he throw into the sea? what charge has he against the waves, the

mass of water and the floating fields? Moreover, if he Does
wishes us to beware of the thunderbolt's stroke, why is he Jupiter wish us to
reluctant to let us be able to see its cast? but if he wishes beware
to overwhelm us with the fire when off our guard, why or not?
does he thunder from that quarter, so that we can shun
it? why does he gather darkness beforehand and rumblings and roarings? And how can you believe that he How can
hurls his bolts at once to many sides? or would you dare he hurl many bolts
to argue that this has never come to pass, that several at once?
strokes were made at one time? Nay, but very often has
it happened and must needs happen, that as it rains and
showers fall in many regions, so many thunderbolts are
fashioned at one time. Lastly, why does he smite asunder Why
the sacred shrines of the gods and his own glorious dwell- destroy his own
ing-places with hostile bolt? why does he destroy the temples
fair-fashioned idols of the gods and take away their beauty and images?
from his images with his furious wound? And why does or scar
he aim mostly at lofty spots, so that we see most traces of mountain peaks?
his fire on mountain-tops?

Next after this, it is easy to learn from these things in 4. Water-
what way there come into the sea, shot from on high, spouts are caused
what the Greeks from their nature have named fiery
presters.[n] For it comes to pass sometimes that as it were
a column let down descends from the sky into the sea,
around which the surges boil, violently stirred by breathing blasts, and all ships that are then caught in that turmoil, are harried and come into great danger. This comes when wind
to pass sometimes when the force of the wind set in cannot break through
motion cannot burst the cloud it starts to burst, but a cloud but
presses it down, so that it is weighed down like a column forces it down to
from sky to sea, little by little, as though something were meet the
being thrust down and stretched out into the waves by sea;

a fist and the pushing of an arm above; and when it has
rent this cloud asunder, the force of the wind bursts forth
thence into the sea and brings to pass a wondrous seething
in the waters.   For a whirling eddy descends and brings
down along with it that cloud of pliant body; and as
soon as it has forced it down pregnant on to the levels of
ocean, the eddy on a sudden plunges its whole self into
the water, and stirs up all the sea with a great roar, con-
straining it to seethe.   It comes to pass also that an eddy
of wind by itself wraps itself in clouds, gathering together
seeds of cloud from the air and, as it were, imitates the
prester let down from the sky.   When this eddy has let
itself down to earth and broken up, it vomits forth a
furious force of whirlwind and storm.   But because this
happens but rarely at all, and mountains must needs bar
it on land, it is seen more often on a wide prospect of sea,
and in an open stretch of sky.

*or else
an eddy
gathers
clouds about
it and drops
to the earth.*

Clouds gather up, when many bodies as they fly in this
upper expanse of heaven have all at once come together—
bodies of rougher kind, such as can, though they be but
intertwined with slight links, yet grasp and cling to one
another.   These first of all cause little clouds to form;
then these grip hold of one another and flock together,
and uniting they grow and are borne on by the winds,
until at last a furious tempest has gathered together.   It
comes to pass, too, that mountain-tops, the closer they
are to the sky, the more at that height do they smoke
continually with the thick darkness of a murky cloud,
because, when first the clouds form, still thin, before the
eyes can see them, the winds carry them and drive them
together to the topmost peaks of the mountain.   There
it comes to pass at last that, gathered now in a greater

*5. Clouds
are formed
(a) as
particles
gather in
the air in
masses
gradually
growing
larger;*

*especially
round
mountain
tops,
whither
they are
driven by
wind;*

throng and thickened, they can be seen, and at once they seem to rise into the open sky from the very summit of the mountain. For clear fact and our sense, when we climb high mountains, proclaim that windy regions stretch above. Moreover, that nature lifts up many such bodies all over the sea is shown by clothes hung out on the shore, when they take in a clinging moisture. Wherefore it is all the more seen that many bodies too can rise to swell the clouds from the salt tossing ocean ; for in all their nature these two moistures are akin. Moreover, we see clouds and vapour rising from all rivers, and likewise from the very earth which, like a breath, are forced out hence and carried upwards, and curtain the heaven with their darkness, and little by little, as they meet, build up the clouds on high. For the vapour of the starry ether above presses down on them too, and, as it were by thickening, weaves a web of storm-cloud beneath the blue. It happens, too, that there come into our sky those bodies from without which make clouds and flying storms. For I have shown that their number is innumerable, and the sum of the deep measureless, and I have set forth with what speed the bodies fly, and how in a moment they are wont to traverse through space that none can tell. So it is not strange if often in a short time storm and darkness cover up sea and land with such great storm-clouds,[1] brooding above, inasmuch as on all sides through all the pores of the ether, and, as it were, through the breathing-holes of the great world all around there is furnished for the particles exit and entrance.

Come now, in what manner the rainy moisture gathers together in the high clouds, and how the shower falls shot down upon the earth, I will unfold. First of all it will

(b) as particles of moisture rise from the sea

or from rivers, or even lands.

(c) as particles fly in from outside the world

6. Rain is caused (a) because the clouds

---

[1] Translating Lachmann's *nimbis* for *montis.*

contain
much
moisture;

(b) because
it rises into
them from
the sea

and the
rivers ;

and is then
squeezed
out by the
force of the
wind and
the mass of
the clouds;

or again,
when the
clouds are
thin, by the
sun's heat.

Rain is
heavy when
the pressure
is violent,
and long
when there
is much
moisture.

The rain-
bow is
caused by
the sun
shining on
the rain.
Similarly
all meteoro-
logical

be granted me that already many seeds of water rise up
with the clouds themselves from out of all things, and
that both alike grow in this manner, both clouds and all
water that is in the clouds, just as our body grows along
with its blood, and likewise sweat and all the moisture too
that is within the limbs. Besides, they often take in also
much moisture from the sea, just like hanging fleeces of
wool, when the winds carry the clouds over the great sea.
In like manner moisture from all streams is raised to the
clouds. And when many seeds of waters in many ways
have duly come together there, increased from all quarters,
the packed clouds are eager to shoot out the moisture for
a double cause ; for the force of the wind pushes it on
and the very mass of the clouds, driven together in greater
throng, presses on it and weighs it down from above, and
makes the showers stream out. Moreover, when the
clouds, too, are thinned by the winds or broken up,
smitten by the sun's heat above, they send out the rainy
moisture and drip, even as wax over a hot fire melts and
flows in a thick stream. But a violent downpour comes
to pass, when the clouds are violently pressed by either
force, their own mass and the impulse of the wind. Yea,
and the rains are wont to hold on long and make a great
stay, when many seeds of water are gathered, and clouds
piled upon clouds and streaming storms above them are
borne on from every quarter, and when the whole earth
smoking, breathes out its moisture. When at such time
the sun amid the dark tempest has shone out with its
rays full against the spray of the storm-clouds, then
among the black clouds stand out the hues of the rainbow.

All other things which grow above and are brought to
being above, and which gather together in the clouds,

all, yea all of them, snow, winds, hail, chill hoar-frosts, phenomena
and the great force of ice, that great hardener of waters, may be
the curb which everywhere reins in the eager streams, explained.
it is yet right easy to find these out, and to see in the
mind in what manner they all come to be and in what
way they are brought to being, when you have duly
learned the powers that are vouchsafed to the elements.

Come now and learn what is the law of earthquakes. B. Pheno-
And first of all let yourself suppose that the earth is below, mena of
just as above, full on all sides of windy caverns ; and you 1. Earth-
must think it bears in its bosom many lakes and many quakes.
pools and cliffs and sheer rocks ; and that many rivers underneath
hidden beneath the back of the earth roll on amain their has caverns
waves and submerged stones. For clear fact demands [n] and rocks.
that it should be in all parts like itself. When these things
then are placed and linked together beneath it, the earth (*a*) When
above trembles, shaken by great falling masses, when some cavern
beneath time has caused huge caverns to fall in ; nay, earthquake
indeed, whole mountains fall, and at the great sudden is caused,
shock tremblings creep abroad thence far and wide. And
with good reason, since whole houses by the roadside just as
tremble when shaken by a wagon of no great weight, and houses are
rock none the less, whenever a stone in the road jolts rocked by
on the iron circles of the wheels on either side.[1] It comes wagons,
to pass too, when a vast mass of soil, loosened by age from or the land
the earth, rolls down into huge wide pools of water, that by an
the earth too tosses and sways beneath the wave of water ; falling into
even as a vessel sometimes cannot stand still, unless the like water
liquid within has ceased to toss with unsteady wave. rocking in
a vessel.

Moreover, when the wind gathering throughout the (*b*) An
cavernous places of the earth blows strong from one point, earthquake

---

[1] The text is uncertain, but this seems to be the sense.

may be
caused by
a great
subter-
ranean wind
blowing
violently
in one
direction.
And yet
men will
not believe
in the
ultimate
destruction
of the
earth, when
it is only
the altera-
tion of the
wind which
restores
equilibrium.

and with all its weight presses on the lofty caves with
mighty strength, the earth leans over to where the
swooping force of the wind presses it.   Then the houses
that are built up upon the earth, yea, the more they are
severally raised towards the sky, bend over in suspense,
tottering towards the same quarter, and the timbers
driven forward hang out ready to fall.   And yet men fear
to believe that a time of destruction and ruin awaits the
nature of the great world, even when they see so great
a mass of earth bowing to its fall.   Why, unless the winds
breathed in again, no force could put a curb on things or
avail to pull them back from destruction as they fell.   As
it is, because turn by turn they breathe in and then grow
violent, because, as it were, they rally and charge again
and then are driven back and give ground, for this reason
the earth more often threatens a fall than brings it to
pass ; for it leans over and then sways back again, and
after falling forward recovers its position to a steady poise.
In this way, then, the whole building rocks, the top more
than the middle, the middle more than the bottom, the
bottom but a very little.

(c) Some-
times the
imprisoned
air bursts
forth,
making a
great
chasm :

There is this cause, too, of that same great shaking,
when suddenly wind and some exceeding great force of
air, gathering either from without or within the earth
itself, have hurled themselves into the hollow places of
the earth, and there first rage among the great caves in
turmoil, and rise, carried on in a whirl ; and when afterwards the moving force driven forth bursts out and at
the same time cleaves the earth and causes a huge chasm.
Even as it came to pass at Sidon in Syria, and as was the
case at Aegium in Peloponnese, cities overthrown by this

issue of air and the quaking of the earth which arose. And besides many walled towns have fallen through great movements on land, and many cities have sunk down deep into the sea, inhabitants and all. And even if it does not burst forth, yet the very impulse of the air and the fierce force of the wind are spread, like a fit of shivering, throughout the riddling passages of the earth, and thereby induce a trembling : even as cold, when it comes deep into our members, shakes them against their will and constrains them to tremble and to move. So men quiver with anxious terror throughout the cities, they fear the houses above, they dread the hollow places beneath, lest the nature of the earth should break them open all at once, and lest torn asunder she should open wide her maw, and, tumbled all together, desire to fill it with her own falling ruins. Let them then believe as they will that heaven and earth will be indestructible, entrusted to some everlasting protection ; and yet from time to time the very present force of danger applies on some side or other this goad of fear, lest the earth, snatched away suddenly from beneath their feet be carried into the abyss, and the sum of things, left utterly without foundation, follow on, and there be a tumbling wreck of the whole world.

[1] First of all they wonder that nature does not make the sea bigger, since there comes into it so great a downpour of water, yea, all the streams from every quarter. Add, if you will, the shifting showers and the scudding storms, which bespatter and drench all seas and lands ; add too its own springs ; yet compared to the sum of the sea all

or remaining imprisoned, causes the earth to shudder.

It is a lesson that the whole world may thus be destroyed.

2. Why does not the sea increase?

---

[1] Either this paragraph is a disconnected fragment, or more probably something has been lost before it, introducing a new section of the paradoxes of nature on earth.

(*a*) Because all that is added to it is but a drop in the ocean ; these things will scarce be equal to the increase of a single drop ; therefore it is the less strange that the great sea does not increase. Moreover, the sun draws off a great part by his heat. For verily we see the sun with its (*b*) because much water is drawn off by sun, blazing rays dry clothes wringing with moisture ; and yet we see many oceans spread wide beneath earth's level. Therefore, although from each single place the sun sucks up but a small part of moisture from the level sea ; yet in so great a space it will draw largely from the waves. by wind, Then again, the winds too can lift a great part of moisture as they sweep the level seas, since very often we see roads dried by the wind in a single night, and the soft mud and by clouds ; harden into crusts. Moreover, I have shown that the clouds too lift up much moisture taken in from the great level of ocean, and scatter it broadcast over all the circle of lands, when it rains on the earth and the winds carry or (*c*) oozes into the earth. on the clouds. Lastly, since the earth is formed of porous body, and is continuous, surrounding on all sides the shores of the sea, it must needs be that, just as the moisture of water passes into the sea from the lands, it likewise filters through into the land from the salt sea levels ; for the brine is strained through, and the substance of moisture oozes back and all streams together at the fountain-head of rivers, and thence comes back over the lands with freshened current, where the channel once cleft has brought down the waters in their liquid march.

3. The eruption of Etna. Now what is the reason that through the jaws of Mount Etna flames sometimes breathe forth in so great a hurricane, I will unfold. For indeed the flaming storm gathered with no moderate force of destruction and ruled tyrant through the fields of the Sicilians and turned to itself the gaze of neighbouring nations, when they saw all the

quarters of the heavens smoke and sparkle, and filled their breasts with shuddering anxiety for what new change nature might be planning.

Herein you must look far and deep and take a wide view to every quarter, that you may remember that the sum of things is unfathomable, and see how small, how infinitely small a part of the whole sum is one single heaven—not so large a part, as is a single man of the whole earth. And if you have this duly before you and look clearly at it and see it clearly, you would cease to wonder at many things. For does any of us wonder, if a man has caught in his limbs a fever gathering with burning heat, or any other painful disease in his members? For a foot will swell suddenly, often a sharp pain seizes on the teeth or makes its way right into the eyes ; the holy fire [n] breaks out and creeping about in the body burns any part which it has seized, and crawls through the limbs, because, as we may be sure, there are seeds of many things, and this earth and heaven has enough disease and malady, from which the force of measureless disease might avail to spread abroad. So then we must suppose that out of the infinite all things are supplied to the whole heaven and earth in number enough that on a sudden the earth might be shaken and moved, and a tearing hurricane course over sea and land, the fire of Etna well forth, and the heaven be aflame. For that too comes to pass, and the quarters of heaven blaze, and there are rainstorms gathering in heavier mass, when by chance the seeds of the waters have so arranged themselves. 'Nay, but the stormy blaze of this fire is exceeding gigantic.' So, too, be sure, is the river which is the greatest seen

Remember the vastness of the universe.

Just as many diseases may come to the body,

so the infinite can supply innumerable seeds of malady to heaven and earth.

The eruption seems 'gigantic', but so

always does
the greatest
thing of its
kind which
we have
seen.

by a man, who has never before seen any greater : so a tree or a man may seem gigantic, and in every kind of thing, the greatest that each man has seen, he always imagines gigantic, and yet all of them together, yea, with heaven and earth and sea besides, are nothing to the whole sum of the universal sum.

The erup-
tion is
caused
because
wind gathers
in subter-
ranean
caverns,

heats itself
and all
around it,
and then
bursts out.

But now in what ways that flame is suddenly excited and breathes abroad from out the vast furnaces of Etna, I will unfold. First of all the nature of the whole mountain is hollow beneath, resting everywhere on caverns of basalt. Moreover, in all the caves there is wind and air. For air becomes wind, when [n] it is set in motion and aroused. When it has grown hot, and as it rages has heated all the rocks and the earth around wherever it touches them, and has struck out from them a fire hot with swift flames, it rises up and so drives itself forth on high straight through the mountain's jaws. And so it carries its heat far, and afar it scatters the ash and rolls on a smoke with thick murky darkness, and all the while hurls out rocks of marvellous weight ; for you must not doubt that this is the stormy force of air. Moreover, in great part the sea makes its waves break and sucks in its tide at the roots of that mountain. From this sea caves stretch underneath right to the deep jaws of the mountain. By this path we must admit that ⟨water⟩ passes in, and the fact compels us ⟨to believe that wind is mingled with it⟩[1] and pierces deep in from the open sea, and then breathes out, and so lifts up the flame and casts up rocks and raises clouds of dust. For on the topmost peak are craters, as the inhabitants name them ; what we call jaws or mouths.

There are
also passages
from the
neighbour-
ing sea,
by which
blasts of
wind
enter in.

[1] A line is lost, of which the words in brackets give the probable sense.

Some things there are, too, not a few, for which to
tell one cause is not enough ; we must give more, one of
which is yet the actual cause ; just as if you yourself were
to see the lifeless body of a man lying before you, it would
be right that you should name all causes of death, in order
that the one cause of that man's death might be told.
For you could not prove that he had perished by the
sword or of cold, or by disease or perchance by poison,
but we know that it was something of this sort which was
his fate.   Likewise, we can say the same in many cases.

*For some
things we
must men-
tion several
possible
causes, one
of which
will be
true in
the given
case.*

The Nile, the river of all Egypt, alone in the world
rises, as summer comes, and overflows the plains.   It
waters Egypt often amid the hot season, either because
in summer the north winds, which at that time are said
to be the etesian winds, are dead against its mouths ;
blowing against its stream they check it, and driving the
waters upwards fill the channel and make it stop.   For
without doubt these blasts, which are started from the
chill constellations of the pole are driven full against the
stream.   The river comes from the south out of the
quarter where heat is born, rising among the black races
of men of sunburnt colour far inland in the region of
mid-day.   It may be too that a great heaping up of sand
may choke up the mouths as a bar against the opposing
waves, when the sea, troubled by the winds, drives the
sand within ; and in this manner it comes to pass that the
river has less free issue, and the waves likewise a less easy
downward flow.   It may be, too, perhaps that rains occur
more at its source at that season, because the etesian blasts
of the north winds then drive all the clouds together into
those quarters.   And, we may suppose, when they have
come together driven towards the region of mid-day,

*4. The rise
of the Nile
may be
caused
(a) by the
north winds
opposing
its stream ;*

*(b) by a
sand-barrier
choking the
stream ;*

*(c) by
excessive
rain in the
interior ;*

there at last the clouds, thrust together upon the high mountains, are massed and violently pressed. Perchance it swells from deep among the high mountains of the Ethiopians, where the sun, traversing all with his melting rays, forces the white snows to run down into the plains.

(d) by the melting of snow on the mountains.

5. Avernian spots; so-called as they are fatal to birds.

Come now, I will unfold to you with what nature are endowed all Avernian places and lakes. First of all, in that they are called by the name Avernian,[n] that is given them from the fact, because they are harmful to all birds, in that, when they have come right over those spots in their flight, forgetting the oarage of their wings, they slack their sails, and fall headlong, drooping with languid neck to earth, if by chance the nature of the spots so determines it, or into the water, if by chance the lake of Avernus spreads beneath them. That spot is by Cumae, where mountains smoke, choked with biting sulphur and enriched with hot springs. There is too a spot within the walls of Athens, on the very summit of the citadel, by the temple of Pallas Tritonis, the life-giver, whither croaking crows never steer their bodies on the wing, not even when the altars smoke with offerings. So surely do they fly, not in truth from the fierce wrath of Pallas, because of their vigil,[n] as the poets of the Greeks have sung, but the nature of the spot of its own force accomplishes the task. In Syria, too, it is said that there is likewise a spot to be seen, where, as soon as even four-footed beasts have set foot, its natural force constrains them to fall heavily, as though they were on a sudden slaughtered to the gods of the dead. Yet all these things are brought about by a natural law, and it is clearly seen

Such as lake Avernus,

a spot by the Parthenon,

and a place in Syria.

All owe their power

from what causes to begin with they come to be; lest *to natural causes, and are not gates of hell.* by chance [1] the gateway of Orcus should be thought to be in these regions; and thereafter we should by chance believe that the gods of the dead lead the souls below from this spot to the shores of Acheron; even as stags of winged feet are often thought by their scent to drag from their lairs the races of crawling serpents. And how far removed this is from true reason, now learn; for now I will try to tell of the true fact.

First of all I say, what I have often said before as well, *Earth contains the elements of all things, both good and bad.* that in the earth there are shapes of things of every kind; many which are good for food, helpful to life, and many which can induce diseases and hasten death. And that for different animals different things are suited for the purpose of life, I have shown before, because their nature and texture and the shapes of their first-beginnings are unlike, the one to the other. Many things which are *And among them many things noxious to each of the senses.* harmful pass through the ears, many which are dangerous and rough to draw in [2] find their way even through the nostrils, nor are there a few which should be avoided by the touch, yea, and shunned by the sight, or else are bitter to the taste.

Next we may see how many things are for man of *Many such exhalations are poison-ous to man. Trees.* a sensation keenly harmful, and are nauseous and noxious; first, certain trees are endowed with a shade so exceeding noxious, that often they cause an aching of the head, if one has lain beneath them, stretched upon the grass. There is, too, a tree on the great mountains of Helicon, which is wont to kill a man with the noisome scent of its flower. We may be sure that these things all grow in this way from the earth, because the earth contains in

---

[1] Reading *forte his* for *poteis* with Munro.
[2] Reading *tractu* with Polle.

itself many seeds of many things, mingled in many ways,
and gives them forth singled out. Again, a light but
newly extinguished at night, when it meets the nostrils
with its pungent smell, at once puts to sleep a man who
is wont through disease to fall down and foam at the
mouth. And a woman will fall back asleep with the
heavy scent of castor, and her gay-coloured work slips
from her delicate hands, if she has smelt it at the time
when she has her monthly discharge. And many other
things too slacken the drooping members throughout the
frame, and make the soul totter within its abode. Once
again, if you dally in the hot bath when you are too full,
how easily it comes to pass often that you fall down, as
you sit on the stool in the middle of the boiling water.
And how easily the noxious force and smell of charcoal
finds its way into the brain, unless we have taken water
beforehand. And when the burning fever has seized
and subdued the limbs,[1] then the smell of wine is like
a slaughtering blow. Do you not see, too, sulphur produced in the very earth and pitch harden into crusts of
a noisome scent? and again, when men are following up
the veins of gold and silver, probing with the pick deep
into the hidden parts of earth, what stenches Scaptensula[n]
breathes out underground? And what poison gold mines
may exhale! how strange they make men's faces, how
they change their colour! Have you not seen or heard
how they are wont to die in a short time and how the
powers of life fail those, whom the strong force of necessity imprisons in such work? All these effluences then

An extin-
guished
candle to an
epileptic.

Castor to
a woman.

A hot bath
after a meal.

Charcoal.

Wine to the
feverish.

Mines to
those who
work in
them.

---

[1] The reading is extremely uncertain: Heinrichsen's suggestion
membra domans percepit fervida febris may be right.

earth sends steaming forth, and breathes them out into the open and the clear spaces of heaven.

So these Avernian spots too must needs send up some fume deadly to the birds, which rises from the earth into the air, so that it poisons the expanse of heaven in a certain quarter ; and at the very moment when the bird is carried thither on its wings, it is checked there, seized by the secret poison, so that it tumbles straight down on the spot, where the effluence has its course. And when it has fallen into it, there the same force of the effluence takes away the remnant of life out of all its limbs. For verily first of all it causes a kind of dizzy seething in the birds : afterwards it comes to pass that, when they have fallen right into the sources of the poison, there they must needs vomit forth their life as well, because there is great store of poison all around them. *Similarly these spots give out an exhalation, which first stops the birds, and then kills them when they fall.*

It may happen, too, sometimes that this force and effluence of Avernus dispels all the air that is situate between the birds and the ground, so that there is left here an almost empty space. And when the birds in their flight have come straight over this place, on a sudden the lifting force of their pinions is crippled and useless, and all the effort of their wings fails on either side. And then, when they cannot support themselves or rest upon their wings, of course nature constrains them to sink by their weight to the ground, and lying in death in what is now almost empty void, they scatter abroad their soul through all the pores of their body . . . . . . *It may be that the effluence dispels the air, and so the birds fall in a vacuum.*

. . . .[1]

moreover, the water in wells becomes colder in summer, *6. Wells are*

---

[1] A considerable passage is lost, in which the poet passed to a quite new subject.

cold in summer, because earth gives out its heat into the air, and warm in winter, because it sends its heat into the wells. The fountain of Ammon grows cold in the day and warm at night for exactly similar reasons,

because the earth grows porous with the heat, and if by chance it has any seeds of heat of its own, it sends them abroad into the air. The more then earth is exhausted of its heat, the colder too becomes the moisture which is hidden in the earth. Moreover, when all the earth is hard pressed with cold, and contracts and, as it were, congeals, of course it comes to pass that, as it contracts, it squeezes out into the wells any heat it bears in itself.

There is said to be near the shrine of Ammon[n] a fountain, cold in the daylight and warm in the night time. At this fountain men marvel overmuch, and think that it is made to boil in haste by the fierceness of the sun beneath the earth, when night has shrouded earth in dreadful darkness. But this is exceeding far removed from true reasoning. For verily, when the sun, touching the uncovered body of the water, could not make it warm on the upper side, though its light in the upper air enjoys heat so great, how could it beneath the earth with its body so dense boil the water and fill it with warm heat? and that when it can scarcely with its blazing rays make its hot effluence pierce through the walls of houses. What then is the reason? We may be sure, because the ground is rarer and warmer around the fountain than the rest of the earth, and there are many seeds of fire near the body of the water. Therefore, when night covers the earth with the shadows that bring the dew, straightway the earth grows cold deep within and contracts. By this means it comes to pass that, as though it were pressed by the hand, it squeezes out into the fountain all the seeds of fire it has, which make warm the touch and vapour of the water. Then when the rising sun has parted asunder the ground with his rays, and has made it rarer, as his warm heat grows stronger, the first-beginnings of fire pass back again into their old abode, and all the heat of the water retires into the earth. For this cause the fountain becomes cold in the light of day. Moreover, the moisture of the water is buffeted by the sun's rays, and in the light grows rarer through the throbbing heat; therefore it comes to pass that it loses all the seeds of fire that it has; just as often it gives out the frost that it contains in itself, and melts the ice and loosens its bindings.

also because the sun's heat breaks up the waters and releases the heat in them.

There is also a cold spring, over which if tow be held, it often straightway catches fire and casts out a flame, and a torch in like manner is kindled and shines over the waters, wherever, as it floats, it is driven by the breezes. Because, we may be sure, there are in the water very many seeds of heat, and it must needs be that from the very earth at the bottom bodies of fire rise up through the whole spring, and at the same time are breathed forth and issue into the air, yet not so many of them that the spring can be made hot. Moreover, a force constrains them suddenly to burst forth through the water scattered singly, and then to enter into union up above. Even as there is a spring within the sea at Aradus,[n] which bubbles up with fresh water and parts the salt waters asunder all around it; and in many other spots too the level sea affords a welcome help to thirsty sailors, because amid the salt it vomits forth fresh water. So then those seeds are able to burst out through that spring, and to bubble out into the tow; and when they gather together or cling to the body of the torch readily they blaze out all

The cold spring, over which torches catch fire, owes its power to seeds of fire, which shoot up separately through the water and unite in flame on the torch.

It is like springs of fresh water in the sea.

at once, because the tow and torches too have many seeds of hidden fire in themselves. Do you not see too, when you move a wick just extinguished near a night-lamp, that it is kindled before it has touched the flame, and a torch in like manner? And many other things as well are touched first by the mere heat and blaze out at a distance, before the fire soaks them close at hand. This then we must suppose comes to pass in that spring too.

Observe how the wick catches before it touches the flame.

For what follows, I will essay to tell by what law of nature it comes to pass that iron can be attracted by the stone which the Greeks call the magnet, from the name of its native place, because it has its origin within the boundaries of its native country, the land of the Magnetes. At this stone men marvel; indeed, it often makes a chain of rings all hanging to itself. For sometimes you may see five or more in a hanging chain, and swaying in the light breezes, when one hangs on to the other, clinging to it beneath, and each from the next comes to feel the binding force of the stone : in such penetrating fashion does its force prevail.

7. The magnet, and how it holds its chain of rings suspended.

In things of this kind much must be made certain before you can give account of the thing itself, and you must approach by a circuit exceeding long : therefore all the more I ask for attentive ears and mind.

Much must be premised.

First of all from all things, whatsoever we can see, it must needs be that there stream off, shot out and scattered abroad, bodies such as to strike the eyes and awake our vision. And from certain things scents stream off unceasingly; even as cold streams from rivers, heat from the sun, spray from the waves of the sea, which gnaws away the walls by the seashore. Nor do diverse sounds cease to ooze through the air. Again, moisture of

(a) From all things bodies are always streaming off, which arouse our senses.

a salt savour often comes into our mouth, when we walk
by the sea, and on the other hand, when we behold wormwood being diluted and mixed, a bitter taste touches it.
So surely from all things each several thing is carried off
in a stream, and is sent abroad to every quarter on all sides,
nor is any delay or respite granted in this flux, since we
perceive unceasingly, and we are suffered always to descry
and smell all things, and to hear them sound.

Now I will tell over again of how rarefied a body all
things are; which is clearly shown in the beginning of my
poem too.[n] For verily, although it is of great matter to
learn this for many things, it is above all necessary for this
very thing, about which I am essaying to discourse, to
make it sure that there is nothing perceptible except body
mingled with void.   First of all it comes to pass that in
caves the upper rocks sweat with moisture and drip with
trickling drops.   Likewise sweat oozes out from all our
body, the beard grows and hairs over all our limbs and
members, food is spread abroad into all the veins, yea, it
increases and nourishes even the extreme parts of the
body, and the tiny nails.   We feel cold likewise pass
through bronze and warm heat, we feel it likewise pass
through gold and through silver, when we hold full cups
in our hands.   Again voices fly through stone partitions
in houses, smell penetrates and cold and the heat of fire,
which is wont to pierce too through the strength of iron.
Again, where the breastplate of the sky[1][n] closes in the
world all around ⟨the bodies of clouds and the seeds of
storms enter in⟩, and with them the force of disease, when
it finds its way in from without; and tempests, gathering

(b) The
bodies of
all things
are porous;

e. g. rocks,

the human
body,

metals,

walls,

even the
circum-
ference of
the world.

[1] The MS. reading *caeli lorica* is probably quite right, and a line is
lost, of which this, as Giussani suggests, was probably the sense.

from earth and heaven, hasten naturally to remote parts of heaven and earth; since there is nothing but has a rare texture of body.

(c) These effluences affect different things differently: e.g. sunlight may melt or harden.

There is this besides, that not all bodies, which are thrown off severally from things, are endowed with the same effect of sense, nor suited in the same way to all things. First of all the sun bakes the ground and parches it, but ice it thaws and causes the snows piled high on the high mountains to melt beneath its rays. Again, wax becomes liquid when placed in the sun's heat. Fire likewise makes bronze liquid and fuses gold, but skins and flesh it shrivels and draws all together. Moreover, the moisture of water hardens iron fresh from the fire, but skins and flesh it softens, when hardened in the heat.

The wild olive is good to goats, loathsome to us. Pigs hate marjoram, and we loathe mud.

The wild olive as much delights the bearded she-goats, as though it breathed out a flavour steeped in ambrosia and real nectar; and yet for a man there is no leafy plant more bitter than this for food. Again, the pig shuns marjoram, and fears every kind of ointment; for to bristling pigs it is deadly poison, though to us it sometimes seems almost to give new life. But on the other hand, though to us mud is the foulest filth, this very thing is seen to be pleasant to pigs, so that they wallow all over in it and never have enough.

(d) The pores and passages in things differ, and let different things pass through them.

This too remains, which it is clear should be said, before I start to speak of the thing itself. Since many pores are assigned to diverse things, they must needs be endowed with a nature differing from one another, and have each their own nature and passages. For verily there are diverse senses in living creatures, each of which in its own way takes in its own object within itself. For we see that sounds pass into one place and the taste from savours into another, and to another the scent of smells. Moreover, one thing is seen to pierce through rocks, another through wood, and another to pass through gold, and yet another to make its way out from silver and glass. For through the one vision is seen to stream, though the other heat to travel, and one thing is seen to force its way along the same path quicker than others. We may know that the nature of the passages causes this to come to pass, since it varies in many ways, as we have shown a little before on account of the unlike nature and texture of things.

Wherefore, when all these things have been surely established and settled for us, laid down in advance and ready for use, for what remains, from them we shall easily give account, and the whole cause will be laid bare, which attracts the force of iron. First of all it must needs be^n that there stream off this stone very many seeds or an effluence, which, with its blows, parts asunder all the air which has its place between the stone and the iron. When this space is emptied and much room in the middle becomes void, straightway first-beginnings of the iron start forward and fall into the void, all joined together; it comes to pass that the ring itself follows and advances in this way, with its whole body. Nor is anything so closely interlaced in its first particles, all clinging linked together, as the nature of strong iron and its cold roughness. Therefore it is the less strange, since it is led on by its particles, that it is impossible for many bodies, springing together from the iron, to pass into the void, but that the ring itself follows; and this it does, and follows on, until it has now reached the very stone and clung to it with hidden fastenings. This same thing takes place in every

We can now turn to the magnet.

It sends off particles which beat aside the air in front and make a vacuum; into this the atoms of the iron rush, and because they are very closely linked together, they draw the whole ring with them.

direction;[1] on whichever side room becomes void, whether athwart or above, the neighbouring bodies are carried at once into the void. For indeed they are set in motion by blows from the other side, nor can they themselves of their own accord rise upwards into the air. To this there is added, that it may the more be able to come to pass, this further thing as an aid, yea, the motion is helped, because, as soon as the air in front of the ring is made rarer, and the place becomes more empty and void, it straightway comes to pass that all the air which has its place behind, drives, as it were, and pushes the ring forward. For the air which is set all around is for ever buffeting things; but it comes to pass that at times like this it pushes the iron forward, because on one side there is empty space, which receives the ring into itself. This air, of which I am telling you, finds its way in subtly through the countless pores of the iron right to its tiny parts, and thrusts and drives it on, as wind drives ship and sails. Again, all things must have air in their body seeing that they are of rare body, and the air is placed round and set close against all things. This air then, which is hidden away deep within the iron, is ever tossed about with restless motion, and therefore without doubt it buffets the ring and stirs it within; the ring, we may be sure, is carried towards the same side to which it has once moved headlong, struggling hard towards the empty spot.

It comes to pass, too, that the nature of iron retreats from this stone at times, and is wont to flee and follow turn by turn. Further, I have seen Samothracian iron rings even leap up, and at the same time iron filings move

The marginal notes (printed in the left margin):

This may happen in any direction.

Further, the air behind the ring pushes it towards the vacuum, where there is no air to beat it back.

The air inside the iron also pushes in the same direction.

When brass is interposed, the magnet repels iron, because the

---

[1] Place ; after *partes* and , after *superne.*

in a frenzy inside brass bowls, when this Magnesian stone
was placed beneath : so eagerly is the iron seen to desire
to flee from the stone.   When the brass is placed between,
so great a disturbance is brought about because, we may
be sure, when the effluence of the brass has seized beforehand and occupied the open passages in the iron, afterwards comes the effluence of the stone, and finds all full
in the iron, nor has it a path by which it may stream
through as before.   And so it is constrained to dash
against it and beat with its wave upon the iron texture ;
and in this way it repels it from itself, and through the
brass drives away that which without it it often sucks in.

effluence from the brass has already filled up the pores in the iron.

Herein refrain from wondering that the effluence from
this stone has not the power to drive other things in the
same way.   For in part they stand still by the force of
their own weight, as for instance, gold ; and partly, because they are of such rare body, that the effluence flies
through untouched, they cannot be driven anywhere ;
among this kind is seen to be the substance of wood. The
nature of iron then has its place between the two, and
when it has taken in certain tiny bodies of brass, then it
comes to pass that the Magnesian stones drive it on with
their stream.

The magnet cannot move other things because they are either too heavy or too rare in texture.

And yet these powers are not so alien to other things
that I have only a scanty store of things of this kind, of
which I can tell—things fitted just for each other and
for naught besides.   First you see that stones are stuck
together only by mortar.   Wood is united only by bulls'
glue, so that the veins of boards more often gape than
the bindings of the glue will loosen their hold.   The
juice born of the grape is willing to mingle with streams
of water, though heavy pitch and light olive-oil refuse.

There are other cases of things with a peculiar affinity and binding power : stones and mortar, wood and glue, wine and water,

And the purple tint of the shellfish is united only with
the body of wool, yet so that it cannot be separated at all,
no, not if you were to be at pains to restore it with
Neptune's wave, no, nor if the whole sea should strive to
wash it out with all its waves.   Again, is not there one
thing only that binds gold to gold? is it not true that
brass is joined to brass only by white lead?   How many
other cases might we find !   What then?   You have no
need at all of long rambling roads, nor is it fitting that
I should spend so much pains on this, but 'tis best shortly
in a few words to include many cases.   Those things,
whose textures fall so aptly one upon the other that
hollows fit solids, each in the one and the other, make the
best joining.   Sometimes, too, they may be held linked
with one another, as it were, fastened by rings and hooks ;
as is seen to be more the case with this stone and the
iron.

Now what is the law of plagues, and from what cause
on a sudden the force of disease can arise and gather
deadly destruction for the race of men and the herds of
cattle, I will unfold.   First I have shown before that there
are seeds of many things which are helpful to our life, and
on the other hand it must needs be that many fly about
which cause disease and death.   And when by chance
they have happened to gather and distemper the sky, then
the air becomes full of disease.   And all that force of
disease and pestilence either comes from without the
world through the sky above, as do clouds and mists,
or else often it gathers and rises up from the earth
itself, when, full of moisture, it has contracted foulness,
smitten by unseasonable rains or suns.   Do you not see,
too, that those who journey far from their home and

dye and
wool,

brass and
white lead.

Whenever
shapes fit
mutually,
a strong
joining
results.

8. Plague
and disease.

When the
seeds of
harmful
things
gather in
the sky,
they
pollute it.
They may
come from
outside the
world or
from the
earth.

So travellers
are affected

country are assailed by the strangeness of the climate by a strange
climate,
and the water, just because things are far different? For
what a difference may we suppose there is between the
climate the Britons know and that which is in Egypt,
where the axis of the world slants crippled; [n] what difference between the climate in Pontus and at Gades, and so
right on to the black races of men with their sunburnt
colour? And as we see these four climates at the four and differ-
ences of
climate
winds and quarters of the sky thus diverse one from the
other, so the colour and face of the men are seen to vary cause differ-
ences of
appearance
greatly, and diseases too to attack the diverse races each
after their kind. There is the elephant disease, which in races,
arises along the streams of the Nile in mid Egypt, and in and produce
special
no other place. In Attica the feet are assailed, and the diseases.
eyes in the Achaean country. And so each place is harmful to different parts and limbs: the varying air is the
cause. Wherefore, when an atmosphere, which chances If then a
to be noxious to us, sets itself in motion, and harmful air noxious
atmosphere
begins to creep forward, just as cloud and mist crawls on moves and
little by little and distempers all, wherever it advances, comes to us,
and brings about change, it comes to pass also, that when
at last it comes to our sky, it corrupts it and makes it like
itself, and noxious to us. And so this strange destruction
and pestilence suddenly falls upon the waters or settles pestilence
even on the crops or on other food of men or fodder of results for
man and
the flocks; or else this force remains poised in the air beast.
itself, and, when we draw in these mingled airs as we
breathe, it must needs be that we suck in these plagues
with them into our body. In like manner the pestilence falls too often on the cattle, and sickness also
on the lazy bleating sheep. Nor does it matter whether
we pass into spots hostile to us and change the ves-

ture of the sky, or whether nature attacking us brings
a corrupt sky [1] upon us, or something which we are not
accustomed to feel, which can assail us by its first
coming.

Such was
the plague
at Athens,
which came
from
Egypt.
     Such a cause of plague,[n] such a deadly influence, once
in the country of Cecrops filled the fields with dead and
emptied the streets, draining the city of its citizens. For
it arose deep within the country of Egypt, and came,
traversing much sky and floating fields, and brooded at
Symptoms
and causes
of the
disease.
last over all the people of Pandion. Then troop by troop
they were given over to disease and death. First of all
they felt the head burning with heat, and both eyes red
with a glare shot over them. The throat, too, blackened
inside, would sweat with blood, and the path of the voice
was blocked and choked with ulcers, and the tongue, the
mind's spokesman, would ooze with gore, weakened with
pain, heavy in movement, rough to touch. Then, when
through the throat the force of disease had filled the
breast and had streamed on right into the pained heart of
the sick, then indeed all the fastnesses of life were loosened.
Their breath rolled out a noisome smell from the mouth,
like the stench of rotting carcasses thrown out of doors.
And straightway all the strength of the mind and the
whole body grew faint, as though now on the very threshold of death. And aching anguish went ever in the
train of their unbearable suffering, and lamentation,
mingled with sobbing. And a constant retching, ever
and again, by night and day, would constrain them continually to spasms in sinews and limbs, and would utterly

----

[1] The MS. text involves an impossible false quantity, but this must
be the sense: possibly, as Housman suggests, the order of the words is
wrong.

break them down, wearing them out, full weary before.
And yet in none could you see the topmost skin on the
surface of the body burning with exceeding heat, but
rather the body offered a lukewarm touch to the hands
and at the same time all was red as though with the scar
of ulcers, as it is when the holy fire spreads through the
limbs. But the inward parts of the men were burning to
the bones, a flame was burning within the stomach as in
a furnace. There was nothing light or thin that you
could apply to the limbs of any to do him good, but ever
only wind and cold. Some would cast their limbs, burn- Attempted
ing with disease, into the icy streams, hurling their naked remedies.
body into the waters. Many leapt headlong deep into
the waters of wells, reaching the water with their very
mouth agape : a parching thirst, that knew no slaking,
soaking their bodies, made a great draught no better than
a few drops. Nor was there any respite from suffering ;
their bodies lay there foredone. The healers' art mut-
tered low in silent fear, when indeed again and again they
would turn on them their eyes burning with disease and
reft of sleep. And many more signs of death were Accom-
afforded then : the understanding of the mind dis- panying
traught with pain and panic, the gloomy brow, the fierce of the
frenzied face, and the ears too plagued and beset with mind, &c.
noises, the breath quickened or drawn rarely and very
deep, and the wet sweat glistening dank over the neck,
the spittle thin and tiny, tainted with a tinge of yellow
and salt, scarcely brought up through the throat with
a hoarse cough. Then in the hands the sinews ceased not
to contract and the limbs to tremble, and cold to come
up little by little from the feet. Likewise, even till the
last moment, the nostrils were pinched, and the tip of

the nose sharp and thin, the eyes hollowed, the temples sunk, the skin cold and hard, a grin on the set face, the forehead tense and swollen. And not long afterwards the limbs would lie stretched stiff in death. And usually on the eighth day of the shining sunlight, or else beneath his ninth torch, they would yield up their life. And if any of them even so had avoided the doom of death, yet afterwards wasting and death would await him with noisome ulcers, and a black flux from the bowels, or else often with aching head a flow of tainted blood would pour from his choked nostrils : into this would stream all the strength and the body of the man. Or again, when a man had escaped this fierce outpouring of corrupt blood, yet the disease would make its way into his sinews and limbs, and even into the very organs of his body. And some in heavy fear of the threshold of death would live on, bereft of these parts by the knife, and not a few lingered in life without hands or feet and some lost their eyes. So firmly had the sharp fear of death got hold on them. On some, too, forgetfulness of all things seized, so that they could not even know themselves. And though bodies piled on bodies lay in numbers unburied on the ground, yet the race of birds and wild beasts either would range far away, to escape the bitter stench, or, when they had tasted, would fall drooping in quick-coming death. And indeed in those days hardly would any bird appear at all, nor would the gloomy race of wild beasts issue from the woods. Full many would droop in disease and die. More than all the faithful strength of dogs, fighting hard, would lay down their lives, strewn about every street ; for the power of disease would wrest

Length of disease.

Subsequent fate of those who escaped.

Unburied bodies avoided by bird and beast.

the life from their limbs. Funerals deserted, unattended, were hurried on almost in rivalry. Nor was any sure kind of remedy afforded for all alike; for that which had granted to one strength to breathe in his mouth the life-giving breezes of air, and to gaze upon the quarters of the sky, was destruction to others, and made death ready for them. And herein was one thing pitiful and exceed-ing full of anguish, that as each man saw himself caught in the toils of the plague, so that he was condemned to death, losing courage he would lie with grieving heart; looking for death to come he would breathe out his spirit straightway. For indeed, at no time would the con-tagion of the greedy plague cease to lay hold on one after the other, as though they were woolly flocks or horned herds. And this above all heaped death on death. For all who shunned to visit their own sick, over-greedy of life and fearful of death, were punished a while after-wards by slaughtering neglect with a death hard and shameful, abandoned and reft of help. But those who had stayed near at hand would die by contagion and the toil, which shame would then constrain them to undergo, and the appealing voice of the weary, mingled with the voice of complaining. And so all the nobler among them suffered this manner of death . . . .[1]
and one upon others, as they vied in burying the crowd of their dead: worn out with weeping and wailing they would return; and the greater part would take to their bed from grief. Nor could one man be found, whom at this awful season neither disease touched nor death nor mourning.

Moreover, by now the shepherd and every herdsman,

Margin notes: Lack of remedies. Despair. Fate of those who avoided the sick, and of those who tended them. Burials.

---

[1] Some lines of connexion seem to be lost here.

The plague in the country. and likewise the sturdy steersman of the curving plough, would fall drooping, and their bodies would lie thrust together into the recess of a hut, given over to death by poverty and disease. On lifeless children you might often have seen the lifeless bodies of parents, and again, children breathing out their life upon mothers and fathers. And The countrymen flock into the town and increase the disease. in no small degree that affliction streamed from the fields into the city, brought by the drooping crowd of country-men coming together diseased from every quarter. They would fill all places, all houses; and so all the more, packed in stifling heat, death piled them up in heaps. Dead in the streets and public places, Many bodies, laid low by thirst and rolled forward through the streets, lay strewn at the fountains of water, the breath of life shut off from them by the ex-ceeding delight of the water, and many in full view throughout the public places and the streets you might have seen, their limbs drooping on their half-dead body, filthy with stench and covered with rags, dying through the foulness of their body, only skin on bones, wellnigh and temples. buried already in noisome ulcers and dirt. Again, death had filled all the sacred shrines of the gods with lifeless bodies, and all the temples of the heavenly ones remained everywhere cumbered with carcasses; for these places the guardians had filled with guests. For indeed by now the religion of the gods and their godhead was not counted for much: the grief of the moment overwhelmed it all. Horrors of burial. Nor did the old rites of burial continue in the city, with which aforetime this people had ever been wont to be buried; for the whole people was disordered and in panic, and every man sorrowing buried his dead, laid out as best he could. And to many things the sudden calamity and filthy poverty prompted men. For with great clamouring they would place their own kin on the high-piled pyres of others, and set the torches to them, often wrangling with much bloodshed, rather than abandon the bodies.

NOTES

BOOK I

1 ff. The introductory invocation to Venus has caused great trouble to the commentators, as it appears to be inconsistent with Lucretius's belief (e. g. II. 646) that the gods live a blessed life apart, and have no concern with the government of the world or the affairs of men. But, though to some extent, no doubt, such an invocation is to be accepted as a poetical tradition, it is much more truly explained as having for Lucretius an esoteric meaning. Venus is to him the creative power of nature, the life-giving force, Lucretius's reverence for which may fairly be regarded as his true religion. (See Martha, *Le poème de Lucrèce*, pp. 61 ff.)

41. *in our country's time of trouble.* The poem was published after Lucretius's death in 55 B. C., and its unfinished state shows that he must have been working at it in the immediately preceding period. During that time Caesar was fighting in Gaul, but Lucretius is more probably thinking of the gathering storm of civil war.

42. *Memmius's noble son.* C. Memmius, to whom the poem is addressed, was an aristocratic contemporary of Lucretius. He had taken some part in public life, and seen foreign service, but was better known as a prominent and somewhat dissolute figure in society, and a patron of letters. He was probably a professed Epicurean, whom Lucretius wished to arouse to a more real faith and a better understanding of Epicurus's doctrines.

66. *a man of Greece*: of course Epicurus, whom Lucretius only once mentions by name (III. 1042). See Introduction, pp. 10 ff.

73. *the fiery walls of the world.* Lucretius conceived of our world as a sphere, of which the outer coat was a circling stream of fiery ether (V. 457–70). The expression here is then to be taken quite literally.

84. *Even as at Aulis*, &c. : for the story of the sacrifice of Iphigeneia at Aulis in order to procure favourable winds for the fleet starting against Troy, see Euripides' play, from which Lucretius has borrowed several details, and even translated phrases in this passage.

the Virgin of the Cross-roads, i. e. Artemis.

95. *seized by men's hands*, &c. Iphigeneia was brought to Aulis on the understanding that she was to be married to Achilles. Lucretius, therefore, here carefully selects phrases which would remind a Roman reader of the ceremonials of marriage.

117. *our own Ennius.* C. Ennius (died 169 B.C.), the first great genius in Latin poetry, who introduced the hexameter, and laid the foundation of nearly all the later branches of Roman poetry. He believed in Pythagoras's theory of metempsychosis, and thought that he himself was possessed by the soul of Homer, whose appearance to him in a vision he described in one of his Saturae.

150. *nothing is ever begotten of nothing.* This first principle shows that the ultimate basis of the universe is a store of matter, to which no addition is ever made. Lucretius's 'proof' has been much criticized on the ground that he argues against 'spontaneous' creation by a denial of 'sporadic' creation. But to his mind they were really the same : if things came into being without a 'seed' or cause, the effect would be that they would appear to spring from alien sources, man from the sea, &c. As this does not occur, we may be sure that things are never created without a 'seed', i. e. are never uncaused additions to matter. Notice that his proof also establishes the law of cause and effect, which was his strongest weapon of attack on religion.

216. *nor does she destroy ought into nothing.* The second principle is complementary to the first. As matter never

receives any addition, so it never suffers any loss : the two together constitute the modern notion of the permanence of matter, and show its existence in the form of particles. Note again the proof : if nature could destroy anything, the whole universe would perish, because (as he explains more clearly in lines 556 ff.) the process of destruction is quicker than that of creation.

330. *there is void in things.* Having established the existence of matter in the form of particles, he proceeds to show that there must also be empty space. To Epicurus's argument that without it motion is impossible, he adds two others derived from the nature of compound things.

370. *which some vainly imagine,* i. e. the Stoics. When Lucretius alludes to opponents vaguely, without mentioning their names, he nearly always has in view his natural rivals, the Stoics (e. g. I. 465, 1053). They held that void did not exist, but that motion was due to the mutual interchange of places between things—a view not unlike that which is now held in conjunction with the conception of ether. Lucretius replies that such interchange of place necessarily implies empty space.

391. *But if by chance any one thinks.* The argument here is rather obscure : ' this comes to be ' is the filling up of the interval between the two bodies with air. Lucretius imagines a view of air as a kind of elastic fluid, which condenses, as the bodies meet, and then expands again when they separate. To it he objects that such condensation and expansion itself implies an admixture of empty space : a thing can only expand because there is more vacuum in it, or contract because there is less.

459. *Even so time exists not by itself* . . . Once more the argument is difficult. The Stoics, against whom Lucretius is, as usual, disputing, held that time was an existence in itself, and even went so far as to call it a ' body '. Lucretius replies that it is only a sensation that we get from things, an 'accident' of things, just as much as their colour or scent or sound, or wealth or poverty.

464. *Then again, when men say...* The Stoics had apparently raised a special difficulty with regard to Epicurus's theory of ' accidents ' in the case of events in the past : the Trojan War, they said, is something of which we are conscious now, but all the persons, of whom you say it was ' an accident ', are long since dead, and we are not conscious of them, much less could we be of their ' accidents '. Lucretius's reply is two-fold: he says first, in a rather frivolous spirit: ' Well, we can say that it is an "accident" of the place, or if you object that that too has changed, of that part of space.' Secondly, he replies seriously : ' of course it was an "accident" of the persons, for, if they had not existed, neither could the Trojan War and its events.'

551. *Again, if nature had ordained . . .* an argument which is more obscure than it looks at first sight. Let us suppose that the rate of destruction is twice as quick as that of creation, and that it takes, e. g. ten years for a horse to be conceived, born, and come to maturity, starting from particles the size of the Lucretian atom : it will then require five for him to grow old and die, and dissolve again into the particles. If at the end of the twentieth year, nature requires to make another horse, the Lucretian atom would, so to speak, be there ready, having lain dormant for five years. But if there is no limit to destruction, during those five years the process of destruc-tion will have been going on at an equal rate, and it will now require not ten but twenty years to put the particles together into a horse : and the next generation would require forty, and so on, creation never keeping pace with destruction. But, as it is, we see that there are fixed periods in which things can be created and come to maturity: there must then be a limit to destruction; in other words, there are ' atoms ' ($\check{a}$-$\tau o\mu o\iota$, indivisible things). (This explanation and illustration come from Giussani's edition of Lucretius.)

599. *since there are extreme points . . .* Another difficult proof of the complete solidity (and therefore indestructibility) of the atom. Lucretius is arguing, as Epicurus had taught

him to do, from the analogy of perceptible things. If we try, e. g. to fix our attention on the extreme point of a needle, we can see a point so small that, though it is perceptible itself, it is the minimum for sight : if we tried to see half of it, it would pass out of the range of vision altogether. The needle itself is composed of a countless number of such tiny points. In the same way then the atom is composed of a few minute parts, which can only exist as parts of the atom, and could not be separated from it ; they are the minimum of material existence, and can have no existence apart from the atom which they compose. The atom then has extension, but not separable parts : in other words, is perfectly solid.

638. *Heraclitus* of Ephesus (about 510 B. C.) held that the primary substance of which the world was created was fire, which gave rise to other things by a perpetual flux ; everything was either streaming upwards to form fuel for the fire, or downwards to the moisture which lay at the other end of the ' path '. Lucretius takes him as typical of the class of early philosophers who believed that the world was made of one element, and introduces ideas which were not actually in Heraclitus's theory : e. g. the notion of rarefaction and condensation really comes from Anaximenes, who believed air to be the primary material. Lucretius's argument holds well enough for any such theory ; if you select one element as the basis, then, if it changes into other things, it ceases to exist as itself ; or if it continues to exist, then other things do not.

716. *Empedocles* of Agrigentum (about 440 B. C.) is selected as the type of the philosophers who held that the world was composed of more than one element ; he himself believed that it was made of all four, earth, air, fire, and water, all eternal and indestructible, but capable by combination and separation of forming the perceptible world. Lucretius again embraces in his criticism two schools of thought, those who held that the elements retained their nature in combination (770 ff.), and those who held that they ' changed ' into other

things (763 ff.). But his general criticism is just: on the one hand, Empedocles is too much of a pluralist, for by his four, always heterogeneous, elements he destroys the fundamental unity of the world; on the other, he is not enough of a pluralist, for the four elements are not sufficient to account for the infinite variety of phenomena.

717. *that island*, i.e. Sicily.

733. *scarce born of human stock*. Empedocles, who practised magic, seems to have laid claim to divine powers.

830. *the homoeomeria of Anaxagoras* of Clazomenae (about 440 B. c.), who held a theory which was an advance on that of the earlier philosophers, whom Lucretius criticizes, and really paved the way for atomism, but Lucretius has not understood him. He held, in the first place, that things were composed of 'seeds', small particles like in substance to the whole. But, as Lucretius points out, this will not account for the phenomena of change, which it was, in fact, Anaxagoras's chief aim to explain. For this purpose he said indeed that 'there is a portion of everything in everything', but explained that these 'portions' were not merely extremely minute, but 'only perceptible by reason', i. e. we know that they are there, but never could see them. He came, in fact, near to the modern conception of chemical change, and the crude criticism of Lucretius from line 875 onwards is therefore beside the mark.

968. *Moreover, suppose now*, &c. This proof by imaginary experiment of the infinity of the universe is a famous one. It is used in much the same form by Locke, *Essay II.* 13.

1052. *Herein shrink far from believing*, &c. This theory, held again by the Stoics, that all things tend to the centre of the world, came, as will be seen, very near the truth, and was an approach to the modern idea of gravitation. Lucretius could not, of course, adopt it, as it was a direct contradiction of the fundamental Epicurean theory that the natural motion of things was always downwards (II. 184 ff.).

BOOK II

40. *the spaces of the Campus*, i. e. the Campus Martius, just outside the walls of Rome, on which military reviews were held, and sometimes an army would be encamped. Munro notes that in 58 B. C. Caesar had his army there for three months before starting for Gaul, and this occasion may well be in Lucretius's mind. Indeed, above, in lines 12 and 13, he seems to be thinking of the rivalry of Caesar and Pompey.

83. *For since they wander through the void*, &c. The account of the movement of the free atoms in the void is a little confused in this and the following passages. Lucretius really conceives of three causes of their movement : (1) the natural fall downwards due to their weight ; (2) the occasional slight swerve sideways (216 ff.) ; (3) the movement due to the collisions originally brought about by this swerve. Here, rather illogically, he only mentions (1) and (3), as he is reserving his account of (2) owing to its special importance.

124. *traces of a concept*. See note on line 744.

127. *such jostlings hint*, &c. A very important passage for Lucretius's theory of motion. All atoms are always moving at the full atomic speed (142 ff.), even in compound bodies, inside which, as they collide with one another, they accomplish tiny trajectories, each moving in the direction which the last blow gave it, until it collides with another atom, and is started in a new direction. This internal vibration in all directions will of course retard the motion of the whole, and we must imagine the atoms forming tiny molecules, and then slightly larger bodies, with ever lessening motion, until, when the bodies are large enough for us to perceive, such as the motes in the sunbeam, the motion is also sufficiently retarded to be visible to us. All this, though not clearly stated, is implied in these few lines.

153. *Nor again do the several particles*, &c. Here the idea of internal vibration and consequent retardation comes out

very clearly ; even the sun's light is so impeded, as well as by the opposition of the air, through which it passes.

185. *no bodily thing can of its own force,* &c.   This is again an important point : upward motion is always the result of external force.   Even among the atoms it can only happen as the result of collisions, when e. g. one atom is squeezed between two others and thus shot up.

219. *push a little from their path.*   The notion of the slight swerve of the atoms and its tremendous result in the free will of man is a supremely important point in the Epicurean philosophy, for it combats Democritus's belief in complete determinism, which Epicurus regarded as a more dangerous enemy to morality than even religion.   See Introduction, p. 17.

225. *But if perchance any one believes.*   This paragraph contains one of Lucretius's most acute pieces of reasoning, that in a vacuum all things fall at the same pace.

269. *so that you see a start of movement,* &c.   The relation between the swerve of the atoms and man's free-will is, of course, to Lucretius's mind not a mere analogy : the former is the cause of the latter.   The mind is composed of a subtle texture of fine atoms (III. 161 ff.), and it is the swerving of these atoms which gives rise to an act of will.

410. *the harsh shuddering sound,* &c.   Sound, in Lucretius's notion, is caused, just like sight or smell, by a body of particles given off by the object, and penetrating the ear (IV. 523 ff.).

485. *For suppose the first bodies,* &c.   For this idea of the inseparable ' least parts ' in the atom see I. 599 ff.

532. *For because you see,* &c.   Here we meet a curious principle of Epicurus, which Lucretius nowhere states, but often acts on, of the ' equal distribution ' (ἰσονομία) of things.   If a certain class is rare in some parts of the world, or even in our world altogether, it will be found in plenty in other parts of the world or the universe : there is, on the whole, an equal number of things of the same kind.   Compare 569 ff. for a similar idea.

598. *the Great Mother of the gods.* This was the title of the earth-goddess, Cybele, whose worship had been brought to Rome from Phrygia in 204 B.C. Lucretius in the next paragraph explains the ceremonial of the cult allegorically.

629. *Then comes an armed band,* &c. There was always in antiquity some confusion between the worship of Cybele in Phrygia and that of the Mother in Crete, which was heightened by the fact that in each place the scene of the worship was on Mount Ida. Modern investigation seems to show that the Phrygian worship was actually derived from the Cretan.

701. *for you would see monsters,* &c. Lucretius returns to this idea of the impossibility of the formation of monsters with parts derived from different races of animals, and supports it with rather different arguments in V. 878 ff.

740. *that the mind cannot project itself into these bodies.* A reference to a rather obscure idea in the psychology of Epicurus. The mind being an aggregation of soul-atoms, its thoughts are caused when these atoms are stirred by images coming from things outside or from its own stores (IV. 722 ff.). But the mind has a power of spontaneously 'projecting itself upon' the images (ἐπιβολὴ τῆς διανοίας), which results in attention, observation, selection, &c., or sometimes, when it so combines more than one image in its grasp, in the creation of a new conception. Here Lucretius imagines his reader as doubting whether it was possible for the mind by such an act of 'projection' to grasp the idea, i. e. to 'visualize', colourless atoms. He replies by the analogy of the blind, suggesting that we must think of the atoms as something which could be touched but not seen. Compare lines 1047 and 1080 of this book.

744. *may become a clear concept.* Another technical notion of Epicurus. The mind had ready in itself general notions or concepts of classes of things, to which it could refer, when any new instance of the class occurred; thus, we know, e. g. that 'this is a horse', because we have the general idea of 'horse' to which to refer (for this reason Epicurus gave the concepts the rather curious name of προλήψεις, 'anticipations').

These general concepts were formed, in the case of perceptible objects, by the storing up in the mind of a series of single impressions, which formed a sort of 'composite photograph'. But in the case of imperceptible things, such as the atoms, he probably conceived of their being formed by a combination of existing concepts by a 'projection of the mind'. So here, by combining the concept of an atom with that of touch without sight, we get the 'clear concept' of a colourless atom. Easier cases of the application of the idea of 'concepts' will be found in II. 124, IV. 476, V. 124, 182, 1047.

865. *It must needs be*, &c.   This proof, that things which themselves have sensation, are yet created of atoms that have not, is of course of immense importance for the next Book, in which Lucretius is going to prove that the soul is mortal.

902. *Next, those who think*, &c., a difficult and very tersely expressed argument.   If there are sensible atoms, they must be like in substance to such sensible things as we know, veins, sinews, &c.   If so, they are soft, and therefore not mortal, which is the very reverse of what Lucretius's imaginary opponents would wish to prove.

908. *still doubtless they must either have*, &c.   Again the argument is put very briefly and obscurely.   He appeals once more to our experience.   We only know two kinds of sensation, (1) the sensation of a complete sentient being, as when 'I feel well' or 'happy', (2) the sensation of a part of such a being, as when 'my tooth aches'.   If then the atoms, which compose sentient beings, have themselves sensation, it must be of one of these two kinds.   But firstly, parts only have sensation as parts of a sentient whole: my tooth only feels as a part of me, and would not feel if it were taken out. In this case the individual atoms, apart from the whole compound, would have no sensation.   Secondly, they may be each of them complete sentient beings; but then (*a*) like other sentient beings they must be mortal (see note on 902), (*b*) they could not by coming together produce one sentient being,

but only a jumble of independent sentient beings, unless (*c*) in uniting they lose their own sense and combine to form the new sense of the compound being; in this case why attribute sense to them as individuals?

931. *But if by chance any one shall say,* &c. A slightly different position to that just dealt with. It may be admitted that the atoms are not sentient when separate, but they become sentient in the compound. No, replies Lucretius; by their union they form a sentient body, but the individual atoms always remain insentient.

975. *whereof the race of men has its peculiar increment,* i. e. the sensible atoms, which, according to the theory Lucretius is opposing, man has in addition to the non-sensible atoms which compose his body. This argument is of course not to be taken quite seriously: Lucretius is fond of finishing a series of serious proofs with a *reductio ad absurdum.* Compare III. 367, 776, and especially I. 918.

1011. *what we see floating on the surface of things* is the 'secondary qualities', and especially colour, as he has explained at great length: what we see *at times coming to birth and . . . passing away* is similarly sensation. This paragraph is a summing up of all he has said from line 730 onwards.

1047. *the unfettered projection of our mind*: see note on line 740. This is clearly a case where the mind, by its own free effort, puts concepts together to form a new conclusion.

1077. *in the universe there is nothing single*: for this argument see note on line 532.

1154. *For it was no golden rope,* &c. A reference to the famous passage in Homer, *Iliad,* 8. 19, where Zeus challenges the other gods to attach a golden rope to him and pull him down from heaven to earth. The Stoics had apparently interpreted the passage allegorically as referring to the creation of life on earth.

BOOK III

19. *which neither the winds shake*, &c.   Again an allusion to a famous passage in Homer, *Od.* VI. 42 ff., which has passed on into English in Tennyson's *Morte d'Arthur*.

43. *that the soul's nature is of blood, or else of wind.*   The theory that the soul was made of blood was that of Empedocles, of wind that of Critias.

94. *First I say that the mind* . . .   All through this book we must distinguish carefully, as Lucretius does, between the mind (*animus*), which is an aggregate of pure 'soul-atoms' situated in the breast, and is the seat of thought and volition, and the soul or vital principle (*anima*), which is made of similar atoms, but scattered throughout the body and mixed with the body atoms, and is the cause of sensation in the body. Sometimes, however, when he is making statements which apply to both, he uses one or other of the terms in an inclusive sense.

100. *which the Greeks call a harmony.*   Lucretius is thinking particularly of Aristoxenus, a pupil of Aristotle, who was a great theoretical musician, and applied his musical theory to the explanation of the human soul.

241. *some fourth nature.*   This idea of the mysterious fourth nature, which is infinitely subtle, and is the ultimate cause of sensation and thought, has often been claimed as a practical admission by Lucretius of something supra-material or spiritual in the mind.   But of course he conceives it as purely corporeal, just like any of the other component elements.

262. *with the motions of first-beginnings.*   See II. 127 and the note on that passage; the idea of the internal vibrations of the atoms there illustrated is what Lucretius has in his mind here.

323. *This nature then of the soul*, &c.   This notion of the very intimate union of soul and body, so that while the body protects the soul, the soul in return lends the body sensation

is not very clearly expressed, but is of course of great importance for the subsequent discussion; neither soul nor body can continue to exist without the presence and help of the other.

367. *if our eyes are as doors*, &c.   Another example of the *reductio ad absurdum* as the conclusion of a serious argument.

371. *Democritus* of Abdera (about 430 B.C.), was, with Leucippus, the earliest exponent of the atomic theory.   He is always regarded with great respect by Lucretius, who carefully notes this point, on which Epicurus differed from him (compare V. 621).   See Introduction, p. 12.

417. *the minds and the light souls* . . .   This is, of course, the main purpose of the book, to prove that the soul is mortal, and that therefore there is no reason to fear its punishment after death.   There follows a rather bewildering series of twenty-eight proofs, which are not well classified or arranged by Lucretius, but we can distinguish three main lines of argument: (1) proofs from the previously described structure of soul and body ; (2) proofs from death, disease, and cure, showing the close parallelism between soul and body ; (3) arguments from the absurdity of the conception of the soul existing alone apart from body.

421. *Be it yours*, &c.: a warning that in this section he means to speak comprehensively of the mind and the soul, and that what is said of the one is applicable to the other. See note on line 94.

430. *by images of smoke and cloud.*   A reference to the theory of ' images ', or ' idols ', as the cause of vision and thought which is expounded in Book IV.

548. *And since the mind is one part of man.*   The mind, whose peculiar sensation, thought, is aroused, just like all other sensations, by touch, is here treated as practically another organ of sense.

597. *the heart has had a shock, or the heart has failed*: these are meant to be phrases of quite common parlance, and to translate them we must, I think, use ' the heart ', though

Lucretius uses his ordinary words for 'mind' and 'soul'. Seeing that he placed the mind in the breast, the change is not so far wrong.

627. *Nor in any other way can we picture to ourselves*, &c.: notice that the test of truth is the possibility of 'visualization', as it must be for the Epicurean, to whom it was the only mode of thought.

679. *Moreover, if when our body*, &c. The argument of this paragraph is not so clear as it might be ; it is really a dilemma. If an already formed soul enters our body at the moment of birth, (*a*) if it keeps its independent existence, it could never become so closely linked and connected with our body, as we see it is ; (*b*) (line 698) if it is dispersed among the limbs, it does not maintain its existence, it perishes, and the soul in the body is a different soul to that which existed before.

741. *Again, why does fiery passion*, &c. An interesting argument in support of heredity as against the notion of the transmigration of souls.

772. *Or why does it desire*, &c. In this and the next paragraph we notice again the *reductio ad absurdum* towards the conclusion ; it has already obtruded itself in lines 725 ff.

784. *Again, a tree cannot exist in the sky*, &c. A new line of argument, that everything in nature has its fixed place, and that of the soul is in the body. Lucretius applies the same argument again in almost the same words in V. 128 ff.

806. *Moreover, if ever things abide for everlasting*, &c. Another general principle, that there are certain fixed conditions for immortality, none of which the soul fulfils. Again Lucretius repeats the argument in Book V. 351 ff. to prove that our world is not immortal.

830. *Death, then, is naught to us*, &c. From here to the end of the book follows a kind of triumph-song over the mortality of the soul. 'We need not fear death, for after it there is no part of us surviving to feel anything.' It is really the climax of the poem.

876. *he does not, I trow, grant*, &c. : perhaps a little obscure.

Such a man professes to grant that his soul does not survive his death on the grounds which Lucretius has just been discussing. But he does not in practice admit either the one or the other, as he half-consciously assumes that some part of him will survive to feel what happens to his body.

891. *and to grow stiff with cold* : this is not an alternative mode of burial, but goes closely with what has just preceded. After embalming, the Romans often left the corpse lying on a rock slab in the vault, or on the bier on which it was brought.

936. *as though heaped in a vessel full of holes.* Lucretius is thinking of the legend of the Danaids, to which he specially refers in lines 1008 ff.

971. *to none for freehold, to all on lease.* Lucretius is here using two technical terms of Roman law : *mancipium* was a full legal process of acquiring a possession, which gave the owner the most complete title to it, *usus*, the mere right of possession by custom, or ' usufruct '. It seems best to accept parallel expressions in English, rather than to introduce their exact equivalents, which would have a very prosy effect, into the text.

1025. *Ancus the good.* Of course Ancus Martius, the legendary fourth king of Rome. Lucretius takes this line from the Annals of Ennius.

1029. *be himself, who once* . . . Xerxes.

BOOK IV

1. *I traverse the distant haunts*, &c. These verses are repeated with a few slight changes, from I. 921 ff.

34. *idols* : it seems best to translate Lucretius's word *simulacra* in this way, as it is itself a translation of Epicurus's word εἴδωλον. The famous theory of vision is clearly explained here by Lucretius himself.

67. *above all, since on the surface of things*, &c. : a passage with more meaning than is at first apparent. When in the

compound body all the atoms are moving at great speed in
their tiny trajectories (see note on II. 527), it is obvious that
those in the inner part are well hemmed in. But those on
the surface have none outside to beat them back, and so are
much more liable to break away from the object; it is these
then that form the films, which produce vision.

193. *first, because it is a tiny cause,* &c. This is a very
esoteric piece of Epicurean physics. We saw (see note on
II. 127) that the speed of the unimpeded atom was much
greater than that of any compound of atoms, however small,
as the latter is checked by internal vibration. For the same
reason the impact of the unimpeded atom is greatest, and it
can therefore impart greater speed to any object which it hits.
The films are sent on their way by the blows of other single
atoms inside the compound, and the 'tiny cause' is therefore
able to impart great speed to them.

199. *Moreover, when particles of things,* &c. Another rather
abstruse piece of theory. Particles coming from deep within
things are obstructed and jostled by the atoms, through which
they have to make their way, and therefore have their speed
diminished. But those which start from the surface, start,
so to speak, without this initial handicap, and therefore attain
a much greater rate of motion.

241. *But because we can see them only* . . . A very confused
statement. Lucretius seems to be combining two points that
he wished to state: (1) that these images are constantly
hitting us in all parts of our body, but we can only see them
with our eyes; (2) as the images are constantly streaming off
bodies on all sides, wherever we turn our eyes, we see them.

246. *For when it is given off,* &c. Not a very satisfactory
account. For (*a*) how can our eyes measure the length of
this 'draught' from objects which passes through them;
(*b*) even if they could, how can they know at what moment
the 'draught' from any particular object, which they are
going to see, begins?

256. *Herein by no means must we deem,* &c. An important

point. We do not see the individual 'idols' of things, but their constant succession gives us a 'cinematographic' impression of the whole object.

311. *flank-curved mirrors*: probably a special name for concave horizontal mirrors.

315. *or else because the image, &c.* : a very ingenious but not very clear explanation. The idea is that with a flat mirror the whole surface of the image meets the mirror at once and is returned as it is, but with the curved mirror one corner of the image would touch it before the rest, and the result would be that the image would be given a twist and turned round so that it reached us again 'right-handed'.

322. *inasmuch as nature, &c.* : as we say in modern scientific language, the angle of reflection is equal to the angle of incidence. These two lines ought possibly to be placed, as Giussani suggests, after line 307, where they would be more immediately in place. Here they give a general principle, which is the real cause of all the last four phenomena.

353. *And when we see from afar off, &c.* The problem of the square tower, which seems round at a distance, was one of the traditional difficulties of the Epicurean school. This explanation, however, tends to destroy our trust in the 'idols' as true evidence of things, and it is doubtful whether it was Epicurus's own.

387. *The ship, in which we journey, &c.* There follows an interesting list of 'optical illusions', in all of which Lucretius holds that the mistake lies not in the sense-perception, but in the inferences made by the mind.

469. *Again, if any one thinks, &c.* This protest against scepticism and vindication of the veracity of the senses is the keystone of the whole Epicurean philosophy: every other part of it really depends on this.

476. *the concept of the true and the false.* The concept, as we have seen (see note on II. 744), must be produced by a series of individual experiences. If a man has never perceived any-

thing true with the senses, how can he have the concept of truth ?

483. *Will reason, sprung from false sensation, &c.* Reason is based on the senses, for its function is to distinguish and correlate the impressions given by the senses. If then the senses are false, much more must reason be : it cannot act as a criterion of the truth of sense-perceptions. The same idea is found in a famous passage of Democritus, quoted in the Introduction, p. 13.

493. *all that goes along with colour* is form in its various aspects of surface-outline, bulk, size, &c.

524. *First of all, every kind of sound, &c.* Sound is in Lucretius's idea a corporeal emission, much like the ' idols ' of vision, which strikes upon the ear.

615. *Nor do the tongue and palate, &c.* The case of taste is easy, because it can be accounted for directly by touch, and it is not necessary to assume the intervention of emissions.

673. *Come now, I will tell, &c.* In the case of smell Lucretius has again to assume the effluence or emission to act as a link between the nose and the object.

694. *Firstly, because coming from deep within, &c.* Compare the argument in lines 199 ff., and the note there.

710. *Nay, indeed, ravening lions, &c.* This curious fact is vouched for by Pliny and Plutarch.

722. *Come now, let me tell you, &c.* The mind being an aggregation of corporeal atoms, just like eye or ear, thought must be produced just like sight or hearing, by the stirring of the atoms of the mind by ' idols '.

777. *And in these matters, &c.* Another obscurely expressed passage. The main idea is simple, if we bear in mind always the Lucretian conception of thought as ' visualization '. The mind can think of whatever it will, because there are at all times present to it ' idols ' of every sort, and it can turn its attention to any one of these it likes by a ' projection ' (see note on II. 740).

823. *Herein you must eagerly, &c.* An argument against

the teleological view of nature, which Lucretius of course dislikes because it might seem to support the theological idea that the gods made the world with a purpose. The eye, says Lucretius, was not made in order that we might see, but because it has been created we do see.

860. *For verily I have shown*, &c. Compare especially II. 1128 ff.

883. *Then comes the will*, &c. : this passage should be read in connexion with the theory of free-will, and its origin in the slight swerving of the atoms in II. 216 ff.

897. *that the body, like a ship, is borne on by sails and wind.* This is almost certainly the sense of this corrupt line, but the parallel does not work out very well. The sails should correspond to the act of will in the body, the wind to the external force, the air entering the pores. But the sails are of no use without the wind. It is possible, as has been suggested, that the 'two things' are the entering air and the parts of the body which it reaches. This would make the parallel more satisfactory, but does not seem likely to be what Lucretius meant, as the distinction would not be important enough.

916. *First of all sleep comes to pass.* Notice again the purely material explanation. Sleep is the absence of sensation, which is due to the soul. It must be then that the soul-atoms in sleep are either scattered about in the body, or driven out of it, or retreat far within below the surface. Even more strictly physical is the account in the next paragraph of how this comes to be.

1063. *it is best to flee those images*, &c. The attack on love was part of the traditional philosophy of Epicurus, who thought it destructive to a man's peace of mind to be too dependent on others, but we cannot help remembering all through this passage the story that Lucretius himself was maddened by a love-philtre, and ultimately driven to commit suicide.

BOOK V

22. *of Hercules* : Lucretius deals at such special length with Hercules because he was adopted as their particular hero by the Stoics.

117. *the giants*, who attempted to assail heaven by piling Pelion on Ossa, and were punished by imprisonment beneath the earth, Enceladus being shut beneath Etna.

155. *all which I will hereafter prove to you* : but he never does. It has been thought, with much probability, that Lucretius's intention was to close the whole poem, after the description of the plague of Athens, with a discussion and picture of the nature and life of the gods, clinching the whole argument of the poem with the proof that they could take no part in the government of the world. He does indeed return to the question of the origin of religion in this book (lines 1161 ff.), but that passage cannot be what he refers to here.

182. *the concept of man*. This is a very good instance of the technical idea of the 'anticipation' (see note on II. 744). If the gods had not in their minds a 'concept' of man, resulting from previous sense-perceptions, how could they have set about to make a man ? One is tempted to reply 'after their own image'.

195. *But even if I knew not*, &c. Lucretius's rather crude contribution to the problem of the existence of evil.

235. *First of all*, &c. : the poet now returns, after the long digression about the gods and the theory of the divine creation of the world, to the point which he left at line 110, that the world had a birth and will be destroyed.

281. *Likewise that bounteous source*, &c. A rather subtle notion : that what appears to us as a continuous stream of light from the sun, or even from torches, &c., on earth, is really a constant succession of small particles of light, the foremost ever perishing, and their place being taken by fresh particles from behind.

320. *as some tell*: of course the Stoics as usual. This passage is interesting, as it is an adaptation by Lucretius of verses in which the tragic poet Pacuvius had expressed the Stoic doctrine.

351. *Moreover, if ever things abide*, &c. Compare III. 806 ff. and the note on that passage.

411. *Moisture likewise*, &c. The story of the flood of Deucalion and Pyrrha was of course familiar in antiquity. Compare e. g. Horace, *Odes* i. 2. 5 ff.

443. *From this mass*, &c. This idea of an original chaos, out of which a world was formed by the union of the like and the separation of the unlike, was, in its main outlines, traditional among the Greek physical philosophers, but Epicurus explained how it might be brought about without the gratuitous assumption of an unaccountable ' whirl' or an arbitrary ' necessity ', such as previous thinkers had assumed.

510. *if the great globe of the sky turns round*, &c. The ideas of Lucretius's astronomy are often curious and complicated,

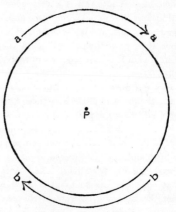

Fig. 1.

but we must always bear in mind that he conceives the world as a sphere, in the centre of the interior of which is suspended the earth; moon, sun, and stars move round it in orbits at ever-increasing distance, and above them, forming the 'walls of the world', comes the ether. The axis of the world he conceived to be inclined. In this passage he first considers the theory that the world as a whole moves round; we must then conceive it as held firm at each end of its axis by the pressure of air at each of the poles (P), and then caused to rotate by a current either flowing above (a, a) in the direction in which the heavenly bodies are seen to move, or below (b, b) in the opposite direction, as a water-mill is moved by the stream flowing beneath it. He then considers other ideas which may be advanced on the supposition that the world does not move round as a whole. He puts them forward as all worthy of consideration on Epicurus's principle, that where our senses do not give us direct information, we ought to consider as possible all explanations which do not conflict with the evidence of the senses.

535. *it is natural that its mass should*, &c. A very curious idea: that the earth on the underside gradually 'thins out' and so forms a light 'second nature' beneath it, which makes a link to connect it with the air beneath it, and so acts as a kind of 'spring-mattress', by which it is continually supported, and does not press heavily on the air.

564. *Nor can the sun's blazing wheel*, &c. This paragraph illustrates a principle of Epicurus complementary to that found in 510 ff.: that, where the senses do give us evidence, we must trust it absolutely. Our sight tells us that sun and moon are of a certain size: they must, then, be of that size. He supports the theory with the curious statements that even on earth fires and lights do not appear to diminish in bulk, so long as they send out light and heat, nor so long as their outline is clear and not blurred.

592. *This, too, is not wonderful*, &c. In this paragraph again, as in many others that follow, we see the principle that all explanations, not contradicted by the senses, are to be considered as possible.

596. *For it may be that from this spot*, &c. : the idea is that the sun is an opening, or breach in the 'walls of the world', through which myriads of particles of light from outside the world stream into it.

614. *Nor is there any single account of the sun*, &c. An obscure section, because Lucretius is guilty of confusion. The apparent path of the sun in the heavens has two notable

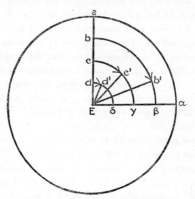

Fig. 2.

features : (1) he appears to make a complete circuit of the heavens in the year, from west to east, just as the moon does in a month, and the planets in longer periods than the sun ; (2) this circuit is not in the same plane as the equator : wherefore it seems that the sun goes up and down as well as round. Of the two explanations given by Lucretius, the first (621–36) would explain the former phenomenon, the second (637–45) the latter, but Lucretius has unfortunately represented them not as concurrent explanations of a complex phenomenon, but as alternative explanations of the whole.

(1) Democritus's theory of the relative orbits of sun, moon, and planets may be explained by the accompanying diagram (Fig. 2). Suppose that in a given time the stars have actually

moved on the outer rim of the world from *a* to *a* : the planets moving more slowly, as they are nearer the earth and thus less influenced by the 'whirl' of the heavens, will in the same time have moved from *b* to *b*¹, the sun from *c* to *c*¹, and the moon, slower still, from *d* to *d*¹. But with reference to the stars, which seem fixed, the planets seem to have moved from β to *b*¹, the sun from γ to *c*¹, and the moon from δ to *d*¹.

(2) But this orbit being set in a different plane to that of

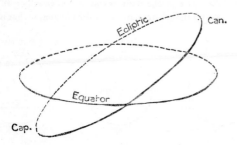

Fɪɢ. 3.

the equator, the effect is of the sun passing down towards the south in the autumn until in winter he reaches the tropic, or turning-point of Capricorn, and northwards in the spring until in summer he reaches the tropic of Cancer. This, it is suggested (637–49), was brought about by winds blowing 'athwart his course'.

643. *those stars which roll through* . . . i. e. the planets.

651. *either when after his long journey*, &c. : this theory, that the sun was extinguished each night, and a new sun lit in the morning, was that of Heraclitus : the other is the normal idea of ancient astronomy.

656. *Likewise at a fixed time*, &c. The two following theories of the dawn correspond exactly to the two immediately preceding theories of the sun's light ; if he completes a circle under the earth, dawn is the advance light of his return ; if

a new sun is created each day, dawn is caused by the light
gathering to form the sun.

Matuta was an ancient Roman deity of the dawn.

682. *either because the same sun*, &c. Another difficult
section, though its general meaning is comparatively clear.
The sun performs apparently both an annual orbit round the
heavens, with which Lucretius has already dealt (614–49),
and also a daily revolution. At most times of the year he
divides the circle of the daily revolution unequally: in the
winter he is for the greater part below the horizon, so that night

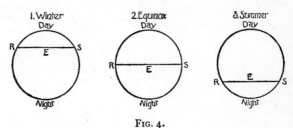

FIG. 4.

is longer Fig. 4 (1); in the summer he is for the greater part
above the horizon, so that day is longer (3); but at the
equinoxes he divides his circle exactly into semi-circles, so
that day and night are equal (2). This occurs twice in
the year, at the equinoxes or 'nodes', the points at which the
sun's orbit cuts the equator (Fig. 5). The exact interpretation
of lines 689–93 has been very much disputed, especially with
regard to the precise meaning of the 'turning-points': are
they a point in the annual orbit or in the daily revolution?
I take the whole passage to depend on what Lucretius has
already said about the annual orbit in lines 614–49: 'the
blast of the north wind and of the south' refers to the theory
that the sun was blown out of his natural course to the tropics:
the 'turning-points' are, just as they were in line 617, the
tropics. The passage means then, that mid-way in the sun's
course from north to south and south to north the sun holds

his ' turning-points' at equal distances apart; i. e. he is on the
equator. The effect of this, Lucretius implies but does not
state, is that day is then exactly equal to night, for when the
sun is on the equator he rises due east and sets due west—in
other words, his daily revolution is exactly along the line of

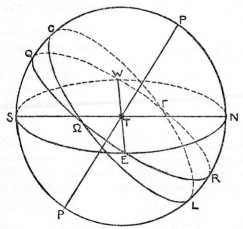

FIG. 5. T=the Earth ; PP=the Poles ; N E S W=the Horizon;
E Q W R=the Equator; Ω C Γ L=the Eliptic ; Ω Γ=the Equinoxes
or Nodes.

the equator, and is therefore performed, as may be seen from
the figure, exactly half above and half below the horizon.

(A fuller description and explanation of Lucretius's idea of
the ' heavenly globe ' may be found in the introduction to Mr.
J. D. Duff's edition of Book v, to which I am much indebted.)

696. *Or else, because*, &c. : this second explanation still rests
on the assumption of ' the same sun ' performing a daily journey
under the earth, whereas the third (line 701) depends on the
Heraclitean notion of a new sun being kindled every day
(compare lines 651 ff. and 660 ff.).

705. *The moon may shine*, &c. Similarly in this paragraph

the first three explanations regard the moon as passing below the earth and re-appearing, the fourth (line 731 ff.) assumes the creation of a new moon every day. Lines 729–730 are a very emphatic expression of the principle that we must accept all explanations equally, if they do not contradict phenomena.

727. *the Babylonian teaching of the Chaldaeans*, especially the theory of Berosus.

737. *Spring goes on her way and Venus*, &c. This description is probably based on some pantomimic representation of the Seasons, or on a picture. Modern readers naturally think of Botticelli's ' Primavera ', and indeed it is not at all unlikely that that picture was actually founded on this passage, as his ' Mars and Venus ' almost certainly was on a passage of Politian in the *Giostra*, which was based on Lucretius's description in Book I. 31–40.

751. *Likewise also the eclipses of the sun*, &c. None of these explanations present any difficulty with the exception of the first theory of the eclipse of the moon (762–4). This is, of course, the correct explanation : the earth, obstructing

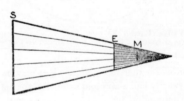

FIG. 6.

the rays of the sun, forms a shadow in the shape of a cone, and when the moon passes into it, it is eclipsed (Fig. 6). But it is, of course, quite inconsistent with the Epicurean theory that the sun and moon are the size we see them, i. e. both very greatly smaller than the earth, for in that case the shadow thrown will not take the form of a cone at all, and the eclipses of the moon would be of much more frequent occurrence and longer duration than they are (Fig. 7). This is the most important of several indications that Lucretius did not really

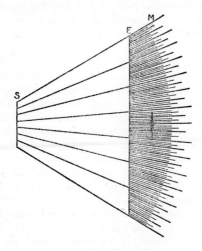

Fig. **7.**

understand his astronomy, and took much of it from the ordinary astronomical hand-books, without considering carefully how far it could be reconciled with Epicurean principles.

808. *there grew up wombs* : a curiously naïve device, by which Lucretius tries to account for the transition from vegetable to animal life. He seems to be a little conscious of its improbability, and is careful just afterwards (813) to supply an analogy for this apparently gratuitous act of kindness on the part of the earth.

837. *And many monsters too earth*, &c. In this idea of the early experiments of nature we get a glimmering of the modern notions of Evolution and Natural Selection, which become more prominent in the next paragraph. It is one of

Lucretius's most remarkable anticipations of modern scientific belief.

878. *But neither were there Centaurs*, &c. The impossibility of the formation of monsters of this sort, combined of parts belonging to different races of animals, has been dealt with already in II. 700 ff.

925. *But the race of man*, &c. Lucretius's study of primitive man, again, has always been admired for its insight, and is all the more remarkable when one remembers the strong prevalence in antiquity of the notion of a Golden Age.

1020. *not to hurt or be harmed.* Here we have the germs of the theory of the Social Compact as the origin of Society.

1028. *But the diverse sounds of the tongue*, &c. There was always a controversy in antiquity as to whether language was made by convention (θέσει) or grew up naturally (φύσει). Lucretius, consistently with the attitude taken up all through this book, decides for the latter view.

1047. *the concept of their use.* See note on II. 744.

1169. *For indeed already the races of mortals*, &c. It is a matter of great difficulty to decide exactly how Epicurus and Lucretius conceived the immortal nature of the gods, and the evidence is very insufficient. But it is certain that they supposed them to dwell in the 'interspaces between the worlds' (*intermundia*), and to become known to men by a constant succession of 'idols', which streamed off their bodies, preserving the 'form unchanged', and, being too subtle to be perceived by the senses, passed through the pores of the body into the mind, and there stirred the soul-atoms.

1198. *with veiled head turning towards a stone*, &c. Lucretius is here carefully recalling the ceremonial of Roman worship. The Roman always veiled his head (as opposed to the Greek), approached with the image of the god on his right hand, and in this position made his prayer. He then turned towards the image and prostrated himself on the ground.

1234. *the glorious rods and relentless axes*, the insignia of the Roman magistrates.

1294. *the form of the bronze sickle, &c.*   Lucretius is probably thinking of its use for purposes of magic.

1302. *the Lucanian kine*, i. e. elephants, which were said
to have been so called because they were first seen by the
Romans in Lucania in the army of Pyrrhus.

1344. *And you could more readily maintain, &c.*   For this
curious argument that if this practice did not obtain on our
earth, it probably did somewhere in the universe, compare
what Lucretius says in 526 ff. about the motions of the stars.

BOOK VI

20. *in part because he saw that it was leaking, &c.* : for this
description of the human mind compare the explanation of
the legend of the Danaids in III. 1003 ff.

31. *be it by the chance or the force of nature.*   One of the few
places where Lucretius in so many words implies that nature
does act by chance, as well as by law.   That there is the
element of chance is probably due to the original swerving of
the atoms ; see Introduction, p. 18.

71. *not that the high majesty of the gods, &c.*   A particularly
interesting passage for the Epicurean conception of the
relation of man and the gods.   The superstitious beliefs of
the old religion are an offence against the majesty of the gods,
living their placid life untroubled by the world.   Yet they will
not lead to direct punishment at the hands of the gods, for that
is impossible.   But they will prevent those who hold them
from approaching the gods with the proper tranquillity of
spirit, and so deriving the greatest benefit from their worship.
The passage shows clearly that the gods were to men a perfect
example of the ideal life, and that their worship should be one
of contemplation ; it also explains how, when, as we are told,
Epicurus himself and his immediate followers scrupulously
attended the ceremonies of religious worship, they may have
done so without inconsistency.

165. *because things always move more slowly, &c.* : another

notable piece of Epicurean observation, that light travels more quickly than sound.

340. *Once again, because it comes with long-lasting impulse, &c.* This conception of the thunderbolt gathering speed as it goes, and the accompanying explanation, are based on the fundamental Epicurean notions of the movement of bodies (see note on II. 127.) In any compound body, even of so rare a texture as the thunderbolt, there is, of course, internal vibration, and though the whole body is moving in one direction the atoms which compose it will be moving in all directions and colliding with one another, and so retarding it. But there is always a tendency that the sideways and upward movement of the atoms resulting from blows should in time yield to their own natural tendency to fall owing to weight. In the case of a falling body this means that more and more atoms are always coming to move in the direction of the whole, and that therefore the speed of the whole body tends continually to increase. Lucretius has not expressed this very clearly, but considering the passage in the light of the general theory of motion, this must be its meaning.

364. *the narrow channel* is not to be thought of as something which separates lands, but rather as something which connects seas and mixes their waters (e.g. the Straits of the Bosphorus). So here, spring and autumn join the cold of winter with the warmth of summer.

381. *the Tyrrhenian prophecies* : it was generally supposed that the Romans obtained their system of auguries and omens from the Etruscans.

387. *But if Jupiter, &c.* Lucretius, in concluding this long section on the phenomena of thunder and lightning, comes back to his main purpose of attacking the traditional religion and its superstitious beliefs.

424. *presters*, i. e. fiery whirlwinds ($\pi \acute{\iota} \mu \pi \rho \eta \mu \iota$).

542. *clear fact demands, &c.* It is not obvious at first sight why this should be so. It may be that here we have another, and rather arbitrary, application of the curious principle of

equilibrium (ἰσονομία). Compare II. 532 and the note there. But more probably he is thinking of his description in V. 492 ff. of the formation of the irregular surface of the upper earth, and argues on grounds of general probability that the same sort of process had taken place on the lower side.

660. *the holy fire* was the name given in antiquity to erysipelas; compare Virgil, *Georg.* iii. 566.

685. *For air becomes wind, when,* &c. This is not such a puerile comment as it looks at first sight, for to Lucretius ' air ' and ' wind ' were two distinct, though kindred, substances. (Compare the account of the composition of the soul, III. 231 ff.) The air, then, by being ' set in motion ', would lose some of its own characteristic atoms, and acquire others, which would convert it into wind.

740. *the name Avernian. Avernus* in its Greek form Ἄορνος means ' Birdless '.

754. *because of their vigil.* The story (told by Ovid, *Metam.* II. 542–565) was that the daughters of Cecrops, against the orders of Pallas, opened the chest containing the infant Erichthonius. The crow, who was on the watch, flew off and told Pallas, but she, in furious anger at what had been done, banished him for ever from the Acropolis.

810. *Scaptensula*: the Latin name for the famous mines of Σκαπτὴ Ὕλη in Thrace.

848. *the shrine of Ammon*: of course of Jupiter Ammon in the Libyan desert. As Giussani remarks, the possession of a thermometer in antiquity would have made considerable difference to these observations.

890. *at Aradus*: an island off the coast of Phoenicia, whose fresh-water spring was famous. The point of the comparison is of course simply that the seeds of fire well up through the water, just as the fresh water does through the salt at Aradus.

937. *in the beginning of my poem too*: he is thinking primarily, no doubt, of I. 329, &c., where he showed that ' there is void in things ', but also of II. 95 ff., where he explained in what manner this occurred.

954. *Again, where the breastplate of the sky,* &c. This passage has been much discussed and very variously corrected and explained, but Giussani's view seems much the most probable. As a crowning instance of the porosity of things, the poet takes the world itself : though it is surrounded with a breastplate (compare 'the walls of the world', I. 73, &c.), yet even through this there penetrate, as he has described in lines 483 ff., storms, tempest, and pestilence.

1002. *First of all it must needs be,* &c. Lucretius's exposition in this paragraph is not quite so orderly or lucid as usual, but it all follows quite directly from his main principles. Ordinarily things are surrounded on all sides by countless moving atoms, which batter against them and are in part the cause of their holding together. The effluence streaming off from the magnet knocks away these particles and creates a void between itself and the iron ring. The atoms on that side of the ring are therefore impelled by the internal air and vibration, and the external air and battering particles on the other sides, to move towards that part, where there is now no opposition. This they proceed to do, but because the atoms of iron are so closely interlaced, they cannot disentangle themselves, but of necessity drag the whole ring along with them towards the magnet.

1107. *where the axis of the world slants crippled.* The ancients conceived that the axis of the earth (and consequently also of the world) was on a slant, rising towards Scythia and sinking towards Egypt. Just the same idea is found in Virgil, *Georgic* I. 240. The idea is characteristic of the atomic school, and is found in Leucippus (*Aet.* 12. 1, Diels, Leucippus, 27).

1138. *Such a cause of plague,* &c. Lucretius here describes the famous plague of Athens in 430 B.C., and very closely follows the account given by Thucydides ii. 47-54.

SET IN GREAT BRITAIN AT THE UNIVERSITY PRESS, OXFORD
REPRINTED FROM PLATES BY
THE CAMPFIELD PRESS, ST. ALBANS

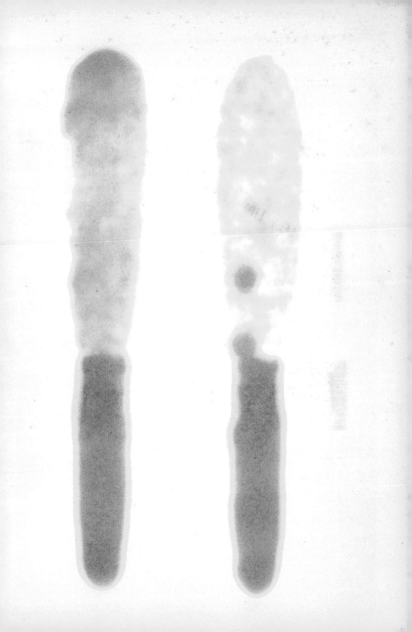